PUNJABI REBELS OF THE COLUMBIA RIVER

Punjabi Rebels of the Columbia River

The Global Fight for Indian Independence and Citizenship

JOHANNA OGDEN

Oregon State University Press   Corvallis

Library of Congress Cataloging-in-Publication Data

Names: Ogden, Johanna, author.
Title: Punjabi rebels of the Columbia River : the global fight for Indian inde-
   pendence and citizenship / Johanna Ogden.
Description: Corvallis, Oregon : Oregon State University Press, 2024. |
   Includes bibliographical references and index.
Identifiers: LCCN 2024000992 | ISBN 9781962645119 (paperback) |
   ISBN 9781962645126 (ebook)
Subjects: LCSH: East Indians—Oregon—History—20th century. | Foreign
   workers—Oregon—History—20th century. | East Indian—Oregon—Social
   conditions—20th century. | Ghadr movement. | Panjabis (South Asian
   people)—West (U.S.)—Politics and government—20th century. | Thind,
   Bhagat Singh, 1892-1967. | East Indians—Legal status, laws, etc.—United
   States | Great Britain--Relations—United States | United States—Foreign
   relations—Great Britain. | Oregon—Race relations—History—20th
   century.
Classification: LCC F885.E2 O334 2024 | DDC 979.5/04300491421—dc23/
   eng/20240215
LC record available at https://lccn.loc.gov/2024000992

∞ This paper meets the requirements of ANSI/NISO Z39.48-1992
(Permanence of Paper).

Oregon State University
OSU Press

Oregon State University Press
121 The Valley Library
Corvallis OR 97331-4501
541-737-3166 • fax 541-737-3170
www.osupress.oregonstate.edu

Oregon State University Press in Corvallis, Oregon, is located within the traditional homelands
of the Mary's River or Ampinefu Band of Kalapuya. Following the Willamette Valley Treaty of
1855, Kalapuya people were forcibly removed to reservations in Western Oregon. Today, living
descendants of these people are a part of the Confederated Tribes of Grand Ronde Community
of Oregon (grandronde.org) and the Confederated Tribes of the Siletz Indians (ctsi.nsn.us).

To our rebel dreamers, then and now

Contents

Notes on Language

Throughout this text I use the word "Indian" to refer to people from the countries known since 1947 as Pakistan and India. Given the inability to immediately define terms, I used the term "Punjabi"—a state and people in northern India that constituted the majority of migrants during this time—in this book's title. In early 1900s North America, they were most often referred to as Hindus or Hindoos. At best, this was a reference to Hindustan, the Indian subcontinent and, more specifically, its northern portion. But Hindu also refers to a religion, and its use thus conflates all Indians with a singular religious outlook. In the early 1900s, the majority of Indian migrants in North America were Sikh (the name Singh is commonly taken by men and Kaur by the women of that faith, with their temples called *gurdwaras*). Hindu/Hindoo was decidedly a racial slur marshaled against the migrants. During the time in which I am writing this manuscript (2014–2022), "Hindustan" and its various derivatives have been employed by ultra-right Hindu nationalists in India as part of a supremacist program. For these reasons, I employ the terms Hindu/Hindoo or Hindustan only as they appear in texts from the time, or when appropriate to a historical period. The vast majority of the Indian migrants were men, and that fact informs my use of pronouns.

I use the terms Indigenous or First Nations people to refer to the original inhabitants of North America.

Indians settled in British Columbia and in Washington, Oregon, and California. I address the area of that broad migratory pattern as "North America," and use Canada, British Columbia, America, the United States, and state names for more specific settlements or events.

There are transliteration issues that affect the spelling of names. The two most common to this text are Dayal/Dyal and Gadar/Ghadar. I use Dayal and Ghadar unless quoting from sources. The popular name for the movement central to this book is Ghadar; I use *Ghadr* to refer to its newspaper. Ghadarites and Ghadris both signify members of the organization.

The Raj was the British sovereign in India. Thind refers to the man; *Thind* refers to his citizenship case.

Race and whiteness are concepts at the heart of this book. Race is a highly unstable concept that exists and morphs within the laws and power relations of humans in which differences in physiognomy—hair, facial features, skin tone, and the like—are assigned social value and power, or their lack.

White is also used throughout this book, often without quotations, to denote Northern Europeans and American-born peoples of that background. Whiteness refers to an expectation of privilege and white supremacy and to the pervasive institutional practices upholding and delivering that privilege. Whiteness relies on inane markers—religion, language, skin tone—as the means to rate peoples' suitability for political inclusion and citizenship. I use "white" with the understanding that people, like the Irish, Italians, Jews, and others, have been excluded and included over time. I employ the term "Asian" as a term of convenience and when referencing the era's belief in the threat of an "Asian other." I do not wish to advance the Orientalist belief that all countries and cultures east of Europe are equivalent, or support the American use of the term as a racial category for purposes of exclusion.

An Introduction to an Unexpected Story

On November 27, 1916, the *Morning Oregonian*'s front page ran multiple hyperventilating headlines declaring "Punjab Rebellion Utterly Crushed," "Uprising Fomented in Oregon Nipped," and "Portland and St. Johns Figure in Story of Plots." Below the last of its six subtitles were the names and fates of specific men: "Solan Lai [Lal], former student at O.A.C. [Oregon Agricultural College] hanged In Mandalay [Burma]. For preaching rebellion, Kanschl Xam [Kanshi Ram] former contractor at St. Johns, Or., where he was known as John Kim, hanged in 1915 for fomenting sedition. Sohan Singh, formerly of Linnton [Oregon], hanged. Kesar Singh, of Astoria [Oregon], sent to prison for life."[1] Unlikely as it might seem today, the headlines were largely true: in the early 1900s, Oregon was a center of Indian revolutionary anticolonial organizing.

The article's author, an unnamed Associated Press (AP) correspondent out of Simla, India, the summer capital for British colonizers, quickly revealed their sympathies. The sole quoted source on the revolt was Punjab's Lieutenant Governor Michael Francis O'Dwyer, who the correspondent credited with guiding the Punjab "ship of state" to "safely weather a storm that might have swept all India."[2] O'Dwyer did indeed supervise the British regime's counterinsurgency in Punjab, and brutally so. He utilized intelligence from a global ring of police agents, much of it centered in North America. He worked with India's central authorities to enhance the state's ostensibly legal suppressive tools and oversaw secret prison trials, death sentences, and imprisonment for activists. Several years after the rebels' supposed defeat, O'Dwyer praised troops who killed hundreds of peaceful civilians whom authorities feared were infected with, and a vector for, the continued dream of Indian independence. As the incident commander

"Punjab Rebellion Utterly Crushed," *Morning Oregonian*, November 27, 1916. Courtesy Historic Oregon Newspapers, University of Oregon Libraries.

explained, the massacre was intended to produce "a sufficient moral effect" throughout Punjab.[3]

While obviously (and murderously) partisan, O'Dwyer nevertheless offered an accounting to the AP reporter of the genesis of Ghadar—the insurgency's popular name—that was largely true. "On a visit to St. Johns, Or., in 1913, Hardial proposed to start a revolutionary paper which should be called the *Ghadr* (Mutiny). This plan met with approval and received moral and financial support in St. Johns, Bridal Veil. Linnton, Portland. Astoria and other places. . . . All told, about 5000 or 6000 were recruited on the Pacific Coast and at Shanghai and Hongkong and these men eventually reached India a considerable time after the war [World War I] had begun."[4] Indeed, from small Oregon towns Ghadar spread to the world, and, during World War I, its partisans challenged and panicked the rulers of British India.

Though O'Dwyer claimed that all was under control in Punjab, he made clear the British remained vigilant. "Plotting among the revolutionary section of the Indians in America undoubtedly continues, but we are keeping a close watch on them because we wish to protect the people of India."[5] On this point, the article was both technically correct and pointedly misleading. While O'Dwyer spoke of "protecting the people of India," centuries of British rule—whether by the monarchy or the privately held East India Company—had plunged the country into crushing famine, epidemics, and poverty. To maintain the highly lucrative colonial regime, the British did far more than keep "a close watch" on US Indians. After imprisoning and executing numerous Ghadris in India, they turned to the United States. There, British officials colluded with the US government to silence nationalists and waged a propaganda campaign, with Britain's message finding a welcome reception in US newspapers.

The AP report gave O'Dwyer a sympathetic platform from which to tell his story in Oregon. It was repeated in the *San Francisco Chronicle*, that city being home to the Ghadar movement's office and newspaper. And it was forwarded by the viceroy of India to British ambassador Cecil Spring-Rice, who in turn dispatched it to US secretary of state Robert Lansing. For both public and governmental audiences, the AP story was tendered as proof of the harm being done to British India by Ghadar nationalists quartered in San Francisco. In effect, if not overt design, it was a hit piece justifying repression.

High-level US and British government agents surveilled, indicted, and prosecuted Ghadar activists, including several from Oregon, in what came to be known as San Francisco's German-Hindu Conspiracy case. Defendants were charged with conspiring to organize a military campaign against England—that is, the revolts in British India—with German monetary and organizational aid. The trial, financially underwritten by the British government, was at the time the most expensive in US history. In 1918, the convicted Indian militants were jailed in a US federal prison, their sentences covered in dailies around the world.[6]

The conspiracy trial's lead prosecutor, John W. Preston, concurrently tried 112 members of the Industrial Workers of the World (IWW) in Chicago. Officially charged with violating the Espionage Act, the radical labor organizers' real crimes were their anticapitalist politics, their internationalist membership, and their strikes and other disruptions of war production. Authorities and the press portrayed the two cases—the IWW and Ghadar—along with others as evidence of America's radical, foreign menace.[7] They were in fact testament to the British and US governments' war—jointly and independently—on multiracial, inclusive democracy. Their urgent goal was to contain the supporters and broad revolutionary impact of the anti-imperial revolts sweeping the world, from Ireland to Mexico, China, and Russia. As an added backstop, the US and British governments sought to block, permanently if possible, nonwhites' access to citizenship and civic power.

In 1920, an Oregon court awarded United States citizenship to an active Ghadar supporter; the decision was appealed by a Portland-based federal prosecutor and advanced to the US Supreme Court. The high court's 1923 opinion in *U.S. v. Bhagat Singh Thind* disqualified Indians from citizenship for not being white. *Thind* was further leveraged by Congress to reach both backward and forward in time. Legislators cancelled the previously awarded citizenship of sixty-five Indo-Americans and barred future immigrants from India for decades. That only a few thousand Indians remained in the United States belies the colonialists' pressing needs. After decades of society-changing immigration, *Thind* extended and reinforced America's whites-only political rule and power. The British government, facing a subcontinent demanding independence, welcomed if not lobbied for *Thind*'s potent and public denial of Indian civic parity. *Thind* also deprived Indian nationalists in America of the gossamer-thin protection of citizenship as they continued to organize against British rule. In short, Indians were officially "free" to work and enrich England and the United States, but barred from social equality.[8]

Globally, Indians' daily lives were shaped by the power dynamics of race and class embedded in citizenship. In Oregon, they challenged their status in profound—and profoundly different—ways. Ghadris sought the overthrow of British rule of India as central to their global civic inclusion. Thind, unlike the Supreme Court justices and many in US society, believed that US citizenship included him. This book traces Indians' differing challenges—collective and individual, revolutionary and legal, in India and the United States—to colonized citizenship and the global governmental efforts against them. I have drawn from and rely on many excellent studies on Ghadar's formation and program, the global anti-Indian suppressive apparatus, and the *Thind* decision.[9] None of these, however, have analytically explored Oregon and the entwined realities of Ghadris who returned to India and the Indians who remained in the United States, for whom Thind was a telling avatar.

As the sensationalist front-page *Morning Oregonian* account of the Punjab rebellion confirms, Indians' presence and history-making organizing was once newsworthy. The article was not the first or last on Indians by the *Morning Oregonian*. The paper reported on the Supreme Court's 1923 citizenship decision, highlighting Thind's reaction and future plans.[10] Years earlier, it had run multiple articles on the 1910 white riot against Indian laborers in St. Johns and the resulting trials.[11] Its sports pages reported on successful Indian wrestlers in the region, and its women's fashion section advertised turbans like "the picturesque turbans worn by the Hindu men one occasionally sees on the Portland streets."[12] Other area newspapers—the *Oregonian, Astoria Daily Budget,* and *Linton Live Wire*—similarly reported, for better or for worse, on Indians' lives.[13]

Yet today their Oregon legacy is largely unknown. Their numbers were small, and their tenure was short. Ironically, Indians' activism worked to erase their contributions as they, under Ghadar's leadership, left the state in droves for India. Bhagat Singh Thind, though better known, has been largely analyzed through his momentous legal ruling, divorced from the myriad of social and legal obstacles he and others navigated, and the radical community that indelibly shaped him.

The erasure and diminution of Indians' Oregon story is also the work of white supremacy and class domination, which mold historical memory in their own image. These were brown-skinned people, many wearing turbans, and Sikhs, Hindus, and Muslims, not Christians. They failed the "whiteness" test for civic inclusion in their times as well as in our historical memory. They were also overwhelmingly laborers in a country that only begrudgingly acknowledges class divisions and radical labor history, let alone America's enduring debt to global workers. In short, Indians' stories have been forgotten in large part because of the very ethnic and class strictures they challenged.

Similarly disremembered and discounted is America's rich environment of global and homegrown radicals, the collective size and synergy of which deeply alarmed authorities. Irish insurgents trumpeted Indians' cause while organizing against their shared oppressor. Ghadris befriended Mexican and Chinese insurgents who strategized and prepared their home-country assaults from the US west. IWW chapters spread across western mines and mills, the very places where Indians labored. Multiethnic socialist lodges dotted US landscapes, with Astoria's Finnish Hall hosting Ghadar's founding. Ghadar leaders and members fraternized in this rich stew of meeting halls, fields, mills, bars, bunkhouses, and, of course, jails. Even there, collaborations continued: authorities dubbed Leavenworth Prison the "University of Radicalism."[14] Colonial power and whiteness internationalized, but so too did resistance.[15]

That Indians' story can be told despite these many archival obstacles is a backhanded testament to the force of their presence. Despite everything arrayed against them, they forged alliances that left enduring traces of their presence. Oregon newspapers, court cases, and censuses offer names and other scraps of details. I am indebted to Indian historians whose work provided me a roadmap for both where to look and how to read these signs.[16] The growing body of North American literature on the Indian diaspora has also aided the sussing out and evaluation of local events.[17] Yet while I rely on all these sturdy cords, Oregon's archives are nonetheless thin. The community was transient, many were illiterate, and altogether little of their own voices were left behind. Moreover, like the men themselves, most of their accounts live scattered across the globe, often in languages I am reliant on others to decipher.[18] I am left to both document and imagine.

Reflecting their lived reality, I have narratively rejoined the trajectories of Ghadar and Thind to give shape to the debates and controversies that transpired in Oregon's bunkhouses, mills, and saloons. Thind, unlike the majority with whom he worked and lived, was a literate, public, and ultimately middle-class figure who wrote letters and books and appeared in newspaper articles and in a momentous national court case. Reading Thind's story together with Ghadar underscores that there was no single response to the racial and class obstacles Indians faced. Instead, the community contested and expressed race and belonging in unexpected and sometimes contradictory ways in the contact zone that was North America. In this push-pull of contending ideas and agendas, people weighed the possibilities and merits of insurrection in India, bending the US racial code and everything in between. Whatever their path, few escaped the punishments of empire.

An Oregon focus also necessitates centering labor and laborers. Unlike other communities in western North America, Oregon had few, if notable, Indian students and nationalist activists. More, British and US economic might were built and dependent on a racialized labor force, of which Indians were one part. The global and local elements of labor dynamics animate this story, including elites' repression and people's resistance and rebellion.

Historian Maia Ramnath beautifully captures the dynamics of Ghadar and the broader Indian nationalist movement, writing that "any dramatic events visible upon the lighted proscenium of the subcontinent were profoundly affected by a multitude of actors in the shadows offstage."[19] This is how I wish to portray Oregon—not as a singular or forever center, but as a place that played a critical role in a specific moment, thoroughly interwoven with world actors and events. Toward that end, I explore a short but dramatic fifteen years, roughly divided into three periods, with World War I its defining juncture: 1907 to 1913 marks Indians' arrival and settlement in North America; 1913 to 1915 brings the founding of Ghadar, England's declaration of war on Germany, and Indians' reverse migration to attempt the overthrow of British colonialism; and 1915 to 1922 is a period of intense government suppression from Punjab to the US Supreme Court. The book's chapters generally hew to these timelines.

Before diving into the Oregon story, chapter 1 provides a broad, global backdrop—an essential, if sometimes dense, context for our story's central characters. Examining British India, Canada, and the United States, the chapter outlines the drivers of migration and the range of political frictions and restrictions Indians faced, from intergovernmental to white laborers' animosity. It also considers Western Oregon's particular policy on race and labor, wherein influential elites opposed communal racial violence as a means of ensuring a labor force, a policy central to Indians' experience.

Chapter 2 explores Indians' lives in Oregon, beginning with the 1907 murder of Harnam Singh in Boring and the prosecution of his killers, which was quietly aided by global British officials. When much of the North American west was convulsed in anti-Asian violence, the conviction of Singh's murderers signaled some measure of safety for Indians. Oregon also had plentiful employment, thanks to a 1905 commercial fair steeped in colonial meanings. Oregon's politics of race illustrates that empire, while eminently global, is also deeply local in its workings, often with unanticipated implications. These hyperlocal politics, embedded in the broader divides of empire, shaped Indian migration to the state and the character of their communities, which are sketched in some detail.

But containing violence in a white settler nation is like expecting water to flow uphill. In 1910, local, regional, and national anti-Indian antipathies fueled a night of white rioting in St. Johns, an industrial river hamlet near Portland, detailed in chapter 3. The attack was perpetrated by both laborers and elites, each with distinct if overlapping motivations. Multiple rioters—including the town mayor, police chief, and numbers of workers—were indicted. With British assistance, Portland authorities secured convictions of two mill men, one in a contentious, highly publicized trial. While the British wished to appear as the protectors of their Indian subjects, Indians drew a different conclusion. With the close of the St. Johns trials, Indians—some of the very men noted by the AP correspondent from Simla—took decisive political and organizational steps toward creating Ghadar.

Chapter 4 focuses on Astoria, a comparatively cosmopolitan coastal town of ten thousand where, with great public fanfare, activists launched Ghadar in the late spring of 1913. Labor and race again loom large in understanding Astoria's political climate and why Indians chose it for their momentous convergence. It was a town of relative racial and labor peace, considerable radical currents, and somewhat self-consciously aware of its financial dependence on global workers. It was also not yet on the radar of the murderous political police agents trailing Indian radicals. By the standards of the day, Astoria afforded Indians a more welcoming home than most. Young, college-educated Bhagat Singh Thind makes his narrative debut here, arriving shortly after Ghadar's formation but laboring and living alongside its many organizers.

Following the Astoria convocation, Ghadris established an office and newspaper in San Francisco and garnered followers across the world. Less than a year later, England and Germany declared war, and profoundly intensified and complicated world politics. From the early weeks of July 1914, Britain's war planning depended on mobilizing Indian troops but was haunted by the memory of Indian soldiers' 1857 revolt. England could ill afford another mutiny while fighting Germany.[20] The United States entered the war three years after England amid a draconian clampdown on domestic civil rights.

Chapter 5 details the growth of Ghadar and its wartime transformation and challenges. Ghadar effectively split, with little to no communication between groups. Several thousand Indians, primarily laborers, sailed home with dreams of overthrowing the British Raj.[21] A cohort of Ghadar students and intellectuals decamped to Berlin in search of German aid, while, in San Francisco, Ghadar staff continued organizing and publishing their newspaper.[22] Others stayed behind, with many, like Bhagat Singh Thind, continuing to support Indian independence.

In Chapter 6 we return to where we began: the AP's report of revolution in Punjab and its rolling repercussions. Though unsuccessful, the Ghadris' revolutionary attempt unnerved British authorities, who responded with violence, not change. For attempting to reclaim their country, Ghadris were executed or sentenced to life imprisonment. The British further pursued Ghadar in US courtrooms with the consent and cooperation of the US government. The San Francisco German-Hindu Conspiracy case involved global heads of state and legions of police, prosecutors, and investigators. It utilized, complemented, and contributed to the US government's clampdown on domestic dissent.

Chapter 7 explores the dangerous US political climate and difficult personal decisions confronting young Bhagat Singh Thind: a virulent anti-immigrant and antiradical political atmosphere and campaign against Indians. In a landscape of terrible options, Thind enlisted in the US military and twice petitioned for citizenship while continuing to publicly support Ghadar. The chapter details Thind's successful Oregon citizenship award and its appeal by a virulently racist prosecutor in an actively antiradical Portland district attorney's office. It further interrogates the trail of British interests in the Supreme Court's denial of Indo-American citizenship in *Thind*.

The postwar state of Indian citizenship in India and the United States appeared bleak, as Indians were officially and unambiguously excluded from the democratic promises of Anglo-America. Ghadar's and Thind's impact, however, played out over decades and within the national liberation movements and shifting geopolitical ground of post–World War II. That war brought realignments to the power and stature of the British and US empires and new necessities for colonialism. In no small measure, this included the demands for self-determination from the people of China, Indonesia, Vietnam, and Cuba, as well as African

Americans and other marginalized groups in the metropoles. In 1947, from a mass movement of millions, Hindustan secured a formal independence seared by the bloody partition of India and Pakistan. Ghadris like Sohan Singh Bhakna, once of St. Johns, remained in the fight for social justice throughout their lives, and their movement inspired a new generation of Indian nationalist activists. Indian American activists continued the struggle for citizenship, successfully reversing *Thind* in 1946.[23]

Ghadar and Bhagat Singh Thind preceded these seismic changes and challenges by decades, contributing divergent strands to the long historical arc of resistance to colonial subjugation. Oregon, founded as a white Eden, was home to both of these momentous expressions of twentieth-century Indian self-determination and civic belonging.

Reflecting both chronology and the driving politics of the times, this book privileges Ghadar. Most simply, Ghadar's formation preceded Thind's arrival and bent his life arc. Most essentially, it is Ghadar that explains an animating mystery of this research: Why, for a few short years, were Indians an integral part of early twentieth-century Oregon, but wholly absent for the next fifty? Here is perhaps the final surprise of an already unexpected history. Indians' exodus was not due to a chilling racial crime. It is instead a radical absence born of monumental, historical agency. Ghadar alone is responsible for that imprint, its influence such that, with World War I, Indians departed the state in droves. Those who did not set sail for India—whether out of fear, disagreement, different life visions, or simply disinterest—moved to communities in British Columbia or California that persevered in the face of the historic leaving. Indians did not meaningfully resettle in Oregon until the 1970s, a discontinuous community largely unaware of its earlier ties to the region.[24] Attempting to account for how and why this happened is the motivation for this book.

1

The Promises of Empire

In the early 1900s, some eight to ten thousand Indians set out for western North America.[1] A few hundred men, one woman, and four children made Oregon home for a decade circa World War I.[2] Living and working in the backwater mill towns of the Columbia River, eight thousand miles from their birthplace and without apparent power, they collectively made an enduring mark on both the twentieth-century Indian imagination and the US racial code.

In many ways Oregon was an unlikely place for such historic, if differing, organizing. The Indian community was small and arrived later than those in California or British Columbia. It comprised almost exclusively laborers who owned little in the way of businesses or land, and who formed no gurdwaras or other cultural institutions. Instead, in Oregon they built more ephemeral and informal community at work, in living quarters, at sporting contests, and, ultimately, in politics.

More pointedly, Oregon was founded as a white Eden, a history that continues to shape its present.[3] Yet the particular ways in which Oregon's state and business leaders and common people exercised white rule, especially in and around Portland, the state's largest city, provided openings and possibilities for Indians.

Oregon's white rule was explicitly enabled by the US Congress' enactment of the 1850 Oregon Donation Land Act. The act was a highly racialized and gendered affair premised on the theft of Native lands that were legally bequeathed in largest measure to married, white citizen settlers. The imprimatur of law sanctified the country's union of race, land, and citizenship, and established some as Oregon "settlers" and the rest as landless outsiders.[4]

White settlers' hopes for ethnic dominance were further aided by the state's foundational law. The Oregon Constitution, ratified just two years before the US Civil War, banned slavery. It also stated that African Americans were excluded from residing in Oregon, although this was unevenly enforced. Black people who lived in the state were barred from owning real estate, making contracts, voting, or accessing the legal system. After the Civil War, Oregon legislators instituted a tax on any nonwhite resident and banned interracial marriages. [5] To the envy of many California politicians and residents, Oregon also became the first state to explicitly apply America's long-enshrined arguments of white supremacy and racial exclusion to Chinese settlers. Oregon's constitutional delegates tagged the Chinese as "almost" like slaves in their living habits and conditions of labor, but ultimately failed to enact an outright ban on Chinese residents. Instead, the state's constitution explicitly denied the vote to any "Negro, Chinaman, or Mulatto," excluded women's vote through pointed omission, and barred Chinese settlers from property ownership.[6] In 1859, the US Congress approved the Oregon Constitution and admitted it to statehood with its exclusionist provisions fully intact.[7]

Oregon's leaders and residents reflected the national views and fissures of their time about race, with statehood granted on the cusp of the US Civil War over slavery. Many of Oregon's settlers were fleeing the fraught racial politics of elsewhere and hoped to legally shut the door not just on slavery, but on a multiethnic, multicultural society.[8] Moreover, Oregon was standing in a solid national tradition. US armies, legislators, and people sought to strip Indigenous peoples of their territory and premised—but did not guarantee—Native citizenship on their relinquishment of sovereignty and/or tribal lands. The country's wealth accumulation and industrial expansion was further capitalized by the chattel slavery enshrined in the US Constitution's designation of African Americans as three-fifths human and noncitizens.[9]

While continuing this legacy and their particular vision of a white homeland, some early Oregon leaders also fashioned a distinct racial politics to ensure a needed workforce. In the late 1800s, powerful men in and around Portland perceived Chinese migrants' flight from ethnic violence in California as a potential boon. They believed in law and order and scorned the spread of vigilante violence. They worked to attract and keep Chinese migrants, forging a management of America's fraught dynamics of race and labor that differed from their counterparts in other areas of the US west. Utilizing their judicial and policing positions and control of the influential Portland *Oregonian* editorial page, they promoted a civic compact decrying and combating ethnic violence. They were largely successful in Portland, and minimized such activities in nearby towns, all while keeping white privilege and power firmly intact. By the late 1880s, Chinese people settled in Portland, often from areas wracked by racial violence, and built a community surpassed only by the Chinese community in San Francisco in wealth and size and, signaling its influence, hosting one of only four Chinese consuls in the United States.[10]

Two key players in effecting Portland's racial policy were Matthew Deady, a judge who presided over Oregon's race-infused Constitutional Convention, and newspaperman Harvey Scott. The men threaded the needle of their own white supremacist views with their belief in the centrality of Chinese laborers in making Portland a prosperous and important imperial hub.[11] Their strategy reflected Portland realities. A bustling commercial center, Portland had well-established civic leadership, diverse institutions, and a broad middle class, served by and supportive of social stability. Deady, Scott, and others were not merely ideologues but also actors, as demonstrated by their role in thwarting two notorious exclusionists, Daniel Cronin and Burdette Haskell.[12]

Haskell's exclusionist credentials hailed from inciting anti-Chinese riots in San Francisco. Cronin, with the Knights of Labor, spearheaded an effort to rid Washington state of Chinese residents. Aided by Tacoma's mayor, Cronin had directed the November 1885 beating and violent expulsion of two hundred Chinese from that town, many of its refugees relocated to Portland by businessman Moy Back Hin. Moving on to Seattle, Cronin organized hundreds to set fires and detonate explosives in the Chinese quarters. Governor-ordered troops quelled the Seattle outbreak, but white violence continued in smaller towns across the state.[13] In the aftermath, Haskell and Cronin, with the backing of organized labor, set their sights on Oregon, a state with a significantly larger Chinese population than Washington.[14]

The two arrived in the area then known as East Portland in February 1886 and gathered followers in Mount Tabor and other burgs

east of downtown. They won the ear of Portland city councilman John
Caples, who had unsuccessfully attempted to ban Chinese laborers
from Portland public works projects. They also had the sympathies of
Sylvester Pennoyer, Oregon's new, pro-(white) labor and strident anti-
Chinese governor.[15]

Despite their local backers and previous successes, Cronin's and
Haskell's schemes did not materialize. There was sporadic violence,
but no expulsion occurred in and around Portland, as Deady, Scott,
and Portland's mayor, John Gates, effectively countered the organizers.
Judge Deady issued legal rulings and Mayor Gates beefed up the police
presence and swore in armed citizens. Central to their success were
Harvey Scott's editorials in the *Oregonian,* the Northwest's preeminent
press and Scott's bully pulpit. Beyond the immediate fight with Cronin
and Haskell, Scott's editorials provided a regional counterweight to the
San Francisco Chronicle, which spread its anti-Chinese opinions and
pro-violence stance across the US west.[16]

Scott believed Chinese laborers could be, as historian Marie Rose
Wong writes, "adroitly exploit[ed] . . . as a state resource."[17] While the
San Francisco Chronicle and other Oregon papers argued that Chinese
workers took white jobs, Scott argued whites should not want such work.
He maintained that Chinese labor, whether clearing land or cleaning
fish, enabled and promoted "white work," such as construction or fishing. Further, he pointed out that having access to cheaper labor would
contribute to the competitiveness of Oregon goods in the world market,
thereby boosting the economy for everyone. Scott summed up these
arguments in "Labor Is Wealth," in which he wrote, "Every person who
can work is an addition to the wealth of our state. Wealth cannot be produced without labor. . . . Labor is capital."[18] In response to the argument
that the Chinese contributed no wealth to the region because they took
or sent their earnings home, Scott illuminated the differences between
social wealth and a laborer's pay. He pointed out that the railroads
and agricultural and mill products that Chinese laborers constructed
remained in Oregon, even if their small wages returned to China.[19]

At a time of pervasive ethnic lawlessness sanctioned by governmental authorities, Scott called for the active punishment of exclusionists like Haskell and Cronin, turning the badge of "undesirables" back
onto them. In 1886 he refused to print an anti-Chinese editorial written

by sitting Governor Pennoyer, believing it might prompt violence and therefore did not comply with *Oregonian* standards. While Scott did not omit news of exclusionist meetings in the newspaper, he framed them in such a way as to argue for the intelligence of Oregonians (as opposed to Californians), who would never jeopardize Oregon's future with such shenanigans.[20]

Importantly, this was a class-based law and order policy. Scott and others argued that the (white) community as a whole benefited from the economic growth enriching the powerful and enabled by Chinese laborers. Further, while the *Oregonian* was a significant persuasive tool, the no-communal-violence policy ultimately rested on state power. The coercive control of the courts and police were wielded against laborers and others who interrupted the Chinese labor stream. Arguably more opposition may have surfaced had Portland not been economically successful. But, as Wong writes, in the late 1800s, "Portland was distinguished from its Northwest counterparts by its unprecedented rate of growth, . . . the third fastest of American cities."[21] The Chinese community was central to that achievement.

Scott's words and the practical, legal efforts of men such as Judge Deady, Portland mayor Gates, and others left Portland and environs largely free from the widespread ethnic violence that engulfed much of the US west. People took note of the city's racial reputation. The relative social peace, combined with a booming economy, drove the sustained growth of Portland's Chinese community as those of California and Washington declined. By 1900, Chinese constituted Portland's second largest foreign-born population.[22]

To be clear, Portland leaders' policy was not a renouncement of white supremacy but instead reveals its shape-shifting skills. It was simply a differing means of managing the country's dynamics of race and labor—and provides a useful object lesson that overt violence is only one measure of a regime of racial supremacy. While these elites did not condone mob violence, they opposed Chinese citizenship and upheld the federal 1882 Chinese Exclusion Act.[23] They also instituted local ordinances that restricted where and how Chinese could set up house, run businesses, be employed, and even the cubic air space required in their living quarters.[24] It was decidedly not a policy of social equity but was for the purpose of attracting and retaining the Chinese laborers considered indispensable to building Oregon to the coveted heights its political and business leaders envisioned.

These powerful Portland-area managers of race and labor were sometimes at odds—tactically if not fundamentally—with local, regional, and national leaders and policy. A 1906 Immigration Service report referred to Portland as a "haven" for Chinese.[25] In the enforcement of the Chinese Exclusion Act, courts were crucial—hearing immigrants' detainment appeals, deportation cases, and ruling on laborers' right to reenter the United States—and federal authorities considered Portland's jurists too permissive.[26] Such frictions were not new in the United States; race and labor management were long entwined on a conflict-laden path. As historians David Roediger and Elizabeth Esch observe, these conflicts reveal their own dramatic story of race and labor, one that can be read in Indians' Oregon saga.[27]

Western Oregon's labor and racial policy unquestionably shaped Indians' experiences, including their motivation for settlement and their ability to politically organize relatively unmolested. More specifically, it played out in the prosecution of the murderers of Harnam Singh in Boring, Oregon, in 1907; in the trials of the 1910 St. Johns anti-Hindu rioters; and likely influenced Judge Wolverton's 1920 citizenship award to Bhagat Singh Thind.[28]

Ultimately, however, preventing ethnic and labor violence, or fielding challenges to white supremacy, was not determined solely by prominent area leaders. Oregon's local dynamics of race and labor were deeply entangled with global necessities and divisions beyond the control of even very influential men. Similarly, Indians' challenges to colonized citizenship evolved across multiple decades and within an array of rivalries and frictions among empires, countries, regions, and people that played out from India to the small Oregon towns of St. Johns and Astoria.

Indian migration and radicalization transpired across two empires, those of Britain and the United States. Each was expanding globally, and each was dealing with tensions between rulers and ruled. Both were reliant on and enriched by colonialism's worldwide circulation of goods and labor governed by white supremacy.[29] Indians traveled within and across these two empires largely along two tracks of labor.

After the British ended chattel slavery in the 1830s, they needed replacement workers in their sugar and rubber plantations of the West

Indies, Mauritius, and elsewhere. Having already subjugated Hindustan, the British shipped off thousands of Indian men and women as contract (or, derogatorily, "coolie") laborers. British mercantilists dictated the duration, locale, and conditions of these desperate peasants' contracts and profited from their labor as both sender and recipient.[30]

By the turn of the twentieth century, Indian laborers were traveling a second track. Indians, overwhelmingly men, migrated as "free" laborers, meaning people without the promise or constraint of a contract, obliged and beholden only to market whims. North America's industrialization fed on global laborers. Noncontract Indians—free laborers—were among the millions who performed the often backbreaking and dangerous work instrumental to US and Canadian economic expansion. Indians' repatriated earnings also provided some hope, and small relief, to the economic devastation and political turmoil British colonialism spawned in India.[31]

While both countries traded in and relied on global laborers, the United States and England were also at odds over a number of issues. High on the list was the relative threat of Indian radicalism. The US government did not countenance anticolonial movements (unless to their advantage), especially after having recently suppressed the Hawaiian, Cuban, and Filipino peoples in pursuit of its own overseas empire. However, India was England's colonial possession, not America's. As Indian radicalism rose in both Canada and the United States, British authorities saw US authorities as undercommitted in their governmental surveillance and suppressive response. Not until World War I did this meaningfully change, when the United States, with substantial British assistance, included Indians on its list of politically suspect and targeted immigrants.[32]

These powers were vulnerable to other political frictions within the global labor systems that supported and enriched them both. Most straightforward were the intergovernmental conflicts among England, the United States, and Canada triggered by Indian migration. Canada was a British Crown Colony in the midst of its own industrial expansion; by early 1900, it was the first and primary site of Indian settlement in North America. Soon after Indians arrived on the continent—for reasons detailed below—they became domestic political liabilities in Canada and the United States. Yet the control measures each government took were often at odds, pushing migrants from one country to another in a perverse game of human whack-a-mole.[33] Further, even if operating within the bounds of the same empire—as England and Canada were—state interests did not always align. Notably, soon after Indians' arrival, Canadians sought to expel them to quiet domestic discontent over its "White Canada Forever" ethos. The British Crown, however, had promised Indians equal status in the empire, and any open abrogation of that pledge endangered colonial rule in India.[34]

These intergovernmental conflicts were driven by more elemental frictions built into colonialism's differing sites of wealth production. There were the colonial regimes, such as England's occupation of India, and settler colonial countries, like Canada, Australia, and the United States. As historian Katrine Barber writes, "If classic colonialism [India] was resource-oriented and circular (colonists lived in the region temporarily to oversee the extraction of natural resources, ultimately returning to their countries of origin), settler colonialism [Canada and US] was a one-way journey motivated by land acquisition that required dispossession and its justification."[35] Each regime was ultimately tied to the riches and powers derived from the international African slave trade.[36] While governments ended their overt trade in humans in the late 1800s, its inheritance endured in, among other things, racial capitalism's "proprietary orientation toward the planet in general and toward 'darker peoples' in particular."[37] In the early 1900s, activist and theorist W. E. B. DuBois captured this: "Whiteness is the ownership of the earth, forever and ever, Amen!"[38]

From its inception, colonialism used impoverished whites globally as "poorly paid shock troops."[39] They built much of the slave system's infrastructure in Africa and staffed the rails and commercial houses of India.[40] In settler colonies like the United States, Canada, Australia, and New Zealand, they cleared land and pursued exclusion, removal, and policing of Native peoples to establish a white-ethno society. Further, the colonies that would become the United States sanctioned and maintained African chattel slavery within their territorial borders. This spawned a particular expectation of white privilege and a particular sense of precarity, given the proximate reality of chained labor.[41] In the colonial United States, poor whites traded backbreaking, dangerous labor to wealthy white landowners for the "possibility of social mobility

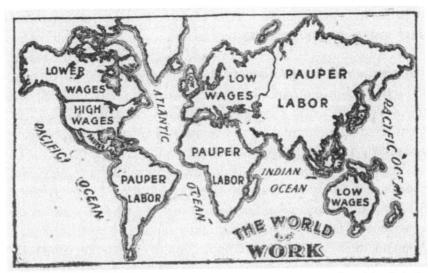

"The Lesson of a Labor Map," *San Francisco Call*, September 30, 1896. An influential exclusionist labor newspaper's visualization of global labor. Courtesy California Digital Newspaper Collection, UC Riverside Center for Bibliographical Studies and Research.

and favored economic, political and social status over indigenous and African peoples," particularly property ownership and *impermanent* bondage.[42]

This social bargain, born of necessity and struggle, shaped white laborers' expectations of privilege from their government and the pervasive institutional practice of upholding and delivering that privilege. As historian Carmen Thompson writes, one of the salient features of whiteness is that it "is an intra-racial struggle as much as *inter*racial."[43] While Thompson's insight arises from her reading of US history, its basic truth also applies to Canada.[44] For both the United States and Canada, Indians' arrival in the early 1900s, like other immigrant waves, further sedimented these regimes of racial supremacy, menaced white laborers' expectations of privilege, and exacerbated white class tensions.

Industrialists' enterprises economically underwrote settler colonies like the United States and Canada, while simultaneously complicating the political promise of ethnic privilege and exclusivity. In times of industrial growth, owners required more laborers than available domestically and employed masses of global migrants. Between 1850 and 1930, more humans traveled the globe than at any previous time in history—some fifty million Chinese and Europeans, and thirty million

Indians—the vast majority of them laborers fleeing privations.[45] Millions met in the rapidly expanding factories, mines, and mills of the North American west. There, labor—and laborers—became the ground zero for the competing forces of industrially driven ethnic mixing and the settler colonial promise of ethnic privilege in political rights, land ownership, and work. Through the decades, capitalists and government functionaries struggled to manage this volatile mix—politically and practically—through a combination of pretext and force.[46]

Legions of laborers in North America resisted the economic instability, inequity, and brutality of industrialization. But many did so with the crude fears and antipathies wrought by a belief in whiteness as privilege.[47] Especially in the west, the main site of North American Asian migration, white laborers' opposition to exploitation commonly became fused with, and arguably diffused by, a hatred of Asians and others, much as in other white settler countries.[48] Too often, fighting for rights as a worker merged with fighting for rights as a white person, as commonly advocated by mainstream labor organizations. Sociologist Jonathan Hyslop dubs labor's particular brand of racism fused with class struggle as "white labourism," arguing it dominated the global organized labor movement and served as a "partner in empire."[49] It played out in exclusivist labor organizing, ugly ethnic riots, and other extralegal attacks on Chinese, Japanese, Indian, and other workers deemed not white. Or, as social theorist Stuart Hall summarized these dynamics, race was "the modality in which class [was] lived."[50]

Certainly, there were exceptions to this rule.[51] The most notable was the Industrial Workers of the World (IWW) or Wobblies, the bold and creative organization in the US west's mines, woods, and mills. Recruiting laborers of all nationalities, the IWW largely rejected and destabilized the racial logic of settler colonialism and its industrialist regime and drew the venom and truncheons of government and private militias alike.[52] By contrast, the American Federation of Labor (AFL) organized workers based on trades, refused membership to workers considered nonwhite, and lobbied for and supported Asian exclusion laws.[53] Neither were socialists exempt from the poison. The Japanese Socialist Party sought censure of the US Socialist Party for its abysmal stance toward Asian workers. [54] Many in the middle class—doctors, teachers, preachers, and others—participated in or condoned violent ethnic outbursts.[55]

Still, North American ethnic riots and other violent expressions were driven largely by laborers entangled in the nexus of industrialization and race-mixing uprooting their lives and threatening their relative entitlement.[56] Their common battle cry was for their rights as "free laborers" against the contract, slave, or coolie workers, all dog-whistle terms for nonwhite immigrant workers. These freighted epithets, studded with white anxiety, expressed the global racial divides of the working class born from, and in the service of, colonialism.

Contract labor was considered degraded labor in much of the world because of its detachment from owning and working land. Countless European peasants had, ostensibly, been freed from the land through law and the rising forces of capitalist agriculture and industry. Many former European peasants became wage laborers, hired as agricultural hands or as industrial factory workers in their homelands. Others migrated to North America as contract, or indentured, workers. Some resurrected their landed status by becoming landowning farmers—for millions the core promise of North America's purportedly unlimited territory. As industrialism increasingly dominated the North American west, their dreams of independence were supplanted by the fact of permanent wage labor, and foreclosed opportunity bred with ethnic animus.[57]

Indians in North America were not indentured or contract workers. Unlike Europeans, however, they remained indelibly marked as such. The word "coolie," if not expressing Indians' actual working conditions in North America, expressed their colonized status and relegation to the lowest tiers of racialized labor in settler colonies.[58] Their religion, ethnicity, skin tone, and turbans further marked their place in the colonial hierarchy of race and labor. In the North American imagination and discourse, they remained "coolie slaves" and cheap and degraded competitors, invectives with even greater valence in the land of former slaveholders.[59] Amid the evaporating dream of western independence, expansive industrial reality, and an entrenched global racial hierarchy, Indians and others were caught in a vice grip of need, revulsion, and civic dispossession.

"True" Americans or Canadians were defined in law and culture as independent whites of self-ruled countries, not ethnically defined unfree laborers. Millions of workers were kept—by law, custom, and force—at the bottom of the wage ladder. In the alchemy of time and place, this racialized labor force stratified further still between nonciti-zen and citizen, a status that writer and activist Arundhati Roy distills to the "right to have rights."[60] The ensuing battles—in mills, courtrooms, street corners, and bars—triggered domestic class frictions within, and regional tensions between, Canada and the United States, and further destabilized British rule of India.

The years between 1907 and World War I were watershed years for Indians in North America. "Promise"—its terms, its power, and its denial—shaped the contours of this formative period and Indians' resistance. They had made their way to North America on the British Crown's promise, and authority, of their equality within the empire. They joined millions of others drawn by the promise of new beginnings. Yet Indians' promise proved cordoned and chiseled by race and class. On North America's stage of millions, promises clashed, shattered, and transformed. How Indians' read and navigated this landscape of prom-ise defines many of the distances and convergences between Ghadar and Bhagat Singh Thind. Entangled in the chaos of empiric dynamics, several thousand Indian migrants became a British nightmare and Bha-gat Singh Thind a signpost for the ugly realities of US inclusion.

Indian organizing in North America—and its particular sense of promise—was long in the making. It was rooted in England's centuries-long plunder of Hindustan. The corporatist administration of the East India Company (EIC), perennially enabled by British troops, underwrote London's spectacular growth, prosperity, and cultural transformations. As England's most successful business for almost two centuries, the EIC was entrenched with power. Nearly a quarter of Parliament mem-bers were stockholders. EIC products and profits fueled London's ship-building and urban expansion, and otherwise built Europe's largest city. Polo from Indian maharajas' courts became England's national sport, tea its drink of choice; cardamom, ginger, and curries became culinary staples, and Londoners walked the streets dressed in a dizzying array of Indian-produced fabrics.

This luxury carried a dirty underbelly. Much as the industrial and political success of the US North depended on its enslaved South, the wealth and democratic traditions of England were shadowed by Indian realities. As journalist Amartya Sen writes, "Those who wish to be inspired by the glory of the British empire would do well to avoid reading Adam Smith's *The Wealth of Nations*, including his discussion of the abuse of state power by a 'mercantile company which oppresses and domineers in the East Indies.'"[61]

For Indians, English imperial extraction produced successive famines, plagues, and the wholesale collapse of indigenous industries. Before the rise of the EIC, England generated about 2 percent of global products, and India 22 percent. "By the peak of the British Raj, however, those figures had reversed, and India, formerly the world's leading manufacturing nation, suffered endemic famine and deprivation."[62] Millions of Indians died, millions more suffered, the breadth of ruin captured in these lines of folk poetry:

> Oh, Uncle Churchill!
> Don't go,
> Until the structure of this house [India]
> Is totally destroyed![63]

Besides looting and dumping products, the British transformed Hindustanees themselves into a commodity. Colonial magnates shipped 3.5 million indentured Indians across the globe to live and work in conditions appallingly similar to the enslaved people who preceded them. Additionally, British colonizers enticed, recruited, and relied on Indian troops, many of them Punjabi Sikhs, to ensure their rule in India and to police and suppress other colonies.[64]

In 1857, Indian troops revolted against the indignities and crimes of British rule, an uprising often dubbed India's first war of independence. Troops mutinied for a multitude of reasons, including food shortages, British takeovers of independent native states, and Christian missionaries' proselytizing among villagers and troops. Most fundamentally, their revolt sprang from a generalized sense of British disrespect for, and ruination of, India.[65] As depicted in this ballad, the Raj responded ruthlessly:

> In the rebellion of 1857, oh young ones, so many atrocities were
>   committed
> The corpses of children were pierced through and paraded
>   throughout open markets

The breasts of uncounted mothers and sisters were cut off,
And innumerable women were killed and thrown into wells.
In the square of Allahabad people were hanged on every
    nim tree.
The Bloody Gate of Delhi, which makes your heart bleed,
Was made red with the blood of those Indians.[66]

Had it not been for the loyalty and intervention of Punjabi troops, many of them Sikh, British rule might well have ended then. The specter of this mutiny—both its very real threat to their power and their utter brutality in suppressing it—haunted British colonial authorities for decades.[67] Indians too did not soon forget this defining event. Some fifty years later the 1857 mutiny, or "ghadar," became an imaginative and rhetorical touchstone for North American organizers facing racial violence in 1907.[68] It symbolized Indian resistance and, for many military veterans, misspent loyalty to British colonizers.

As part of resecuring British authority in the mutiny's wake, the British government reorganized the Indian military, rewarding and enshrining the loyalty that had saved them. Half of the reconstituted forces deployed domestically and to other Crown Colonies came from Punjab. The British government also ended the East India Company's corporatist administration and brought India under the direct political rule of Queen Victoria, now the Empress of India. [69] Indians' relation to the queen was codified in her proclamation of 1858, in which she conferred British imperial membership on her new Indian subjects, its benefits ostensibly colorblind and equal throughout her empire.[70] The queen's 1858 proclamation advanced the quid quo pro of state belonging: protection of its members conditioned on their loyalty to its governing power. Not surprisingly then, besides granting Indians' membership in the empire, the proclamation promised retribution for the 1857 mutineers and no mercy to those who gave them quarter.

After 1858, thousands exploited Queen Victoria's pledge of equal standing in her empire and sought work abroad, often to save family farms. The majority of Indian migrants to North America were Sikhs from Punjab, a breadbasket for Hindustan and source of many troops. Besides Queen Victoria's promise, Indians' notion of their right to live and travel in North America was bolstered by Canada's British Crown membership and the United States' avowal of equal opportunity for all comers. Military veterans, nearly half of all Indians in North America, carried an added sense of entitlement, given Punjabi Sikh troops' role in saving British rule in 1857.[71]

As subjects of a British Commonwealth country, Indians were formally free to enter Canada under Queen Victoria's edict. By 1905, Indians were migrating in meaningful numbers to British Columbia, which quickly became home to the largest Indian community in the hemisphere. Many British Columbians also quickly became hostile to Indians' presence. In their view, the queen's pledge to Indians regarding their right to travel and live throughout the empire violated Canada's ability to maintain itself as a white republic. Within a few short years, Indian migration had triggered tensions between England and Canada over the entwined principles and promises of self-governance and white right.

"White Canada Forever"[72]
1900s popular Canadian bar song

This the voice of the West and it speaks to the world:
The rights that our fathers have given
We'll hold by right
and maintain by might,
Till the foe is backward driven.
We welcome as brothers all white men still,
But the shifty yellow race,
Whose word is vain, who oppress the weak,
Must find another place.
Chorus:
Then let us stand united all
And show our father's might,
That won the home we call our own,
For white man's land we fight.
To oriental grasp and greed
We'll surrender, no never.
Our watchword be "God save the King"
White Canada for ever.

In 1906, white British Columbians perceived Indians as a threat to the province's racial balance of power and, with a vote, disenfranchised them through World War II.[73] This was followed by a series of draconian measures against Indian migrants over the following years. Australia and New Zealand, British settler colonies similarly opposed to nonwhite migration, instituted similar measures. The administrative body for white settler colonies, the British Imperial Council, succinctly expressed the colonies' collective viewpoint: "Merely being the subjects of the British government does not give Indians the right to settle in British colonies. The white *owners* of these colonies have the right to permit or not to permit the Indians to settle [emphasis added]."[74] London was left to finesse its promises to the white dominions with those made to Indians. These waters were further complicated by rising anticolonial sentiments in India that risked destabilizing a peerless colonial possession.

Most immediately, however, British Columbians' sentiments and proscriptions against Indians spurred migration southward. Indians, like millions of others, were also independently drawn to America's booming western economy, and entered its San Francisco and Seattle ports.[75] Once in the United States, Indians found themselves in a country that had thrown off British rule, but not British imperial custom, belief, and law, especially with respect to those considered not white. For two hundred years, whiteness formed the explicit legal prerequisite for US belonging. The country's race-based citizenship laws dictated voting rights, land ownership, marriage, and other fundamentals of building influence as equal members of society. Indians were promptly enveloped by America's house rules.

In 1907, a wave of anti-Asian violence washed across the North American west. From Southern California to British Columbia, white laborers and others attacked people from Japan, China, India, and elsewhere. In Bellingham, Washington, several hundred Indians were effectively and violently driven out of town largely by fellow millworkers. A few days later, in Vancouver, BC, with the encouragement of local leaders and US anti-immigrant labor organizers, one of the largest race riots in Canadian history was carried out by upward of ten thousand people from all walks of life.[76] Yet no matter the province or state, perpetrators went unprosecuted. Instead, national, labor, and town newspapers disparaged the Indians and other victims as dirty, unfit neighbors and fellow workers.

In 1907, Indians were handed a bitter lesson on the implications of self-rule. While rulers of sovereign sending countries like China and Japan profited politically and economically from out-migration, they did not silently suffer the humiliation of their migrants being attacked overseas. These governments intervened on their nationals' behalf in Canada and the United States. The British did not defend their subjects, leaving many Indians feeling like "slaves and orphans" as later Ghadar poems expressed it. [77] Instead, the British marshaled a variety of governmental actions to prevent Indians continued migration to, and settlement in, Canada. For Indians who remained in North America, British colonial authorities, in league with their Canadian and US counterparts, initiated a political policing unit to monitor and disrupt their radical organizing.[78]

The first restriction against Indians came in January of 1908, with the Canadian government's passage of an amendment to its Immigration Act, commonly known as the Continuous Journey provision. It ostensibly required all migrants entering Canada to have traveled directly from, and with a ticket purchased in, their country of birth. Later amendments added the condition that all migrants land with $200 in hand, or roughly $5,000 a hundred years later.[79]

The Continuous Journey provision was not employed against all, or even most, migrants. First, it was simply ignored with respect to Europeans who migrated to Canada by way of the United States or elsewhere. The Chinese were already subject to a $500 entrance tax, thanks to an earlier government attempt to stem their migration to Canada. Japanese migrants paid $40 to enter Canada because of treaty protections negotiated by their government, a rising imperial power. Importantly, both China and Japan controlled well-established steamship service, allowing them dependable, direct travel to Canada as the new law required. Thus, none of the Continuous Journey provisions affected either Chinese or Japanese immigration, other than the relative few Japanese entering Canada from Hawai'i. This was not the case for Indians.[80]

The 1907 attacks on Indians in Canada and the United States generated troubling headlines and commentary in the Indian wire service and various journals. Given India was brimming with dissent, especially in Bengal and Punjab, the British Raj carefully considered its moves.

The overseas Indian community from Australia to South Africa also intently awaited colonial authorities' response to the mistreatment of its putative citizens. British authorities sought an outcome that would undercut Indian nationalist agitation yet pacify Canadian citizens' demand for a white dominion. The Continuous Journey provision was the empire's resolution.[81]

By design and intent, the Continuous Journey provision was aimed solely and directly at Indians while equally intended to conceal that very fact. Its cash requirement was without doubt a high bar on an already costly journey. More ominous, however, was the requirement that Indians travel directly from their country of birth to Canada. Canadian government officials working with their British and Indian counterparts knew there were no direct passenger ships between India and Canada. Even if travelers could raise the passage and the $200 landing fee, there were no ships for them to legally board. In a final doubling-down, the British Raj implemented in-country passport controls that choked off Indian passage to Canada.[82]

The combined effect of this multipronged effort was immediate: by 1909 it had effectively ended new Indian migration to Canada.[83] With the Continuous Journey provision, British Canadian and Indian authorities quietly and efficiently enacted a ban on Indian migration without ever mentioning race or ethnicity. This seemingly colorblind law was critical to maintaining the empire's claim to equal membership of all its subjects—and thus to undercutting Indian nationalist organizing—while effectively banning Indian subjects from further migration to Canada and quieting white unrest.

The British Home Office, a ministerial department of the Queen of England, had concluded that it was a grievous political mistake to have enabled Indians' passage to the West. Indians presence inflamed British Columbians' want of ethnic homogeneity and destabilized its labor politics. Further, although this migration was once considered a safe outlet for India's rural poverty and rising radicalism, British authorities had inadvertently enabled a troublesome community of banned radicals and disquieted laborers to coalesce in the North American west and out of direct British control. Globally, agitators seized on the post-1907 measures to further expose the sham of Britain's promise of Indian equality and the degradations of colonial rule.[84]

Much to the irritation of the British, US officials were not equally concerned about Indian migration and their threat to colonial rule. Still, as evidenced by 1907's popular violence, many Americans wanted no more Indian immigrants, and Canada's institution of the Continuous Journey provision promoted exactly that. Indians in the United States— whether entering from India or Canada—could no longer legally cross into Canada, given the newly enacted Continuous Journey provision.[85]

If not concerned per se about the small number of Indian migrants, controlling the so-called Hindu problem intersected with broader calls by US citizens and politicians to close the immigration doors that had been wide open for so long. America's western industrial expansion was slowing, and demands to reassert ethnic exclusivity and power were growing. In 1905, the Department of Commerce and Labor began construction of the Angel Island Detention Center to help stem the tide of so-called undesirable and increasingly unnecessary laborers from the East. Opened in January 1910, Angel Island made extensive use of detention and interrogation to exclude thousands of Chinese, Japanese, and Indian immigrants. Nationally, measures such as literacy tests were promoted as a means to curtail other unwanted migration. The anti-immigrant movement gained momentum but did not fully prevail until the draconian measures enacted around World War I, which essentially barred all Asian, and drastically restricted European, immigration.[86]

After 1907, and until the 1917 passage of the Asiatic Barred Zone, America's control of Indian immigration was largely left to, and effected through, the prejudices and whims of western immigration enforcement agents, especially in the major port of San Francisco. The policy proved effective: Indians had the highest rejection rate of any Asian immigrant. Immigration agents, directed by their national superiors, claimed Indians would be unable to secure work and would thus become public charges. They were also directed to consider Indians as carriers of disease, resulting in long quarantines and/or costly medical interventions. These measures were fiercely contested by migrants and their allies. Indian farmers, labor contractors, intellectuals, and other laborers appeared at the many hearings to attest to the availability of jobs and to guarantee their support should that prove to not be the case. Yet agents persevered in the lie about the lack of work, adding that, even if there was demand, Indians would remain unemployed, given westerners' prejudices. Aided by consulate employees in India and other parts of the empire discouraging Indians from migrating to the United States by 1909, San Francisco immigration officers had reduced legal Indian entries to a few hundred people.[87]

The American measures were still far short of British ambassador James Bryce's request that the US government ban Indian migrants, as it had done with the Chinese in 1882. Radical activist Taraknath Das, then of British Columbia, publicly thanked the US government for declining the British request. It was a commitment, however, that proved short-lived: US authorities moved pitilessly against Indians with the outbreak of World War I.[88]

The multiple British, Canadian, and US immigration measures in the wake of the 1907 violence were enacted by distinct national entities with differing political necessities. For Indians, however, the

Indian Entrants by Year

Year	Canada	USA	Event
1905	45	145	
1906	387	271	
1907	2,124	1,072	Anti-Asian riots across the West
1908	2,623	1,710	
1909	0	337	Continuous Journey in Effect
1910		1,782	St. Johns riot March 1910
1911		517	
1912		165	
1913		188	
Total Emigres:	5,179	6,187	

The above chart is not static; people crossed and re-crossed borders. The estimates below differ due to so-called legal and illegal migration, how people were categorized upon entry, and the overall infancy of border controls.

Figures for Canada from Puri, *Ghadar Movement*, 15–16; figures for USA from Jogesh C. Misrow, "East Indian Immigration on the Pacific Coast" (master's thesis, Stanford University, 1915), 11, https://www.saada.org/item/20120123-599.

- January-October 1907: 11,440 Asians, including 8,125 Japanese, 2,047 South Asians, and 1,266 Chinese disembarked in B.C. (Lee, "Hemispheric Orientalism," 25–26).
- Indians estimated in Canada after 1908: 3,500. Some Indians left for the U.S. for work and due to the political atmosphere in B.C. (Puri, *Ghadar Movement*, 16).
- 1899-1913: 6,656 Indians officially entered the U.S. (Ramnath, *Haj to Utopia*, 17).
- Estimates of the total number of Indians in North America range from 6.000-7, 000 to 10,000. 200-300 of these migrants were likely students (Ramnath, *Ghadar Movement*, 17).
- For comparison, 25,000 Chinese were estimated to reside in Vancouver in 1906 (Jensen, *Passage from India*, 62).

measures fashioned a singular, hemispheric racial cordon and political jolt; its impact both deeply personal and, ultimately, collectively transformative.[89]

Most immediately, the meaning and effect of the Continuous Journey measure was not fully apparent to Indians. Straightaway, hundreds were caught in transit. In Canada, people disembarked ships from Hong Kong in full keeping with previous immigration rules and after raising heartbreaking amounts of money, only to be turned away. Others found themselves suddenly stuck in global ports, scrambling to trade or book new passages as Canada's doors slammed closed. Often those new tickets were to the United States, where, unknown to most, entrance had become as tenuous as the prejudices and mood of a US immigration officer.[90] But as Indians pieced together the stories and implications of the Continuous Journey provision, it became a moment of truth: they had again been betrayed by the very empire that had promised them equality.

As Indians' anger rose, government officials added still more fuel to the fire. In 1909, not content with a de facto ban on Indian migration, British Columbian officials, in consultation with British colonial authorities, moved to rid Canada of Indians altogether. They proposed that Indians in British Columbia voluntarily relocate to Honduras, a British plantation state. A highly skeptical delegation of Indians accompanied British Columbian authorities to investigate the country's conditions firsthand. What they found were Indian contract laborers— coolies—in destitute conditions begging for assistance and cautioning their Canadian brethren to never set foot in the country. When the enraged delegates returned to British Columbia, they and the wider Indian community resoundingly denounced the proposal.[91]

Unable to remove all Indians from Canada or to control US policy with respect to Indian migration, British authorities considered how to mitigate its political effect in and out of Hindustan. British fears were strikingly specific: they were worried Indians would experience, and then expect, political freedoms. As Taraknath Das argued, the British Honduras scheme exposed British willingness to export Indians by the shipload to British plantations but its *fear* of Indian settlement in lands with broad democratic rights.[92] Punjab Lieutenant Governor Michael O'Dwyer, who presided over the vicious wartime clampdown on Ghadar, agreed that "the atmosphere of freedom was false and the atmosphere of slavery was a healthy one."[93]

Historian Harish Puri cites exchanges between Indian government officials and their counterparts in Canada and London, detailing fears that: (1) close familiarity with white laborers would undermine British prestige, given the myth of white supremacy was fundamental to British colonial rule; (2) Vancouver had socialists, and Indians might become imbued with the doctrine; and (3) any discrimination or violence against Indians abroad would fuel nationalist sentiment in India. Or as British Brigadier-General Swayne warned, immigrants in North America would "go back to India and preach ideas of emancipation which would upset the machinery of law and order." [94] British fears were borne out, and authorities scrambled to contain the rising threat to colonial law and order. Their answer was to surveil, disrupt, and murder Indian radical organizers.[95] As Canada was ultimately under British rule, it did so with a freedom it did not enjoy in the United States.

At the bidding of British colonial authorities, Canada formed a police unit initially focused on Indians in British Columbia. The unit was headed by William Hopkinson, a multilingual former Calcutta police officer of European and Indian descent who became a BC immigration agent. Hopkinson, who accompanied the Indian delegation to British Honduras, began his job spying on and disrupting the increasingly enraged Indian community upon his return to Canada. Hopkinson's reach enlarged further when he was hired as an agent for the US Bureau of Immigration to assist in the US detention of Indian migrants and detection of Indian radicals, especially at Angel Island. This one man, and the network of informants he recruited, inaugurated a West Coast–wide spying apparatus against the restive community.[96]

One moment captures the tenor and threat of Indians' rising discontent. Like many Sikhs in British Columbia, Bhai Bhag Singh, a leader in the Vancouver gurdwara, was a veteran of the British Indian Army. In October 1909, after years of loyal service, Bhai Bhag Singh, Natha Singh, and other veterans fueled a bonfire outside the temple with their military papers, uniforms, and photographs. As Natha Singh avowed, "Our uniforms and medals show that we have fought for the British as mercenaries against our own countrymen and to enslave other Asian nations. The uniforms and medals are the symbols of our slavery."[97]

With the flames, they publicly severed their ties with the Crown, and the gurdwara thereafter banned the wearing of British military regalia on the premises.[98]

It is hard to overstate this act of political symbolism. In British Columbia's climate of antipathy and suppression, it was courageous. It also signified a rejection of previous loyalties, rights, and privileges (preserving one's paperwork was a requirement for continuing veteran payments and other benefits).[99] Their act also highlights the rapidity of political changes in the community. After a racial attack just two years earlier, an Everett, Washington, newspaper described Indians walking the town's streets, "tall, erect, decorated with medals awarded for signal bravery while in the British military service in India," and so asserting their value to the empire.[100] Certainly not all Indians in Vancouver had come to a similar conclusion, but it marked a turning point. That these veterans, supported by their major cultural institution, would repudiate their military service foreshadowed Ghadar—which translates as mutiny or revolt—in both timing and content. The 1907 North American riots occurred fifty years after the 1857 troop mutiny against British rule, which was saved, in large measure, by the loyalty of uniformed Sikhs.

The protest also underscores the importance of Vancouver as a militant Indian center. Nationalists Taraknath Das and Gurdit Kumar were part of Vancouver's radicalized community before being forced to leave the country due to their politics. Once in Seattle, Das and Kumar organized study groups of students and Indian millworkers, and directly aided the radicalization of the St. Johns community.[101] Das, Kumar, Natha Singh, Bhai Bhag Singh, and others exemplified what the British feared about Vancouver radicals' effect on Indian migrants in the West.

It is perhaps not altogether remarkable then that, in 1914, inside the Vancouver gurdwara, veteran Bhai Bhag Singh was murdered by Bela Singh, a Hopkinson informant. Bhai Bhag Singh was, by then, a leader in the Ghadar Party, and his murder occurred amid a dramatic and bitter Canadian immigration fight. Police informant Bela Singh was tried for killing Bhai Bhag Singh in Vancouver's downtown courthouse. During the trial, Mewa Singh—on the courthouse steps and in broad daylight—assassinated Agent Hopkinson in retribution. Hopkinson's 1914 funeral procession was that of a state dignitary, one of the largest in Vancouver's history. On the day Mewa Singh was executed by state authorities, Indians gathered in solidarity outside the prison walls, and four hundred attended Mewa's funeral.[102] It was a sign of things to come: of Indians refusal to be cowed or subjugated, and authorities' brutal response.

In sum, in the aftermath of the 1907 white riots, global politicians purposefully moved to control the threat of Indian radicalism to the British Empire, a path they would escalate during and after World War I. Following 1907, their many stratagems were focused on Canada, home to the largest Indian community in North America, a country founded on white supremacy and beholden to the British Empire. But their impact defied borders and flowed through the global community and back to India. Taken together, colonial authorities' reaction spurred a game-changing reckoning in the Indian community. It fully flowered a few years later among laborers in Oregon, in the wake of the 1910 St. Johns riot and with the formation of Ghadar in Astoria in 1913.

Oregon's Indian community blossomed from the secondary migration of those relocating from British Columbia, Washington, and California, largely after 1907. Oregon did not completely escape the storm of anti-Asian violence that year; there was an attack at a mill camp in rural Boring. However, what made Oregon notable was that, unlike in Bellingham or Vancouver, BC, local authorities with British assistance tried and convicted the perpetrators. Western Oregon's relative peace—and the prosecution of its violators—is symptomatic of the region's social accord regarding race and labor and made the state understandably appealing to Indians, especially after 1907.

Oregon also had work. In both Washington state and British Columbia, Indian employment contracted substantially after 1907.[103] Not so for Western Oregon, particularly after Portland's 1905 world's fair, the Lewis & Clark Exposition. After the exposition, Oregon experienced one of its greatest economic booms—a decade of growth in commerce, real estate, and industry. The state's population grew an unprecedented 63 percent, and Portland's more than doubled.[104] New industries sprang up, old business expanded, and the economy boomed. Indians were among the tens of thousands of newcomers attracted to the region in its wake. Oregon's economy, long tied to San Francisco's fortunes, was further fueled by the devastating 1906 earthquake and fire and its subsequent rebuilding.[105] Mills across the Pacific Northwest, including in Oregon, cranked into high gear to provide construction materials; Oregon's farm products could not be shipped south fast enough.

Though records are thin and dispersed, they suggest that five hundred to seven hundred Indians resided in Oregon from roughly 1905 to 1915. All were men, except for Rattan Kaur of Astoria, wife of Bakhshish Singh Dhillon, and mother of their four children, Kartar, Karm, Budh, and Kapur.[106] Overwhelmingly, Oregon's Indian community was composed of Sikh military veterans and Sikh farmers from Punjab. Smaller groups of Muslim and Hindu intellectuals and laborers also called Oregon home, and Oregon Agricultural College (now Oregon State University) in Corvallis hosted some six students.[107]

Ranging in age from eighteen to sixty-two, Indians lived and worked from Medford to Portland, and from Astoria to The Dalles. In The Dalles, with a climate similar to Punjab, several men bought land seemingly to farm. The effort did not go well, with Bishn Singh imprisoned over a land deal gone bad, and records providing no further clues or context for his case.[108] In 1909, a crew of Sikhs worked out of Medford building rail lines.[109] In Portland, Beer, Ginga, Hardit, Kader, Mar, Masav, Nathu, and Sarvan Singh found employment in a cordage factory.[110] Portland also became home to a few small entrepreneurs, like popcorn vendor Herman Singh, who married Pearl Lilly Kahn, also a popcorn vendor, and they had a child together.[111]

Overwhelmingly, however, Indian men lived along the expansive Columbia River and labored in its many lumber mills that utilized the river as a highway to regional and international ports. Sometimes only a handful worked and lived together in small river towns like Goble, Rainier, Bridal Veil, and Hood River. Like many western workers, they were highly mobile, given the boom-and-bust nature of the western economy. They were not the worst-paid mill workers, but enjoyed some of their best wages in Oregon.[112] Records also suggest that some river mill managers passed the word about Indians' stamina and reliability, unlocking opportunities for them in Linnton and elsewhere. The largest communities, with upward of one to two hundred people each, were in St. Johns and Astoria. There most Indians were employed in the Monarch and Hammond mills, respectively, lived collectively in bunkhouses or other mill housing, with a few renting rooms in town.[113]

If not for the 1910 St. Johns "anti-Hindu" riot, Indians in Oregon might have been remembered as only a historical anomaly, if at all. Instead, local racism in St. Johns had global implications.[114] Conditioned by experiences from across the diaspora, Indians beat back their attackers that night and fought them in courtrooms of law and public opinion for the next two years. They also began studying—with the aid of Taraknath Das, Gurdit Dutt Kumar, and Pandurang Khankhoje—the reasons for their disrespect everywhere. With the timely intervention of prominent nationalist Har Dayal, then of San Francisco, they began organizing. As they mobilized up and down the Columbia River in advance of their 1913 formation of Ghadar in Astoria, they were relatively undetected by Hopkinson's fearsome political police. By 1914, when Ghadar put out the call to return to India and drive out the British, the vast majority of Indians in Oregon boarded trains and ships bound for home and inspired generations.[115]

Bhagat Singh Thind also left his mark, though not by joining those who returned. An earnest and devout college student from Amritsar, Punjab, by way of the Philippines, young Thind arrived in Astoria shortly after Ghadar's formation. He worked in Oregon mills and lived among its Indian community, including its many Ghadar activists, forming lifelong friendships and commitments. His brother Jagat was to have joined him, but was one of hundreds ensnared by the Continuous Journey provision, his ship forced back to India. Although Thind did not heed Ghadar's 1914 call to return, he assisted the organization strained by the departure of hundreds of activists and government suppression.

Thind was one of several thousand Indians who, with a variety of attitudes toward Ghadar, stayed behind and pursued an American future. While Thind continued to advocate for Indian independence, he also purchased US war bonds, enlisted in the US Army, and twice applied for citizenship. How much these actions expressed American loyalties or simply his concern for his safety and future is difficult to parse. What is certain is that the US government and much of the populace were actively engaged in depriving Indians and others of any prospects or power.[116]

As historian Adam Hochschild details, in the United States, the world war reputedly fought to make the world safe for democracy became a domestic war against democracy. It was a time marked by rampant racism, suspicion, and targeting of radicals and "foreigners," especially those not white or Protestant.[117] The specific campaign against Indians by the US and British governments was part and parcel of this broader national crusade, and Portland was no exception. Lester Humphreys, a strident nativist in the Portland federal district attorney's office, challenged a local judge's citizenship award to Thind. Feeding on entrenched colonial prejudices and laws, Humphreys kick-started an era-defining Supreme Court decision that for decades barred all Indians from US citizenship and, eventually, from even entering the country.[118]

This momentous Oregon story of Ghadar and Thind, rooted in the promises and disappointments of empires crossbred with local racial and labor politics, begins in an otherwise unremarkable timber camp, with the 1907 murder of Harnam Singh.

2

A Murder, a Fair, and Community-Building at the Margins

On the night of October 31, 1907, brothers Harnam Singh and Sporan Singh, along with an unnamed third man, were asleep in their quarters at the Jarl & Pagh Bros' Mill in rural Boring, a timber encampment about twenty miles east of Portland.[1] A day earlier, Harnam had been hired to unload the mill's ripsaw. His companions were waiting to be taken on and boarding on mill grounds in the meantime.[2]

A few miles away, J. M. Dickinson and his sons John and William, along with John Riley, Earl Ransler, Walter St. Clair, and Vernon Hawes, were out drinking in a Sandy, Oregon, saloon. The Dickinsons were well-known Boring residents and woodcutters; the others were described in newspapers as transient laborers, as lumber workers of all ethnicities often were. That Halloween night, the men's conversation turned to resentments about the Pagh's hiring of a "Hindu," and the possibility of two more joining the crew. Whatever triggered their hatred of Indians—petty jealousies, rampant anti-Indian western headlines and rumors, or a putrid mix of both—they hatched a plan to "run them out" of Boring.[3]

The gang left the bar, loaded up on guns and ammunition in Sandy, and took off for Boring. Back at the lumber camp they posted on a hill and opened "fire on the shack of Hindus." Volleys flew over the sleeping Singhs' cabin but failed to provoke the hoped-for panic. Someone then shot directly into the roof of the Singhs' cabin, but still got no response. Finally one man, likely William Dickinson, aimed directly into the Indians' quarters.[4] The rifle bullet pierced the back of Harnam Singh's thigh, shattered his femur, and exited the front of his leg. The vigilantes fled into the night, leaving Harnam critically wounded, his bunkmates horrified, and the area littered with revolver, rifle, and shotgun shell casings.[5]

Sporan Singh, Brother of Harnam Singh, the Wounded Hindu.

M. Ram, Interpreter.

"Hindu Fears Knife," *Sunday Oregonian*, November 3, 1907, p. 11. Sporan Singh, brother of Harnam Singh (left); Munshi Ram, interpreter (right). Courtesy Historic Oregon Newspapers, University of Oregon Libraries.

Widespread reports about the Boring and other western attacks underscore the reach of 1907's anti-Asian hysteria and the appetite for violence. As far away as Butte, Montana, the *Anaconda Standard* described the Boring "assault by an unknown band of Halloween hoodlums . . . with the apparent purpose of assassinating three Hindus," with "repeated volleys . . . from revolvers and rifles, about 30 shots in all being fired."[6] Unlike other cities, Portland-based newspapers reported on those who aided the Singhs, detailed the investigation into and prosecution of their attackers, and gave some limited voice to Indians' account of events.

The *Morning Oregonian*, then the Northwest's largest newspaper, reported that one of the mill owners, having either heard the shots or been summoned by Sporan or the other uninjured man, rushed to fetch the local doctor.[7] Dr. McElroy kept Harnam alive through the night, and transferred him to Portland on an Oregon Water Power and Railway car the next morning.[8] Local policing authorities met and transported Harnam to Portland's Good Samaritan Hospital. Once in the hospital, M. Ram from Portland, described as "a Hindu, who was educated in the British school in Lahore," translated Harnam's story to reporters and authorities, including the Singhs' willingness and ability to identify the attackers. The victims stated that they clearly saw their assailants, who were not fellow mill workers, but choppers seen working near the mill.[9] Doctors informed Harnam that saving his life required amputating his badly injured limb. Dependent on his physical capacities to earn a living, Harnam chanced death over the loss of his leg.[10] His gamble failed, and Harnam died on November 5, 1907, a week after the attack, a US resident for all of three weeks.[11]

Oregon governor George Chamberlain apprised Multnomah County authorities "of the enormity of the offense, and recommended prompt action in apprehending the guilty men."[12] At the scene of the crime, Constable Johnson, Justice of the Peace Jonsrud and his son, Constable Jonsrud, recognized the shell casings and a tobacco pipe as belonging to the Dickinsons.[13] *Oregonian* articles reported on the prompt arrest of all but one of the suspects (who fled town) on charges of assault and shooting with an attempt to kill.[14] With Harnam's subsequent death, murder charges were lodged, bail was revoked for the Dickinsons, and for the next six months the defendants awaited trial from inside the county jail.[15] The *Morning Oregonian* reported Harnam Singh's "friends and countrymen" hired state senator and prominent trial attorney Dan J. Malarkey to prosecute the case alongside Multnomah County district attorney Hedges.[16] The *Sunday* and *Morning Oregonian* continued their coverage in the lead-up to and during the spring 1908 murder trial.

On April 25, 1908, after deliberating thirteen hours, the jury convicted J. M. Dickenson and his son William of second-degree murder and three others of manslaughter, with penitentiary sentences of life for Dickenson and his son and one year for the others. Reportedly, the jury "believed all of the prisoners participated in the crime and the only thing that prevented a speedy verdict was a failure to agree as to what degree of murder should be assessed."[17]

With the verdict, the *Morning Oregonian* revealed its core beliefs in a brief, unsigned editorial. After disparaging Harnam Singh as a "dirty Hindu," the piece went on to chastise white workers: "The verdict rendered at Oregon City Saturday ought to have a wholesome effect on that class of individuals who are always interfering with inoffensive Hindus and other Far Eastern aliens."[18] It was a perfect encapsulation of Deady, Scott, and other elites' racial and class policy honed years earlier with the Chinese. Area industries needed those "dirty Hindus," and the writer welcomed the punishment of "the class" who interfered with their profitable labor stream.

Harnam Singh's murder was of a piece with—and a different order of magnitude of—western anti-Asian violence that year. Just two months before the Boring shooting, two hundred to three hundred Indians living and working in Bellingham, Washington, were beaten, robbed, and driven from their homes and work by hundreds of people toward the end of the Labor Day weekend. In the wake of Bellingham, violence cascaded across the state.[19] Many Indians escaped north, often on foot, to nearby British Columbia, hoping for the protection of the British Crown. Within days, however, some ten thousand Vancouverites demonstrated against Asian migrants and migration. The Vancouver rally devolved into a rampage that destroyed Japanese and Chinese homes and businesses across the city, reported by news services across China, India, and Japan. From spring through the late fall of 1907, thousands of men, women, shopkeepers, preachers, and laborers demonstrated against and attacked Chinese, Japanese, and Indian migrants in towns and camps from California to British Columbia.[20]

The hostilities of 1907 were driven by a spate of fear-mongering press reports about Asian migration in mainstream, labor, and explicitly exclusionist newspapers triggered by a spike in immigration of Chinese, Japanese, and Indians to western Canadian and US cities. Nativist organizers like the Asian Exclusion League fanned laborers' anxieties arguing that migrants, not the capitalist economy, complicated or caused western financial and employment insecurities.*

---

* Theodore Roosevelt was the US president during the many 1907 riots. Long an advocate of the white religion, he used the prodigious power of his office to defend and police whiteness. Shortly before the 1907 riots, he wrote "it is idle to blind ourselves to the fact that the English-speaking commonwealths of the sea coasts on the Pacific will not submit to the unchecked immigration of Asiatics, that they ought not to be asked to submit to it, and that if asked they will refuse" (Lee, "Hemispheric Orientalism," 35). In the wake of the 1907 West Coast violence, he made clear his solidarity with exclusionists' goals, if wanly criticizing their methods. He engaged in extensive international consultations with Canadian and English authorities in the hopes of forging a multinational response

1908 Bellingham Greets the Great White Fleet: a seamless fusion of domestic, regional and global white right. Whatcom County Historical Society.

Adding to the mix was Japan's 1905 military victory over Russia, the first modern military victory of an Asian power over a European one, and one that thrilled the colonized world. Together, Japan's victory and North America's migrant influx became a sign, as American historian, journalist, and eugenicist Lothrop Stoddard preached, of the world's "rising tide of color" that threatened white civilizations.[21]

All charges against the Bellingham rioters were dismissed because, as the *American Reveille* reported, "Not a single person in the city could be found who would positively swear in court that he saw any one of the defendants at the impromptu mass meeting held in front of the Hindu quarters on the particular night when the young men

to Asian migration. Roosevelt's greatest demonstration of white solidarity and designs on Pacific power came in December 1907; he transferred sixteen battleships, dubbed the Great White Fleet, from the Atlantic to the Pacific. After rounding South America, the ships' first ports-of-call were San Francisco and Bellingham, sites of the two largest 1907 US riots. Hundreds of thousands turned out to celebrate the fleet's arrival before the battleships continued on to Hawai'i, Australia, and New Zealand. As historian Margaret Werry writes, the fleet's message was of "national and racial solidarity on the one hand, and imperial advancement" against emergent Japan on the other (Lee, 37–38). Roosevelt's move fused white right domestically, regionally, and globally.

were alleged to have been participating in a riot."[22] Or as Portland British consulate James Laidlaw stated in his internal report, Bellingham authorities "found [it] impracticable to secure a conviction of those who were arrested for the riot, owing to the popular feeling against Hindu labour."[23] Further, in the wake of the Washington riots, most Indians found themselves locked out of millwork through World War I, an especially damaging white victory and economic blow, given the timber industry's rising dominance in the state.[24]

There were also no prosecutions in Vancouver, BC. There, authorities focused on preventing Indians' continued migration, settlement, and organizing with the establishment of special policing and surveillance officials and a series of globally crafted laws restricting immigration and settlement. Moreover, due to pervasive prejudice and its governmental endorsement, Indians were plagued by significant unemployment in British Columbia for the first time since their arrival.[25]

In the hours, days, and weeks after the 1907 violence and blowback, Indians across the Canadian and US west agonized over the cause of the hostility against them and what to do in its face. Some, despite having crossed oceans and gambled significant monies, chose to return to India. Others scrambled to navigate the dangerous and rapidly changing western conditions, but did so with little or conflicting information. Where could they work? Where was it safe? Paradoxically, Harnam Singh's story was a credible positive in Indians' calculations of a landscape of bad options. That a murder and its prosecution might attract Indians to Oregon is a damning testament of the broader realities of their lives. Yet in 1907, it was the only known case of anti-Indian violence in Oregon, and the only instance of decisive action by authorities against its perpetrators.[26]

High-level British governmental intervention factored into Oregon's emergence as a potential destination for Indians. British officials were deeply concerned about the political impact of 1907's widespread western violence not on the migrants, but on the growing anti-British sentiments in India and the diaspora. In early September, Portland British consul James Laidlaw was deployed to Washington state to assist with a riot postmortem, and his reports were transmitted, with comment, by US British ambassador James Bryce to superiors in London. Consul Laidlaw was somewhat more critical of authorities than Ambassador Bryce's cover remarks; however, both men assessed that local Washington state officials had acted appropriately in quelling the violence and protecting the Sikhs, but were constrained by, or in agreement with, the pervasive anti-Hindu sentiments.[27] Both men also acknowledged that, despite its (self-serving) desires, the British government's "powers of intervention in a State are limited" owing to the protocols of intergovernmental relations, an assessment agreed to by England's secretary of state for India, John Morley.[28] This was, of course, a colonizer's respect for approved channels and authority, one not extended to Indian people.

In Oregon, by contrast, the interests of powerful Oregon political figures and British authorities better aligned. Regional political differences with respect to matters of race and labor, while still rooted in white supremacy and class exploitation, provided options the British did not enjoy in Washington state. With Harnam Singh's death, Consul Laidlaw "called upon Oregon's Governor who immediately telegraphed the local authorities to prosecute the perpetrators of the outrage to the utmost, and six men and boys are now in gaol [jail] charged with murder."[29] Secretary of State for India Morley urged, through consulate channels, that "His Majesty's government should be represented in the forthcoming trial."[30] Seeking to intervene in local affairs without stirring parochial passions, the British government was likely the "friends and countrymen" local newspapers reported as having hired Oregon attorney Malarkey.

Consul Laidlaw, who was at the center of and lauded for his efforts, discounted Boring's impact on Indians: "This case has, however, little significance beyond showing the widespread feeling against the influx of Hindus into the country."[31] On that account he proved quite wrong.

Just days after the Boring attack, Portland was clearly on Indians' radar. A November 4 headline from Everett, another Washington town where Indians were attacked without legal consequence, stated "Hindus Are Leaving City, Aliens Alarmed by Saturday's Demonstration, Are Taking Departure. Many Going to Portland." The article reported they were "seeking new and more friendly pastures."[32] Enjoying no protection in Everett, they sought out the places where headlines and community networks told them they might work in greater safety.[33] Consul Laidlaw's reports partially track their movements, noting "some passed through here [Portland] on their way to California."[34] He noted the small group who made their way to the southern Oregon coastal town of Marshfield (now Coos Bay), where they were again expelled by laborers with the assistance of local authorities.[35] Laidlaw, however, did not report on the emergence of budding communities.

While Oregon was new to Indians' information networks, given how few by then had passed through its territory, they nonetheless noted and navigated state and regional differences.[36] Through an active and experimental process, they crafted decisions that shaped both their daily lives and, ultimately, their organizing. Arrival routes, censuses, and local patchy sources read through the lens of regional violence and constricted employment sketch the genesis story of the Columbia River settlements that became sites of historic Indian resistance.[37]

Most of the eight-thousand-some Indian migrants entered North America through the major ports of Victoria, Vancouver, Seattle, and San Francisco. These large immigration checkpoints generated records. Photos of docked ships waiting processing capture Sikh, Muslim, and other Indians on board. Logs riddled with inaccuracies nonetheless provide names, entry dates, ages, or professions of Indians who came ashore and a baseline for tracking a mobile community. Agents in these major immigration control centers later became critical actors in the multigovernment campaigns against Indian anticolonial organizing.

While hundreds of "Singhs" entered the port of San Francisco from 1900 to 1910, none were recorded in Oregon harbors.[38] For Indians, Oregon ports never grew to the bureaucratic scale and importance of other western cities. Additionally, in the eyes of federal authorities, the Oregon immigration apparatus was tainted by the area's racial politics, particularly its judiciary. Altogether, this produced an unexpected upside for Indians by reversing the dominant surveillance dynamics. The leaner immigration organization left fewer records documenting Indians' arrival in the state but weakened the surveillance and policing apparatus soon arrayed against them. What Oregon did offer, and Indians utilized, was a broad, navigable river running from the Pacific Ocean to Idaho, and well connected to regional rail lines.[39]

Indians arriving in Oregon by train, foot, or river steamer were overwhelmingly secondary migrants from California, Washington, and British Columbia. The US government census—the primary official records that document their presence—reveal no Indians in Oregon in 1900, a community by 1910, and only seventy-five to a hundred men remaining in 1920. Census reports are marred by language differences, and the misunderstandings and prejudices of door-to-door canvassers. The trepidations of interviewees also skewed information about names, birthplaces and parents, age, language abilities, or education. For their part, tasked with fitting these newcomers into the US racial hierarchy, but unclear how to do so, census workers recorded Indians as white, black, mulatto, or even octoroon.[40] Detailing early Indian communities is further complicated by their frequent movement from job to job, town to town, state to state, and globally. Still, in 1910, canvassers documented, and likely undercounted, Indian communities, mostly in mill towns along the Columbia River from Astoria to The Dalles.[41]

Despite their copious details and big-picture view, the censuses are utterly silent on the political transformations and agency shaping Indian demographics, let alone capturing how they felt upon arrival in the state. Yet buried within the documented years of the community's growth between 1900 and 1910 are two events with particular salience for Indians: Portland's 1905 world's fair, and the Boring murder prosecution. Read in the practical necessities of Indians' lives, the 1905 world's fair meant jobs, and the Boring conviction suggested a measure of safety. Both were in short supply for Indians of the west, and both were significantly shaped by Portland newspaperman Harvey Scott.

In the late 1800s, newspaperman Harvey Scott stood tall among the prominent leaders in Portland who welcomed Chinese migrants, not as equals and fellow citizens, but as needed laborers. He and other powerful men reasoned that riots, beatings, and murders were bad for business and by opposing such—with laws, policing, and his newspaper editorials—they could attract and retain Chinese laborers as a needed local labor force.[42] Indians' position in Western Oregon was intimately tied to this policy toward Chinese immigrants, with the trial and imprisonment of Harnam Singh's murders testament to local officials' commitment to their anti-communal-violence strategy.

Scott also served as a president of Portland's ponderously named world's fair, the Lewis & Clark Centennial and American Pacific Exposition and Oriental Fair, which opened on June 1, 1905. Over the next four months, one to two million people walked through its grand doors

Astoria

	Esr Singh	Marre Singh	
	Ganga Singh	Metz Singh	
Amr Singh	Gasava Singh	Munshi Karim Ram	
Argensa Singh	Gerbachen Singh	Munshi Ram	
Babo Singh	Gudid Singh	Narian Singh	
Bahader Singh	Hagara Singh	Pakker Singh	
Ban Singh	Hajour Singh	Pakhr Singh	
Bar Singh	Hardet Singh	Peter Singh	
Basnt Singh	Hookam Singh	Pohauen Singh	
Boga Singh	Inder Singh	Ram Singh	
Bud Singh	Jager Singh	Ri Singh	
Butra Singh	Jenda Singh	Santa Singh	
Butte Singh	John Singh	Saporn Singh	
Butte B.S. Singh	Jowanda Singh	Sarin Singh	
Caser Singh	Kesar Thathgarh Singh	Shanker Khan	
Dahna Singh	Ksai Singh	Singh, Marre	
EA Singh	Lal Singh	Sunder Singh	
Esar Singh	Mala Singh	Surain Singh	
Esor Singh	Manga Singh	Tota Singh	
		Tova Singh	

Clatskanie

Bhagat Singh
Bhawan Singh
Bita Singh
Bleagot Singh
Boor Singh
Dewa Singh
Ganda Singh
Indor Singh
Jaget Singh
Jaget Singh
Jai Singh
Labh Singh
Narain Singh
Rud Singh
Samand Singh
Sunder Singh
Sunder Singh
Surain Singh
Surain Singh
Surain Singh

Goble

Chanda Singh
Fanj Singh
Jawand Singh
Karbant Singh
Ofagar Singh
Sohn Singh
Sunder Singh
Suraien Singh
Wasawa Singh

John Day

Ahmed Khan	Dovna Singh	Jowala Khan	Natha Singh
Ajmat Khan	Fattah Khan	Kan Singh	Niamat Khan
Arjan Singh	Firman Singh	Kartar Singh	Nowab Khan
Bashanta Singh	Ganda Khan	Kehr Singh	Omar Singh
Bhag Singh	Ganda Singh	Lan Singh	Pakher Singh
Bhan Singh	Ganga Singh	Marain Singh	Rulia Singh
Budh Singh	Gurbachan Singh	Massa Singh	Santa Singh
Chanda Singh	Gurbachan Singh	Mastan Singh	Sikander Khan
Chanda Singh	Harman Singh	Moti Singh	Sunder Singh
Chet Singh	Ishar Singh	Naram Singh	Umar Khan
Dalel Khan	Jhanda Singh	Nassrulla Khan	Usaf Khan
Dogar Singh	Jindo Singh	Natha Khan	Wamdar Khan
			Wasan Singh

Rainier

(Punjabis located at this site. Detailed records unknown)

St. Johns

Ali Mahamed	Hazara Singh
Ali Raka	Indar Singh
B Singh	Jagal Singh
Basant Singh	John Kim
Batan Singh	John Sandi
Ber Singh	Konah Singh
Cashar Singh	Mahamed Alah
Chand Kim	Sanda Singh
Chand Khem	Singh Singh
D. Singh	Suba Singh
Ganga Singh	Succha Singh
Harnan Singh	Surin Singh

Seaside

H. Khan
Krem Khan
M. Khan

Portland

Beer Singh	Kader Singh	Masav Singh	
Boggit Singh	Kanshi Ram	Mat. Singh	Sohan Bhakna Singh
Hardit Singh	Lahna Singh	Matah Singh	Sunder Singh
Ganda Singh	M. Singh	Naidu Singh	Thakar Das Dhuri
Gings Singh	Makand Singh	Nathu Singh	Udham Kasel Singh
Hernan Singh	Mar Singh	Noud Singh	Wasava Singh
Jawnar Singh	Marca Singh	Ron Singh	Wasawa Singh
John Singh	Masas Singh	Sarvan Singh	Wasawa Singh

Linnton

Hun Khan
Mahamond Khan
Unerak Iphsahan

100

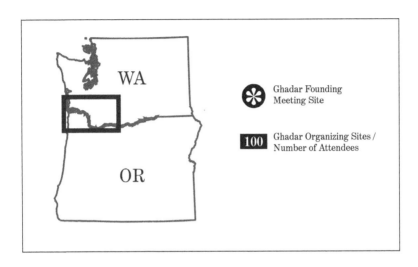

Ghadar Founding
Meeting Site

100 Ghadar Organizing Sites /
Number of Attendees

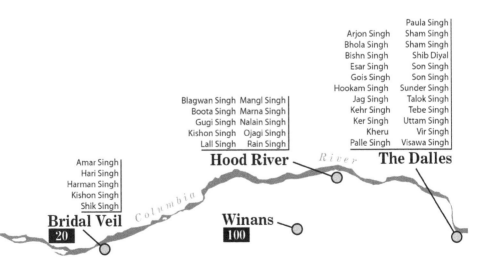

Paula Singh
Arjon Singh   Sham Singh
Bhola Singh   Sham Singh
Bishn Singh   Shib Diyal
Esar Singh   Son Singh
Gois Singh   Son Singh
Hookam Singh   Sunder Singh
Jag Singh   Talok Singh
Kehr Singh   Tebe Singh
Ker Singh   Uttam Singh
Kheru   Vir Singh
Palle Singh   Visawa Singh

Blagwan Singh   Mangl Singh
Boota Singh   Marna Singh
Gugi Singh   Nalain Singh
Kishon Singh   Ojagi Singh
Lall Singh   Rain Singh

Hood River   *River*   **The Dalles**

Amar Singh
Hari Singh
Harman Singh
Kishon Singh
Shik Singh

Bridal Veil   *Columbia*
20

Winans
100

emblazoned with the watchword "Westward the Course of Empire Takes Its Way."[43] Following the US west's frenzied industrialization, businessmen were hungry for new outlets for their products. Powerful Portlanders were also worried about rising competition from Washington ports and lumber barons.[44] In 1905, exposition backers aimed to promote and build Portland as the peerless commercial capital for the US empire, its gaze firmly set on the lucrative markets across the Pacific Ocean.[45] The exposition's glistening, if impermanent, complex conveyed Portland boosters' designs on what they rightly saw as the dawning new age of Pacific trade. It was Portland's grand, international advertisement for the settlers and investors required to create that hoped-for reality.[46]

Organizers' dreams were met a thousand fold, netting a tidy 21 percent rate of return on investment.[47] More enduringly, the exposition proved to be Portland's gateway to the twentieth century, and the Pacific trade it envisioned still dominates the state's economy.[48] The exposition delivered unrivaled economic and population growth that boomed for seven long years.[49] Tens of thousands were hired by newly minted or expanded industries, and real estate sales boomed.[50] If Portland and environs generally felt like opportunity, it was perhaps doubly so for Indians, given their constricted racial and economic status elsewhere. Oregon's economic expansion was, however, wrapped in the exposition's unapologetic racial playbook, expressive of the global and regional politics that shaped Indians' lives.

Scott, with others, framed and promoted the exposition in impeccably imperial terms. His July 1905 *Pacific Monthly* magazine article, titled "Momentous Struggle for Mastery of the Pacific," was overlaid across photographs of the exposition grounds and opening ceremonies, illustratively situating the Oregon exposition in the schema of America's larger imperial project. In it Scott wrote, "Our own interest in the Pacific, which started with the establishment of our cordon of states on this western verge of the continent, has been prodigiously increased and magnified by the acquisition of the Hawaiian and the Philippine Islands." Omitting the horrors of American "acquisition" for the people of the Philippines, Scott argued the possessions were only the beginning of US designs on Asia. He described the 1905 conflict between Japan and Russia as simply "fighting the preliminary battle of all nations that want an equal chance on the Pacific," especially the China trade.[51] For Scott, it was America's fate to take up this challenge; Western colonization, led by Portland, must continue across the Pacific to ensure America's promise. One lobbyist, seeking federal exposition funds, argued the sole obstacle in meeting its historic destiny was Portland's lack of "enough people to break the soil and fell the trees," which promoters hoped the exposition would solve by attracting new residents.[52] In an irony born of global colonialism, Indians escaping British subjugation and the 1907 racial violence and economic constriction helped fulfill the exposition's mission.

From promotional materials to the in-person exposition experience, organizers sought to enlist Oregonians and visiting westerners in their vision of the economic expansion, jobs, and consumer goods to be had through continued westward colonization and its underlying racial outlook. The exposition tied local prosperity and national expansion to America's civilizing mission. Its built environment was highly curated, reflecting the racial hierarchy of the times. Europe and Asia each had stand-alone buildings.[53] Over the "Oriental Building" (as the publication called it), however, was affixed an American eagle and inside were goods, primarily from Japan, all displayed in a sea of American red, white, and blue. As the *Oregon Daily Journal* reported "the idea one received immediately [of the Oriental Building] . . . is America looking toward the orient. Below are the nations of the orient with their old ideas and customs, while above, looking over the whole, is America, extending to these countries her civilization through the medium of education." The "East" was seen through the imperial gaze and for the sole purpose of America's gain.[54]

Once inside the gates, millworker, butcher, seamstress, and doctor walked shoulder to shoulder through the exposition's symbolically composed paths.[55] Along them, thousands of daily visitors not only encountered global products and goods, they also observed Native Americans, Filipinos, and Chinese displayed, zoo-like, on the entertainment trail as objects of global Western progress, not as fellow builders of an entwined future. Fairgoers' close-up inspection of nonwhite peoples in the staged and hierarchical portrayal of difference promoted "a collectivity of sameness among white visitors" in contrast to the staged "other" before them. As historian Emily Trafford further writes, the fair and its exhibits "visualized the progress of the American nation from its indigenous past to its imperial future and plotted the position of various non-white races in relation to its own achievements. . . . It was a performance of white supremacy that would continue to influence their thoughts and actions long after the fair gates had closed."[56]

This was the present and imagined Oregon into which brown-skinned, often turbaned Indians arrived in the years after the exposition's close in the fall of 1905. In the pages of the *Oregonian,* Indians inhabited the journalistic world of the exotic, racialized, "picturesque representative" of global peoples, ever distinct from the "average" American. In the exposition's schema, they were the peoples and of the lands to be exploited for the benefit of Oregon's white Eden.

Not surprisingly, the exposition's script of unfettered white progress did not play out so neatly in the day-to-day reality of Oregon life. Its dreamscape was erected atop a global dynamic of industrial expansion premised on white supremacy and class exploitation. And laborers—white and nonwhite alike—consistently failed to stay on point. The events in Boring illuminate the basic predicament for Oregon's elite: their efforts to control white violence—for example, the Boring prosecution—attracted Chinese, Indian, and other nonwhite, and often underpaid, workers, the very people who triggered white laborers' panic. It was an arrogant striving to control laborers' competing notions of, and claims to, standing and personhood that the powerful, of course, fostered. The exposition's aftermath threw these dynamics into high gear.

As one small part of the tide of thousands who arrived in Oregon after 1905, Indians labored in lumber mills and lived and shopped in towns up and down the mighty Columbia River. They did so among others similarly driven by the racial and economic necessities and possibilities of the day. Together people navigated and negotiated the shared spaces of towns, mills, and bunkhouses, but without the exposition's curated racial and class guardrails. Some whites—like the Dickinsons in Boring—grew angry or anxious when faced with the many nonwhites in post-exposition Oregon enabling its rapidly expanding industries.[57] They found themselves sharing jobs and towns not with dioramic set pieces, but with actual Indians and others who, metaphorically, had jumped the exposition's ropes and claimed their right to be. There were frictions, large and small, but also unexpected alliances and newfound visions.

Amid these discordant Oregon realties, Indian laborers built community and wrote an unscripted chapter to the playbook of their times. Their very suppression in North America helped nurture a collective identity, softening any divides among Muslims, Sikhs, and Hindus.[58] As Hindu M. Ram translated and helped raise funds for the Sikh gunshot victims in Boring, they acted as "Indians" against a besieged "Hindu" other, a scenario repeated across the North American west.

This "Indian-ness" resonated with other communities around them and became woven into their resistance. In North America, Indians moved among thousands of other global workers in an era of nationalist revolutions in Mexico, China, Ireland, and Egypt; the radical labor and internationalist organizing of the Industrial Workers of the World (IWW or Wobblies); and the many North American multiethnic socialists. As simultaneously socially reviled yet economically essential peoples, Indians lived segregated from the mainstream, and as integral members of this expansive global workforce. In these new lands, among new people and in a new social nexus, Indians fashioned means to cope and endure, and to ally and resist.

In important ways, Oregon's Indian community took shape in an environment distinct from other enclaves across the North American west. California's Indian farm owners and agricultural workers were scattered across miles of fields; in Oregon, Indians lived and worked in close proximity, possessed little or no land, and harbored few landbased dreams of permanence. Washington's massive lumber mills dwarfed those of Oregon and spawned a treacherous political atmosphere. Grays Harbor, just north of Astoria, was the world's leading lumber port from 1906 to 1910, and its mills created semi-dystopian landscapes riven by internecine class warfare accompanied by statesanctioned violence and industry-hired thugs.[59] Oregon laborers did not experience the scale of violence that accompanied much of Washington and western labor organizing, a fact that aided Indians' budding resistance. Crucially, by living outside of Canada, Indians were out from under the immediate thumb of the British and the lethal political police stalking the community in British Columbia. This was helped by Oregon being overwhelmingly an Indian laboring community. Though

Consul Laidlaw tracked laborers' movements, his and others' notes
and reports make clear he did not consider them any real threat, unlike
students or overt nationalists. It was a mistake repeated by other officials through the years.[60]

Within the psychic and social space Oregon afforded, Indians navigated and utilized its openings and varied social tolerances and built
community and tools of resistance with what they had. Fewer Indians
migrated to Oregon, and they arrived later and were largely millworkers, not property owners or businessmen; they established no temples,
mosques, or other formal cultural institutions. In Stockton, California,
and Vancouver, BC, such establishments were epicenters of cultural
continuity and resistance open to all faiths and creeds. Indians were
not, however, culturally impoverished in Oregon. They sustained their
faith without dedicated structures, and they built essential bonds utilizing both familiar tools and those newly at hand. Bunkhouses, politics, and sports were more informal, ephemeral, and left fewer records
than built institutions, but proved to be vital hubs of Indian persever-
ance and resistance. These more fleeting forms also proved nimble in
culture and expectation and, eventually, in evading authorities' eyes.

The Indian community left little of their own voices behind; activists' later memoirs are devoted to accounting for their political movement, not their everyday.[61] They inhabited countries that mythologized
permanence, settlement, and whiteness. Canadian and US historical
archives replicate that bias and silence the diverse, lived reality of the
global community at the heart of their respective national expansions.
Long are property, marriage, and business records, but few are the
details of the west's transient millions who mined, milled, lumbered,
and made community where and with whom they might.[62]

Before Indians in Oregon forged a resistance movement, they
gradually and organically constructed what activist and writer Janet
Dewart Bell terms a "cultural architecture for change."[63] Sketching its
contours requires desegregating Indians from accounts of their multinational coworkers and stirring Indo-Canadian and autobiographi-
cally informed fiction into Oregon's few archival scraps. It is in part
a construct, yet less imaginary than a community without bonds and
activism without foundation.[64]

Work was at the center of Indians' collective lives across the North American west, and they banded together in self-selected crews. Those with the requisite language skills and self-assurance negotiated their terms of hire. They sustained one another if work was scarce. While they had staid businessmen and political and religious thinkers in their midst, Indians lacked a sizable overlay of conservatizing elements. In this, Indians were markedly different from Chinese workers, who were often beholden to powerful contractors.

The Six Companies was an association of Chinese organizations, headed by merchants rooted in Chinese provinces, which amalgamated to regulate life in the new world, including as labor contractors. San Francisco's Chinese Six Companies often advanced laborers' overseas travel costs, negotiated employment terms, sometimes intervened with western industrialists, and required the repayment of all debts before laborers could return to China. The company was deeply entangled with the Chinese monarchy, had an enormous financial stake in the maintenance of a malleable and available workforce, and, frequently, if not always successfully, worked to counter nationalist influences in the Chinese overseas community. Many Chinese businessmen also amassed fortunes by providing goods and services to North America's Chinese laboring community.[65] In contrast, Indian businessmen, like Oregon labor contractor Kanshi Ram/John Kim and California potato farmer Jawala Singh, became Ghadar organizers and financial backers.[66]

Similarly, Indians were not subject to a significant conservatizing religious hierarchy. In North America, gurdwaras became centers of resistance; in India much of the Sikh religious hierarchy allied with the British during World War I and considered the returning radicals apostates.[67] British consulate records reflect government agents' cognizance of the impact of differing cultural and labor organizations. Reports from police agent Hopkinson discussed the merits of establishing groups similar to those of the Chinese and Japanese as a means of undermining the influence of Indian nationalists on immigrants.[68] Instead, in North America, Indians lived as an unmediated community of a few banned radicals and thousands of racialized workers relatively free from a suppressive labor and religious hierarchy.

Bunkhouses were important to laborers of all ethnicities, who lacked the solid homes and family life afforded by higher paid and more stable working-class jobs. Tens of thousands of men and women occupied the bottom rungs of working-class life, expected to move on when work dried up or a mill shut down. Laborers faced keeping body and soul together in the chaos surrounding them, yet were never lionized as symbols of rugged western individualism. Instead, the tumult of their lives became another confirmation of their lack of respectability; their transitoriness further branding them as outsiders.[69] For many laborers, bunkhouses, often crowded and lacking rudimentary comforts, became a staple of life and were key to labor organizing such as that done by the IWW.

Indians were no different. Many in Astoria and St. Johns—towns central to later Ghadar organizing in Oregon—lived in and carried out their day-to-day lives in mill bunkhouses and other constellations of collective housing. The most well-known Oregon community of Indians congregated along the waterfront near the Hammond mill in Alderbrook, a district on the eastern edge of Astoria, where Indians occupied bunkhouses and a few small stand-alone houses. From about 1906 until the mill burned down in the fall of 1922, that area of Birch Street between Fifty-First and Fifty-Second Streets was known as Astoria's Hindu Alley.[70] In St. Johns, Indians were employed by Monarch Mill, which operated a bunkhouse on the northern margins of town that was home to Indians and others. In both towns, men also lived in small apartments above downtown businesses or, like Kanshi Ram/ John Kim, rented rudimentary quarters near the mill and the town's center or, like wrestler Dodan Singh, lived on the edges of Astoria's Chinese neighborhood.

Theirs were predominantly communities of Punjabi Sikhs, joined by Hindus and Muslims, some from different regions of India, but all laboring men from nineteen to sixty-plus years in age. Beyond their numbers, the conditions of their lives shaped a hypermasculine culture. Work, politics, and sport all inspired laborers' physical contests with the environment or with athletic, class, or national rivals. Although the mills employed few women, St. Johns and Astoria were filled with women working as domestics, mothers, laundresses, gardeners, prostitutes, shopkeepers, and printers. The politics of labor and nationalism,

Indian Residents of Astoria, Clatsop County Historical Society (CCHS), Photo 10,506-00D

however, were too often male purviews. With the notable exception of the IWW and Astoria's Finnish and other Socialists, few political alliances had explicit concern for women's rights in the workplace, suffrage, or reproductive rights and domestic equality.[71]

It is difficult to imagine Indians did not sometimes dream of home, including of lives with the mothers, wives, or children some left behind. Looking out at the Columbia or Willamette Rivers perhaps

triggered their memories. Punjab translates as "the land of five rivers" and, like home, the mighty waters flowed and made life happen
in Oregon. But now they saw and smelled towering Douglas firs, not
mango trees or cotton and rice fields. Instead of shopping in lanes
filled with familiar people, brightly colored clothes, and a common
tongue, in Oregon they walked cool, gray, rain-filled streets and
heard a myriad of unaccustomed languages—Greek, Italian, Chinese,
Gaelic, Finnish, and more. They labored in both lands, but the rou-
tines of the farmer or the vendor were traded for the regime of an
industrial worker. Maybe some old ways crept in—someone kept a
cow nearby for milk or tended a garden. But their work and social lives
had changed dramatically.[72]

In their new lives, the mill whistle called them to work. Frequently,
an ex-military man gathered the dungareed and often turban-clad crew
and marched them into the mill armed with leather aprons and gloves,
passing other gangs with other languages.[73] Their days were immersed
in the noise of the saws and chains. Known for their animated speech
and spirit, amid the din of work the Punjabis likely raised their voices
to talk or joke with friends, braiding their words into the soundtrack
of industry. Among industry managers, they held a solid reputation.
They also quickly learned that, no matter their efforts or skills, some
positions and wages would never be offered to them. Walking home at
day's end, they saw the solid homes of men better rewarded than they.
But they also saw the Turks, Greeks, Finns, Swedes, or Irish returning
to bunkhouses or perhaps worse—broken-down shacks in the nearby
forest. Relatives in Punjab likely never imagined the day-to-day realities that generated their remittances. [74]

At the end of the day, they had the comradery of the bunkhouse,
where their language and ways could hold sway.[75] Like other migrants,
they remade home among the unfamiliar, adapting old to new and making both change and continuity part of their personal landscape. Many
formed a cooperative kitchen, pitching in for food and paying a man
to cook with a wage equal to their mill earnings. At the end of a ten-
or twelve-hour shift, they were assured of a ready meal and familiar
smells. In their cramped quarters, ample space was given over to the
pile of dirty, wet coats and boots from work and to spaces for sleep.
Yet surely, and however modestly, they decorated, making housing into

a semblance of home. Memories brightened their rooms, with drawings or photos of beloved fields, rivers, and family. Aspirations adorned their walls, whether religious saints or nationalist heroes, life-affirming scripture or stirring words of banned activists and poets.[76]

Come dawn, the ambrosia hour for Sikhs, an observant's recitation formed many Indians' first morning sounds, as people still practiced their faith without formal temples. Other homes filled with Muslims' early morning remembrances of God or a Hindu's personal offering to a deity. The patting out and cooking of chapatis and making of tea soon followed. The morning meal was quiet and efficient as they dressed and readied for work. But in the evening, like most of us who work, they surely decompressed from the demanding day. They complained to those they trusted. They gossiped. They told stories of ludicrous situations, idiot coworkers, hilarious occurrences or near misses on the green chain and loading docks. Boots were tossed and water splashed while they cleaned up as they could. There were petty squabbles and ongoing jokes, and men's shouts and laughter could be heard outside the walls. They sought advice on money, love, family, or legal matters. Some nights, they tended to the wounds from the day, as all the work associated with the once-towering trees was dangerous except for that done by its accountants or owners. But with appetites born of strenuous labor, they sat and ate together, some drinking tea, some whiskey, but all adding the clinking of plates, cups, and cleanup to the sounds of the evening.[77]

Some nights featured readings or debates. Most of the men, but not all, had little formal schooling and never learned to read or write. But here too, people pitched in. Literate laborers read to others. College students joined them at the mill to earn tuition and living expenses for their school year, like Pandurang Khankhoje, soon a Ghadar leader, and Bhagat Singh Thind, soon famous for his US citizenship case.[78] At the invitation of Hammond workers, Ram Chandra, a principal propagandist for the Ghadar press soon to come, visited, talked politics, and convalesced for some months in Astoria.[79] Those competent in one or more of the numerous languages they navigated read aloud to their compatriots from newspapers, the teachings of their faith, or labor and political tracts, whether from Punjabi, Urdu, Hindi, English, or other sources.[80] From the homeland they learned of boycotts and bombings and rising new leaders. They might have shared accounts of local labor struggles like that in nearby Grays Harbor, Washington, where their countrymen refused to be used against a strike.[81] Articles from Taraknath Das's *Free Hindusthan* brought radical insights from the Vancouver, BC, community.[82] In this way, the news and politics of home merged with those of the new lands and became the property of all who cared to take part.[83]

Their debates morphed and changed, and the collectives were enriched or impoverished by those who moved in and out, as mobility was a constant. Opinions vied, and the like-minded of whatever persuasion found one another, grew apart, and regrouped as the times, spaces, and sentiments demanded. Amid this flux and flow, the bunkhouses and shared houses remained critical to the crescendoing debates about the way forward for India and for Indians. Before the divide between those who departed for India with Ghadar and those who sought acceptance and a life in America, their contending voices and concerns were heard through the thin walls and amid the sound of the rivers and its mills.

Weekends brought a different rhythm. They slept later and lingered over the morning meal. Hair and clothes were washed. Some wrapped freshly laundered turbans, while others donned hats over neatly shorn hair.[84] Dungarees were traded for street clothes, and they walked or hopped a trolley into town to shop or to simply meander. Some sought diversions of drink, games of chance, or sex. Others might have attended Christian churches out of curiosity or to better integrate into town. For those not interested in venturing out, the pleasures of the flesh or of salvation could still be enjoyed, as their vendors often came door to door. Men stayed home to play musical instruments and practice with those who sang or danced. Some composed, perhaps with others more literate, letters home to young wives they could now support with their wages, but not with physical closeness.[85]

For fun and exercise, Indians often grappled with one another in outdoor wrestling matches during off-hours.[86] Historian Harish Puri suggests that wrestling became a part of militants' covert physical training-in-plain-sight regime in North America. [87] The wrestling talents of some were likely also useful in the more mundane settings of barroom scraps or shop floor disputes.Wrestling was also entwined in the larger backdrop of Indian colonial politics and associated notions of dominant and subjugated manhood, North American race relations, and small-town rivalries.

With a long tradition in many cultures, wrestling was a part of Astoria's social life, with public matches attended by men and women alike. Indians competed with Finns and others in the local scene. Records are thin and sometimes contradictory, but wrestler Dodan Singh made his home in Astoria for significant periods between 1910 and 1913.[88] Like others, he moved back and forth between Oregon and Vancouver, BC.[89] One seeming constant wherever he lived was his work in the lumber mills, which sports writers often explained as the source of Dodan's uncommon endurance and strength.[90] How and where he otherwise trained is unclear.[91] In one highly publicized match, Dodan Singh bested prominent Portland wrestler Eddie O'Connell. While O'Connell did his best to trade in ethnic intolerance, Dodan was treated in local papers as Astoria's hometown champ.[92]

The wide popularity of Astorian wrestlers Dodan Singh and, later, Basanta Singh is suggestive of sports' ability to challenge entrenched relations of power such as class or race by focusing on the training and abilities of discrete individuals.[93] Indians' competition in a sport requiring close, sustained, and intimate body contact helped counter their portrayal in mainstream culture as dirty and diseased "others." It proved an avenue for Indian recognition and acceptance—as men and as celebrated town members—and where communities made space for diverse populations, seemingly with Astoria particularly open in this regard.

Finally, there can be no question that, in their off hours, Indians pursued overt politics and associations with activist laborers of many ethnicities. These were times of global nationalist and labor stirrings, and Indians found and made community among their many adherents. Indians attended political lectures and convened in the Finnish Socialist Hall. They compared experience and talked strategy with Chinese, Irish, and Mexican nationalists. Sohan Singh Bhakna was a member of the IWW in Portland and "spoke regularly about the exploitation of migrant workers and the formation of race- and class-based hierarchies along the Pacific Coast."[94] Descendants of the Bakhshish Singh Dhillon family recount tales of Finns and IWW representatives meeting in their grandfather's house in Astoria.[95] British surveillance files describe that Bhagat Singh Thind "kept company with a bunch of socialistic I.W.W. anarchistic Finns."[96]

Politics proved Indians' most vital, enduring, and eventually most public means of resistance. But it was tightly nested within an array of relations, supports, and alliances that nurtured and sustained them in big and small ways. The thin, surviving historical record of Indians in Oregon provides some names, ages, and a rough idea of the years when men arrived. It reveals they were involved in wage strikes, sued one another in court, got in fights with fellow employees, were arrested for drinking, became well-known wrestlers, filed for citizenship, filed for divorce, played with the few Punjabi children in the state, cared for one another, and talked and otherwise entertained themselves in the times they were not working. [97] What such records tell us about what Indians faced in Oregon, how they lived, and what they accomplished is difficult to document, let alone imagine, from such thin and scarce sources. Still, certain essentials are clear.

Compared with their countrymen in British Columbia and California, Indians came to Oregon later and in smaller numbers. Many arrived after experiencing harrowing racial attacks. They came as laborers, assigned to the lowest rungs of industry's divides, with few, if notable, students and radicals in their midst. Indians settled in a state specifically imagined as a white Eden, open to others to the degree they served that higher purpose. Yet in Oregon Indians found the means and spaces to persist. They built community with each other and others. They found openings, allies, and new imaginings. Many of their day-to-day concerns soon fell to the wayside as the times and conditions tested them as individuals and tested the alliances and bonds they had forged in a few short years.

Most immediately, in the spring of 1910 in St. Johns, Western Oregon's racial script faltered, and Indians were targeted by an inflamed white mob. In response, Indians rejected the 1905 exposition's presumed passivity and fought back in the streets, courtrooms, and press. More profoundly, they came to reckon with the global class and racial structures that shaped their lives wherever they settled. Indians demanded their rights to equality, citizenship, and self-rule, and transformed themselves from objects of Western colonizers to agents of their own future.

THE HINDUSTANEE

The Official Organ of the United India League

Volume I   Vancouver, B. C., Wednesday, April 1, 1914   Number IV

BIG WRESTLING MATCH

Pat Connelly is training with the elite of Vancouver wrestlers at the Commercial Club. As a champion of Great Britain, a home ruler Irishman, and a well-known grappler in this city, his match with Dalbagh Singh is awaited with keen interest.

Dalbagh Singh hails from Raipur Dubba, a wrestling haunt in Punjab. All Punjabees indulge in the sport of wrestling, it being a national sport with them. Dalbagh Singh is the favorite champion of his district, having secured titles in many a center in Punjab. He is training with a bunch of Hindus as assiduously as Pat Connelly, and both are full of confidence.

The Vancouver public will have an opportunity of witnessing the most exciting and skillful grappling match ever seen in this city.

Pat Connelly weighs 182 pounds, whereas Dalbagh Singh tips the scales at 170 pounds.

The British champion undertakes to gain two falls in sixty minutes from the Hindu champion. The match takes place on Friday, April 3, at 8:30 p. m., in the Dominion Hall. Each party has already posted $200.00 with the Sporting Editor of the Daily News-Advertiser.

Tickets, general admission $1.00, and ringside $1.50, can be had from the office of The Hindustanee, 516 Main St., Room 1, or the Commercial Club, Dominion Hall.

CHAMPION OF INDIA

DALBAGH SINGH

PAT CONNELLY, Champion of Great Britain

The Hindustanee, April 1, 1914. Courtesy South Asian American Digital Archive (SAADA). *The Hindustanee*, an important nationalist press published in Vancouver, BC, showcased a "Big Wrestling Match" between local Dalbagh Singh and Pat Connelly, champion of Great Britain. Notably, while the match filled the front page, Taraknath Das's report on the arrest of Har Dayal and coverage of a Canadian Parliament debate about "Hindus," ran inside.

Interlude
Wrestlers Dodan Singh and Basanta Singh

Astorians Dodan Singh and, later, Basanta Singh were covered by Astoria's and the region's press, taught wrestling, and competed in regional interethnic matches. Three thin and sometimes contradictory regional snapshots of Dodan Singh provide intriguing glimpses of the public side of his career and its interplay with global and local events.

In September 1910, the Portland press began reporting on an October match between Dodan Singh, then of Astoria, and Eddie O'Connell, the wrestling instructor at Portland's elite Multnomah Athletic Club.[1] The *Morning Oregonian* reported that O'Connell was "fresh off wins against the Russian champ on the East Coast" and that he pledged to throw Singh twice in the first hour. To underscore his confidence, O'Connell "wagered the dark-skinned man $500," an enormous bet, given that millworkers in Astoria then made $2 to $3 per day. In October, the paper began publicizing the contest, scheduled in downtown Portland's Merrill Hall, billing it as "beef and brawn [Dodan] against brains [O'Connell]."[2] An earlier match in Astoria in July between O'Connell and Al Singh, "a Hindu," had also garnered considerable interest, with around $2,000 in bets pooled before the match.[3]

In its coverage, the *Oregonian* noted an international match two months earlier between India's wrestling champion Ghulam Hussein, aka the Great Gama, and Stanislaus Zbyszko of Poland, the reigning European wrestling champ. Their heavily followed bout took on overtones of the Indian nationalist struggle, with dominated India (Gama) challenging Europe (Zbyszko) in the colonizer's home turf of London. The match itself did nothing to undercut those meanings. After more than two hours with Zbyszko largely prone on the mat, resisting a pin and angering the crowd for his lack of play, referees called a break. Zbyszko then refused to return to the ring, quickly left the country, and evaded calls for a rematch. Gama was named the new World Champion to the joy of Indians globally.[4] Singh noted Gama's victory days before his match with O'Connell.[5]

The *Morning Oregonian*'s coverage of the Singh-O'Connell match can be read as revelatory of more local politics. First, the paper intimated that Singh had a following in Astoria that extended beyond Indians. Reporting that he expected to beat O'Connell, the paper went on to say, "Dodan Singh put on the finishing touches to his training yesterday afternoon before a large crowd of wrestling fans in Astoria. . . . The Hindu's opinion of himself voices sentiment of the sporting fraternity of Astoria, a large number of which will be at ringside on Tuesday evening to wager their money on the Hindu."[6] Many of Astoria's "sporting fraternity," besides the Indian community, were rooting for, and likely wagering on, Singh.

The next day, the newspaper reported a $1,000 side bet on the match. Highlighting hometown competitor O'Connell with a photo, but not one of Singh, the article acknowledged Singh as the advantaged, heavier wrestler. It also quoted O'Connell as saying that "the turbaned wonder from the trans Pacific shores will not last."[7] O'Connell's quip can be taken simply as a competitor's taunt. But the O'Connell-Singh bout took place six months after the nearby St. Johns anti-Indian riot. Portland papers had reported on the disturbance off and on for months, including about the suspected riot ringleaders' upcoming trials in Portland. Rioters had declared their intention to rid St. Johns of "Hindus." Was O'Connell echoing their aims in his pledge that "the turbaned wonder would not last"?

Match night brought a large crowd, estimated at more than a thousand people, including many Indians.[8] O'Connell's optimism about the match was not borne out. Singh won handily. Yet reporters could not altogether concede Singh's competitive merits. Echoing the broader discourse of European superiority over Indians, the *Morning Oregonian* argued that, while O'Connell had lost, he was "more scientific." The paper conceded that, if not mentally equal, the "Hindu was popular," and that the "brown-skinned man was heavier and stronger of body" and "showed endurance and his gameness won many friends." Continuing its graceless coverage, the paper also cited Indians' supposed propensity to sweat as a disadvantage for the Irish-descended O'Connell.[9]

The drama after the match was also compelling. The confident, big-betting O'Connell reportedly absconded with the purse. O'Connell

Dodan Singh.
Courtesy Clatsop Co
Historical Society

refused to give Singh a cent from the more than $700 in gate receipts, let alone pay up on his large challenge bet. In response, a furious Dodan Singh and friends went to the Portland police headquarters, declared he'd been robbed, and demanded O'Connell's arrest for felony robbery. If the Multnomah district attorney would not issue a warrant for O'Connell's arrest, Dodan pledged to enlist the local British consul.[10] Any stiffed competitor would likely seek justice within available channels. But Singh's response is resonant of the St. Johns riot aftermath, when Indians successfully demanded authorities intervene on their behalf and prosecute their attackers.

How the O'Connell theft resolved is unclear, but it seems the event wasn't forgotten. O'Connell wanted a rematch in Astoria. In 1913, the *Daily Astorian* reported that Dodan Singh would not meet O'Connell because Astoria sheriff Burns didn't trust the Portland grappler to "be on the square."[11] One could speculate that if O'Connell had been convicted of the theft, he'd be unable to continue public, competitive matches. But at a minimum, Sheriff Burn's statement reflects his belief in Singh's account of events and not O'Connell's. Notably, this was two months before Ghadar's historic Astoria gathering.

In 1911, a year after the Portland Singh-O'Connell match, a Seattle paper reported on a wrestling coach in Bellingham, Washington, looking for someone to beat Dodan Singh, then of Vancouver, BC. The paper quoted Coach Perry as saying, "Vancouver sports want to see this little Hindu cleaned but there is no one in sight to do the trick."[12] The wrestling world had no shortage of racialized titles—The Terrible Swede, Kid Savage of Mexico, the Manilla Fighter, the Japanese Bone-Crusher—reflecting sport's part in ritualized interaction and organized spectacle between newly coexistent and often exoticized peoples. But in this instance, the coach's "this little Hindu cleaned" invective has the distinct feel of a rather specific racial grudge.

Coach Perry did not include Singh among "Vancouver sports" members and appears less interested in an exciting match than knocking the racialized Singh down a peg. That this report originates in Bellingham and references "Vancouver sports'" desire to see Dodan Singh defeated also seems germane. Both cities were sites of significant racial violence against Indians in 1907, and ethnic animosity continued to pollute their air, seemingly including the sporting world. Singh was reportedly cheered by large crowds in Astoria, and the local sheriff intervened against the crooked Portlander O'Connell. While there is a danger in overburdening these slight records, the contrast seems notable.

Ten years after Dodan Singh's tenure, and long after most Indians had left town, Basanta Singh took up residence, at least for a time, in Astoria. In Oregon, Basanta launched a wrestling career beginning with bouts in other small towns such as Pendleton, Cottage Grove, and La Grande. Some of these towns, including Pendleton, a cattle town three hundred miles upriver from Astoria, had a surprisingly welcoming tone to their coverage of his bouts, including outlining their good fortune in hosting such a talented grappler. In a nod toward community connection and largesse, Basanta offered to wrestle in town any time for a charitable cause. In 1922, he undertook a national, multi-bout tour, which was announced by the *Oregonian*, and returned to Oregon claiming a national welterweight title. Perhaps because of his positive reception and success, he announced plans to the press, in perfect English and ambassadorial from-my-people-to-yours language, to bring other wrestlers from India to compete. His plan, however, proved impossible with the 1924 passage of the Johnson Reed Act, which effectively banned all Indian immigration.[13]

3

St. Johns, the "Hindu City"

St. Johns, Oregon, sits on the banks of the Willamette River, near its convergence with the Columbia River, a few downstream miles from Portland's center. Today St. Johns is just another city neighborhood. In the early 1900s, this otherwise unremarkable town was home to an ugly ethnic riot and to the critical beginnings of a radical Indian independence movement.

In 1910, St. Johns had freshly blossomed from a few hundred souls living in and among a collection of tents, shanties, and docks to a bustling town of four thousand. It boasted a new city hall and school, streetcar service to Portland, telephones, sidewalks atop muddy roads, hotels, boardinghouses, and a lively real estate market. The town's transformation was one measure of the economic boom that Portland's 1905 Lewis and Clark Exposition had delivered to the region. In the wake of the exposition, industries swelled and new residents, including tens of thousands of laborers, flocked to the area.[1]

At least a hundred Indians were among those who had arrived and worked in St. Johns' new or newly expanded industries. The Monarch Lumber Mill and St. Johns Lumber Company were their primary employers, and many lived in Monarch's bunkhouse on the northeastern outskirts of town. Others shared apartments above downtown businesses or lived a few blocks down the hill in workers' shacks near St. Johns Lumber and the Willamette River. Years of articles in the local booster newspaper, the *St. Johns Review,* had reported on the town's growth and promise, urging residents to recruit friends and family to resettle in St. Johns and contribute to its glorious future. The *Review* almost never mentioned the Indians living in town. One exception was in the summer of 1907, a time of rampant anti-Asian sentiments in the North American west. The paper reported on the unspecified

Group of Hindu laborers forced by mob to leave work in St. Johns lumber mill.

HINDU ASSAULTS LEAD TO ARREST OF 23 PERSONS

Seven of Alleged Rioters Furnish Bail in Sum of $2000, Remaining Sixteen Languish in City Jail.

A rare photo of some of the Indians living and working in St. Johns. The use of the word "persons" with respect to those arrested for the riot was not a respect applied to Indians, the St. Johns Review in particular preferring terms like "cloth tops," "greasy cloth wearers," and "dirty Hindus." Photo: "Hindu Assaults Lead to Arrests of 23 Persons," *Oregon Daily Journal*, March 23, 1910, p. 5; terms are from "The Hindu Situation," *Review*, April 8, 1910, 1. Courtesy Historic Oregon Newspapers, University of Oregon Libraries.

criminality of one "I. Wilson," deeming him representative of the "gang of Hindoos . . . temporarily" located in St. Johns who needed to be "given an emphatic invitation to move on."[2] Their invitation was forcefully delivered on March 21, 1910.

That Monday night, downtown St. Johns erupted in anti-Indian violence perpetrated by a crowd of two to three hundred, including many laborers, a *Review* reporter, the town's mayor, the night police chief, two police officers, a prominent business owner's son, volunteer firefighters, and others.[3] Collectively, they attempted to terrorize and violently expel the Indians living and working in their midst. The riot's repercussions reverberated far wider and longer than any participant likely ever dreamed or desired.

St. Johns exploded many Indians' hopes for peace and employment in Oregon. Portland authorities' dreams of managing racial and labor animosities also took a hit, and they scrambled to reassert their control by arresting and trying multiple participants. Great Britain, through its Portland consul, James Laidlaw, rushed to contain and redirect the seething anger of the Indian community. Urgent cables passed between the US State Department and British authorities in London and Delhi, the US attorney general's office, and local prosecuting authorities. Federal authorities dispatched Secret Service agents to aid the local investigation. In the riot's wake, neighbors testified against neighbors, an accused felon served as mayor, a local judge was censured, and prosecution dragged on for two years. Eventually a kind of peace was restored in town, but one in which Indians emerged as an anticolonial hub. A seemingly local riot of perhaps two hours embodied the confluence of colonial economic, race, and labor politics that shaped Indians' lives and drove their global organizing.

In early 1910, Indians' presence in St. Johns was a simmering undercurrent. While rumor's power is certain, exactly how and where it gets translated into daily thoughts and actions is unpredictable and difficult to trace. It is clear, however, that multiple anti-Indian crosscurrents infected St. Johns.

In February, about five weeks before the riot, Portland Manufacturing Company, an up-and-coming plywood company showcased at the 1905 exposition, burned to the ground.[4] Despite proof being "scant," the *Morning Oregonian* reported the arrest of a "Hindu," on suspicion of having set the fire.[5] In fact, the evidence was wholly unreliable, unable to substantiate charges. Portland Manufacturing was within blocks of St. Johns Lumber Company, where many Indians were employed and lived close by. St. Johns Lumber was rumored to have plans to employ more Indians, and according to the *Review*, this rumor triggered the March 21 unrest.[6] In this atmosphere, it is not difficult to imagine mill men's conversations during lunch breaks or at the bar after work veering toward "Hindu-hating," especially when Indians worked close by. Local rumors that an Indian had maliciously burned down the plant and were poised to take over lumber mill jobs gained even greater traction amid broad rumblings of a "Hindu invasion" and "tide of turbans" making headlines across the US west.

Accounts vary, but all put Gordon Dickey, a mill foreman, at the center of events and Condon's Saloon as the jump-off point for the night's drama.[7] By some reports, Dickey had gone to the downtown bar to present a petition demanding that Indians no longer be served.[8] Others claim Dickey was simply drinking with friend Frank Jones, an employee of Portland Manufacturing, and they had words with, or threw beer on, two "Hindus."[9] Either way, a dustup between several white and Indian men spilled into the downtown streets, and a crowd of hundreds immediately assembled.

Dickey reportedly addressed those gathered and set them off on their task for the night: "to seek out the British subjects and banish them from St. Johns forthwith." [10] One group rousted the Indians living above Bitgood & Cole butcher shop, a few blocks from Condon's. Others moved down the hill and targeted Indians still at work at St. Johns Lumber or at home in the nearby mill shacks and boardinghouse. As the *Review* wrote, "Every Hindu that was encountered was peremptorily ordered to stop work and get out of town at once."[11]

If the *Review* was to be believed, what saved the town it described as "bordering on anarchy" were the actions of night police chief Bredeson and Mayor Hendricks. It reported that Chief Bredeson was summoned and his entreaties to stop were taken up by the crowd and that Mayor Hendricks arrived quickly and deputized multiple firemen to help quell the situation. The mayor was also said to have gone to the mill, where he delivered a "stirring address" and told the men they were doing wrong and to desist. [12] (The next day the Multnomah County district attorney and the sheriff served warrants on Hendricks and Bredeson.) "Cheers were given to the mayor and the crowd quickly dispersed."[13] The newspaper claimed that none of the Indians had been robbed of valuables or cash, but describes them as having been treated "roughly" or even "decidedly rough." One man's leg was "reportedly broken" and others "slightly wounded." Finally, the *Review* reported that numerous Indians were "escorted" or "placed" on the streetcar and told not to return. Guarded by Milton Unger, a prominent local merchant's son, forty some Indians were forced—not "placed" or "escorted"—onto the Portland-bound, union-run streetcar with orders to never return.[14]

Portland newspapers were more inclined to depict the night's actual violence, describing windows broken, doors off hinges, bits of clothing scattered, "Hindus [pulled] out of their beds," and "everywhere the evidence of riot, and in a fw [*sic*] cases, bloodshed." The *Morning*

Oregonian also reported that one *Review* reporter had participated in the riot.[15] Neither the *Review* nor the *Oregonian* interviewed Indians—despite the presence of English speakers and multiple translators—until well into the trials some months later. In court, Indians testified to being robbed at gunpoint of valuables and hundreds of dollars, being beaten, sometimes with a gun, that one man was pushed out of a second-story window, and that local authorities either passively watched or actively participated in the attacks.[16] Mr. Lauthers, the owner of the shacks, testified that the riot's aftermath looked like a "Kansas cyclone had struck."[17]

Indians were not cowed by the rioters or by newspaper opinions. That night, and over the next two years, they fought for respect and for the right to work and live in St. Johns. On the morning of March 22, a group of Indians led by Kanshi Ram, aka John Kim, an Indian labor contractor running a crew at St. Johns Lumber, went directly to British consul James Laidlaw in Portland to demand action.[18] Consul Laidlaw, on behalf of the British subjects he represented, formally petitioned the Multnomah County district attorney's office to intervene. By that afternoon, Indians walked the streets of St. Johns with Deputy District Attorney (DDA) C. W. Garland and pointed out their attackers. DDA Garland was armed with 190 warrants and a deputy who took suspects into custody on the spot.[19]

Consul Laidlaw also lodged a complaint with the US State Department, which in turn instructed the US district attorney's office to assist local prosecutors. US Secret Service agents soon appeared in St. Johns, questioning and arresting area residents.[20] To aid the prosecution, Consul Laidlaw hired local attorneys, including Dan J. Malarkey who prosecuted the murder of Harnam Singh in Boring.[21] Within a week, personnel from these many agencies converged on St. Johns, ratcheting up tensions even further.

By Friday, March 25, most Indians had returned to their homes and jobs or were expected soon.[22] Some came armed. Kanshi Ram/John Kim, Inder [Indar] Singh, Rakha Ram, Ram R, George Frank, and Delee Singh were arrested in Portland on March 24 for buying and carrying concealed weapons.[23] The *Daily News,* a pro-white labor newspaper, reported that they armed at the direction of Consul Laidlaw, who "advised the men to purchase guns, but to carry them in holsters about the waist."[24] Whatever the idea's source, its rationale was clearly stated by Kanshi Ram/John Kim: "We have no protection."[25] Underscoring Ram's concern, the following day's front-page article in the *Daily News*, a piece that reads as more hope than fact, argued Indians' return could trigger a bloody "race war."[26]

The *Review* was incensed that DDA Garland came to St. Johns with a "horde of deputies and a band of dark skinned British subjects, . . . arresting citizens left and right without the least regard to innocence."[27] The paper took to referring to the district attorney's role as "czarist justice" or "bowing to the British lion." [28] It also argued that DDA Garland's vigorous prosecution was simply to further his own career, and perhaps it was, in part. But it was also in keeping with the area's policy against communal racial violence. The district attorney's office intended to arraign all those arrested under the warrants before the local St. Johns Justice Court. That plan quickly went awry amid the competing interests of, on the one hand, the St. Johns city and court officials and, on the other, the many state, local, and international authorities involved.

At the direction of the St. Johns City Council, sitting city attorney (CA) Henry Collier and private attorney George J. Perkins defended many of those arrested, including members of the St. Johns volunteer fire department.[29] Both lawyers were also running for St. Johns city attorney. Mayor Hendricks was up for reelection in the same election, set for early April. The attorneys, "keen in their efforts to act for their constituents" reportedly did not charge for their services."[30]

DDA Garland accused CA Collier and other St. Johns officials of "absolutely" refusing to identify anyone associated with the riot, given the upcoming election.[31] DDA Garland stated it had, "so handicapped us that we have been unable to secure many of the ringleaders of the squabble," and might necessitate bypassing local court in favor of the grand jury.[32] A day later, in open court, CA Collier accused DDA Garland of "maligning the character of the good citizens of St. Johns." The prosecutor responded he would prove CA Collier as "guilty in the riot case as many others" and again raised the possibility of removing the matter from local court.[33] DDA Garland also reported having received threats of physical and political harm unless he released all of those arrested.[34] Local Justice Conrad Olson stated that the riot was a stain

on St. Johns and the entire country, and found it lamentable that city
authorities seemed inclined to screen the guilty ones. He also made
clear that he personally "did not favor the Hindus," but nonetheless
sought justice.[35]

The many St. Johns Justice Court hearings were packed with
supporters of the accused. Indians were also present, but reportedly
stayed outside.[36] In deference to the workingmen, proceedings were
held at night and on Saturdays, with sessions sometimes lasting until
midnight. Justice Olson feared the hearings would consume the entire
summer, given the sheer number of cases, witnesses, attorney fights,
and necessary translations. Besides the attorneys' fireworks, every day
seemed to add new drama. Kanshi Ram/John Kim, a plaintiff and the
acting interpreter, was accused by CA Collier of influencing testimony,
despite CA Collier's inability to understand Punjabi or Hindi. Consul
Laidlaw suggested a replacement for Ram, someone who was already in
the courtroom, and the hearings proceeded.[37] Later that day, a brazen
Mayor Hendricks took the stand and admitted to watching an Indian
being beaten but claimed to be unable to identify the perpetrators.[38]

A major turning point came with Justice Olson's remarks on the
testimony of St. Johns Lumber Company manager, N. E. Ayer. Piqued
by Ayer's testimony in support of Indians and his holding of their jobs,
the *Review* reported that Justice Olson said, "If the wife and children
[who were in the courtroom] of Mr. Ayer of St. Johns Lumber Co. were
forced to mingle daily with the Hindus, the lumberman who is assisting the prosecution would soon change his opinion regarding them."
Justice Olson also accused Indians of lying in their testimony, including
falsely accusing men of having taken part in the riot.[39] Indians immediately gathered in the hallways in protest. They threatened to drop
the case if Justice Olson was not removed, potentially leaving Portland
and British authorities unable to make a fitting political example out
of the affair and creating the appearance they had been bested in a
small-town courtroom.[40]

DDA Garland, already experienced in the city's obstructionism,
declared Justice Olson's remarks the final straw. He ordered the matter immediately transferred to the Multnomah County grand jury.
This took the St. Johns prosecution out of the hands of the local court
and put it firmly into the hands of the district attorney's office, adding

significantly enhanced powers. First, the punishment for any witness refusing to appear in front of the grand jury was, and is, jail. While witnesses can consult with counsel, no lawyer can advise their client during, or even accompany them to, grand jury questioning. Further, the district attorney summons all witnesses and conducts all questioning and document review in the presence of the empaneled jury members. The district attorney also decides whether to issue an indictment, its issuance dependent on the vote of jury members. All of this was done in and remained secret, particularly given that, in 1910, a stenographic record of the testimony was legally barred. Only the ultimate charges, if any, are known outside of the grand jury and only when sent on for prosecution in open court. Justice Olson may not have been entirely unhappy with this turn of events. Just days earlier, he had requested the grand jury take charge. He was, after all, in the unenviable position of agreeing with the sentiments of the rioters but charged with prosecuting them in clear public view.[41]

Indians' outrage over the incident likely factored into DDA Garland's decision, but they did not restrict their pushback to the courtroom. Four days after Justice Olson's remarks, the *Morning Oregonian* published a lengthy excerpt of a piece penned by noted Indian radical activist and then University of Washington PhD student, Taraknath Das. The article appeared on the first day the Multnomah County grand jury convened in Portland. In it, Das thanked manager Ayers and his family for their support and commended Consul Laidlaw for his actions on behalf of the British subjects who, Das reminded, were entitled to all the same rights as other of its subjects, whether English, Irish, or Australian. He then rhetorically asked whether the present discrimination against Indians, who he stated were Caucasians, was based on race prejudice. Das declared that Indians' former high regard for America as the "land of liberty" stood in the breach of this trial.[42]

Das's article revealed an intimate knowledge of the courtroom proceedings. If he wasn't already in the Portland area, he likely arrived shortly thereafter. Either way, he clearly was in close contact with local people and well versed in events. For the Indians of St. Johns, Das's university credentials were helpful. He lent eloquence and credibility to their fight, especially in the battle for public opinion. He spoke Punjabi, Hindi, and English.

His political credibility, however, was likely most important to them. Das had been living in Vancouver in late 1907 during the watershed Bellingham and Vancouver anti-Asian riots.[43] He was a firsthand witness to the enormity of the changes that occurred in the wake of those events. In response, many of British Columbia's Indian community had embarked on radical organizing in earnest, and Das was an integral part of that work.[44] Based on experience, Das and others in St. Johns had a keen sense for the stakes of the battle they were engaged in and the need to meet it head-on.

In the politically charged atmosphere, Indians and non-Indians alike awaited the grand jury findings, most especially whether city officials would be indicted for participating in and/or not attempting to quell the riot. The grand jury worked for three weeks, and local newspapers speculated on their findings and release date.[45] On April 27, 1910, the *Morning Oregonian* announced indictments brought by the State of Oregon on behalf of sixteen Indian Sikhs, Hindus, and Muslims: B. Singh, Khem Chand, Ali Raka, Indar [Inder] Singh, Kanshi Ram/ John Kim, G. Frank, Ali Mahamad [Mahamed], C. A. Dass, N. Box, F. Mahamad, Succha Singh, Ber Singh, Scandee Jan, Suba Singh, Hernam Singh, and Me Ha.[46] For failing in their duty to disperse the rioters or stop the disturbance, Mayor J. F. Hendricks; G. W. Dunbar, the night chief of police; O. R. Downs, justice of the peace; and G. W. Etheridge, a policeman, were indicted. Dunbar and Etheridge were also indicted for assembling to drive the Indians out of town (aka riot), assault, battery, robbery, carrying weapons, and disturbing the peace. City attorney Collier was implicated by the grand jury's official report but escaped indictment.[47] Charges against the city officials carried penitentiary or jail terms and hefty fines if convicted.[48] Besides Gordon Dickey, laborers Ray Van de Bogard, John N. Groves and Dan Herrold, along with Milton Unger, the sweetshop owner's son, were charged with riot.[49]

Dickey was indicted as the ringleader. As the *Morning Oregonian* wrote, Dickey "is accused of having dragged one of the terrified Hindus from the very presence of Mayor Hendricks by the hair of his head, while the dusky skinned native of India screamed for protection. The Mayor was at that time presiding in the City Hall at a meeting of the firemen, and the Hindu had fled to him for protection, it is charged."[50] The newspaper also noted that, while only the theft of $185 was

"Hindu Turban Latest Idea in Fashionable Feminine Headgear," *Sunday Oregonian*, May 29, 1910.

charged, "the mob is said to have taken everything of value the Hindus possessed, looting their houses, . . . about $700 in cash, . . . and some 30 Hindus were driven from town."[51]

Two Greek men, neighbors of the Indians, were charged in the riot but stressed they should have been protected, not arrested, as the mob was rumored to be after "all foreigners" that night. Greeks, Italians, and Turks organized several nights of watches after the March 21 fracas.[52] Given the contentious nature of this case, and that St. Johns was a small town, it is noteworthy that the hundred or so local witnesses interviewed by the grand jury, and thus responsible for the formal charges being made against their neighbors and city officials, were named in the indictment.[53]*

---

*Symbolically, Indians in St. Johns were attacked for their turbans. Shortly before Gordon Dickey's trial opened, the *Sunday Oregonian*'s fashion page (see image above) featured a different sort of assault on the turban, one emblematically more in keeping with Portland elites' policy towards immigrant laborers. The "Woman's Department" described the new style amongst Portland women in part by referencing Indians in town. "This little turban follows strictly the lines and styles of the Hindu headdress . . . . exactly after the manner of the picturesque turbans worn by the Hindu men one

In June of 1910, Gordon Dickey, whose case was considered the strongest, was tried in Portland for assault and robbery with a dangerous weapon and felony rioting.[54] Dickey was represented by three attorneys.[55] The British consulate's attorneys assisted with the state's prosecution as did the US district attorney's office.[56] Dickey's defense team called more than twenty witnesses, and the state called almost ninety, Indian and non-Indian alike.[57] Throughout, the *Review* editorialized about the autocratic legal tactics being employed against the town's citizens and officials.[58] Taraknath Das, despite 1908 British reports that he was the ringleader of North American Indian anticolonialists, was appointed the proceedings' interpreter. His appointment raises questions as to how closely Oregon authorities were attuned to Indian nationalist politics or were looped into the anti-Indian policing apparatus, and also about the authorities' confidence in containing Indians' outrage.[59]

Mayor Hendricks refused to testify in Dickey's trial, arguing that because he was under indictment he wouldn't risk incriminating himself. Not so for Officer Downs, who "spoke freely," saying he knew he should have attempted to stop it. He also clearly implicated city attorney Collier, Officer Etheridge, and a previous mayor as all present and restraining Indians, some of whom he described as weeping, bleeding, and being forced to the trolley cars.[60]

Dickey took the stand and attempted to paint himself as a friend and protector of "the Hindus."[61] Indians' testimony remains the best rejoinder to Dickey's claims. Kanshi Ram/John Kim testified that Dickey and others broke into his home and asked, "Who's boss here?" to which Ram replied that he was. At that, Dickey held a loaded revolver to Ram's head while Officer Dearlove searched him and took $50 from his pocket. Ram asked Dickey whether he held "the whole United States Government" in his hand, and Dickey answered, "No, but

---

occasionally sees on the Portland streets." The turban was by then a national fashion trend, one art historian Jaimee K. Comstock-Kipp describes as "sartororientalism" that served "to build American women's image of themselves as civilized while dismissing other cultures as savage." (Comstock, "Art Deco Sartorientalism," 23). By dubbing the turban as "fashionable feminine headgear" the *Sunday Oregonian* article also promoted the cliché of Indian men as feminine as compared to their white counterparts. This both domesticated the supposed "Hindu" threat to white womanhood and provided an objectifying flipside to the explicitly ethno-exclusionist and masculinist press. (Paye, "the Anti Hindu Riot").

I'll fix you. I will blow you up." Dickey then handed Ram to the mob, who loaded him onto the streetcar, while others threw rocks at Indians' homes. Ram asked a policeman for help, who replied he would help if the crowd wasn't so large.

Ali Mahamed [Mahamad] testified that he watched one white man push a Hindu out of a second-story window. Mahamed was robbed of $43.25 while Dickey kept guard and then pocketed the money. G. Frank showed a scar by his ear made when he was struck with the butt of a gun. After being robbed, Frank ran to City Hall for protection but was beaten again by men there. Frank escaped on the trolley. [62]

After a seven-day trial, Gordon Dickey was convicted on June 15, 1910, of felony riot.[63] The jury deliberated five and a half hours and found Dickey "guilty as charged in the Indictment," and asked that he "receive the extreme clemency of the court."[64] The *Review* continued its bombast about autocratic justice sparing nothing in its quest for a conviction. It also amplified the jury's mixed verdict about Dickey, expressing the "regret of its citizens" about the conviction. The paper concluded that, although the trial had seemed fair, and Dickey, by law, had been judged guilty, it was unlikely that he would ever be considered guilty in the eyes of the people of St. Johns, as "the provocation and incentive for the 'outbreak' is here well appreciated and understood."[65]

After his conviction, and angling for leniency, Dickey confessed to his role in the riot and promised to implicate others.[66] He also petitioned for a new trial. The court postponed Dickey's sentencing for two months while prosecutors assessed the value of Dickey's admissions for their cases against the others, including the police officers and Mayor Hendricks.

In consultation with Crown attorney Dan Malarkey, Deputy DA Fitzgerald prepared an internal Multnomah County district attorney office memorandum. They opined it would be "mightily hard to convince a jury that he [Dickey] was now telling the truth," given Dickey had "so discredited himself by his former [court] testimony." The report calculated that, beyond Dickey's confession, evidence was "otherwise meager," but provided no further details. Ultimately, Dickey's was the only conviction sought and secured. [67]

However, an earlier report from attorney Malarkey to Consul Laidlaw, which wound its way up through the British global chain of command, sheds light on the difficulties of securing other convictions.

Malarkey had hoped to use Dickey's felony riot conviction to scare other indictees to turn state's evidence in exchange for lesser charges. The strategy failed, as Malarkey writes, "because of fear or sympathy [people were] unwilling to tell what they knew, and though we did everything in our power to force out of witnesses . . . to such an extent we were denounced in local newspapers."[68] Witnesses simply denied their sworn testimony before the grand jury that had issued the indictments. As that testimony was not recorded, prosecutors had no rebuttal. British officials were particularly disappointed they would be unable to prosecute any police.[69]

Consequently, both Malarkey and the Multnomah district attorney's office advised against going forward with other cases and lobbied against any new trial of Dickey. However, they observed that the "conviction of Dickey after a hard fought trial accompanied by great newspaper exploitation . . . accomplished what . . . your government desired, i.e. to make the people of this district understand that Hindoos, subjects of your government, will be protected by the Courts and law from persecution and abuse to the same extent as our own citizens. . . . If we tried others and lost, that would undue this effect" and might revive "bad feelings against Hindoos which, as near as I can learn, has entirely subsided since Dickey's conviction." Malarkey noted that any acquittals would have a particularly bad effect on "the very class of people" who would attack Hindus but for the fear of punishment." One assumes Malarkey was not referring to the mayor or police, particularly as this was the same class-based language used after the Boring convictions of Harnam Singh's murderers. The attorneys' appraisal was approved by British ambassador Bryce in Washington, DC, the Secretary of State-India office in London, and the Viceroy of India.[70]

Dickey's request for a new trial was heard November 14, 1911, and the court ruled against him.[71] On January 15, 1912, he was sentenced to five years in the Oregon State Penitentiary for felony riot. The court immediately suspended his entire sentence, and he was released on parole without bond "pending his good behavior."[72] On February 6, 1911, Van de Bogard, Dickey's half-brother, pled guilty to simple riot (not felony) charges and was sentenced to one year in the county jail. He too was paroled and released without bond, never to do time.[73] While no further prosecutions occurred, charges were allowed to "drift," as Malarkey put it, as a deterrent, but all were eventually abandoned. [74]

Mayor Hendricks's case vanished from area papers, his name mentioned only in the context of trials under way or in his capacity as mayor. Still, St. Johns had an indicted felon as mayor for close to a year. He had been the town's first mayor elected for two terms, but was not reelected in 1911.[75] Hendricks sold his business in 1911, gave up other city appointments, and reinvented himself as a local real estate agent. By 1912, he had moved out of the area entirely.[76] According to the *Morning Oregonian*, all charges against the mayor were formally dropped on March 6, 1912, the last of the legal actions resulting from the riot.[77] He promptly petitioned the St. Johns City Council to pay his legal fees, which, in a two-to-three vote, they agreed to do.[78]

In March 1910, the collective fears, and fearmongering, of many St. Johns residents were expressive of a national wave of anti-Indian hysteria filtered through hyperlocal anxieties. Exclusionist reports on the threatening "tide of turbans" ran hot in national and local presses in 1910, and news from the St. Johns riot added more grist to the animosity mill.[79]

In February 1910, the Asian Exclusion League (AEL) warned that, in just one week, 327 Hindus had arrived in San Francisco. *Colliers*, a popular magazine with national distribution, published its "Hindu Invasion" article with a photo spread spotlighting the men's turbans. It repeated AEL's absurd claim that "10,000 Indians lived in California," and that, because of this, "there is no doubt that popular sentiment in California is behind the League's appeal to Washington, DC for relief from this Hindu invasion which is beginning to assume alarming proportions."[80]

The *Colliers* article was followed by two more, similar in tone and content, in national magazines: the *Forum*'s "Tide of Turbans" in June and the *Survey* in October. The *Survey*, featuring a photo spread to help identify the problem people, claimed five thousand Indians had entered San Francisco that year and raised concerns about the "ability of the nation to assimilate this class of Hindus."[81] Many local presses followed suit, as did trade union newspapers, including in Portland. Beyond these formal outlets, whispers, grumblings, and worn exclusionists handbills spread anti-Indian vitriol from one mill, bar, and boardinghouse to the next. Promoted by government representatives, hate groups, mainstream sources, and rumor mills, hysteria over the menace of Indians was rampant in 1910. Fueled by fear, loathing, and ignorance, and wholly dismissive of fact, it was the fake news of its day.

The national furor was occasioned by a seeming lapse in San Francisco immigration officers' clampdown on Indian in-migration. In response to the 1907 ethnic unrest, US immigration officials selectively enforced their administrative rules and slashed the entry of Indians by roughly 80 percent between 1908 and 1909. Several immigration agents in San Francisco refused to abide by this policy promoted by agency superiors and local nativists and argued that agriculturalists needed workers. By the close of 1910, these agents had briefly restored Indian immigration to previous years' levels.[82] The resulting landings that year—a mere 1,800 Indian among a million some migrants nationally—constituted what newspapers railed against as "nothing more nor less than a threatening inundation of Hindoos over the Pacific Coast."[83] This political hurricane of national headlines and western labor agitation made landfall in St. Johns on March 21, 1910, turning local rumblings and an otherwise routine Monday night explosive.

On its face, branding 1,800 Indians a menacing tide is ludicrous. Yet in small-town St. Johns, it may well have seemed that Indians were growing by the "alarming proportions" claimed by the AEL. Especially for those steeped in Oregon's foundational white Eden ethos, Indians' presence symbolized the town's dramatic economic and demographic transformations wrought by the 1905 exhibition: burgeoning manufacturing, commerce, and prosperity for many, accompanied and enabled by an influx of nonwhite workers. Those who acted out on March 21, 1910, or defended their actions after, feared or opposed the cultural implication of industrially fueled globalization on their town and their lives. Or, more simply put, they believed St. Johns was becoming a "Hindu city."

The *Review* gave clear voice to local white anxieties and bigotries. After years and months of silence about Indians in St. Johns, post-riot the newspaper positioned itself as the community champion of all things "anti-Hindu." It consistently demeaned Indians as "an undesirable class of human beings" that "all" townspeople agreed were a problem. Its only riot critique was that, because it was unlawful, it brought trouble to the city:

We all want them to go and mingle with their own kind. If they were cleanly in their own habits, conform to American dress and customs, be of some good to the country, no objection to their remaining and becoming useful citizens would be made. . . . They love to parade up and down the public thoroughfares. Strangers coming to town get an impression that it is a Hindu city, and it is a great incentive for them to make a hasty exit. But to remove them, mob methods are not the way.[84]

In fact, not "all" people in St. Johns supported or took part in the riot. The mob made up perhaps 5 percent of the town's population, not accounting for outsiders. More than a hundred white and Indian residents enabled formal charges, testified at trial, and were publicly named, if also legally compelled, for doing so. Mr. Ayers maintained Indians' jobs at St. Johns Lumber and testified on their behalf.

Still, the riot and its aftermath revealed a convergence of some whites from differing social strata who, at a minimum, were out to rid St. Johns of visible Indians, a goal articulated and amplified by the *Review*. Besides assailing Indians for "parad[ing] up and down the public thoroughfares," the *Review* specifically noted Indians downtown residency as a riot trigger. [85] Participants bonded over a ruination narrative: Indians burned down up-and-coming businesses and jeopardized jobs, while their visibility threatened the town's growth. Symbolically and practically, their outrage converged on St. Johns' city center and sought to transform it into an Indian no-go zone. Indians might work in the area, but unlike other community members, it was unacceptable for them to live or socialize in the town's heart. It was an enforcement, and reinforcement, of a cultural geography of whiteness.

The mob's first target was a prominent downtown St. Johns saloon and nearby Indian housing. They did not target the Monarch bunkhouse on the town's outskirts, perhaps out of simple convenience. The *Review*, otherwise so specific in its recitation of the threats posed by Indians, never mentioned the Monarch Mill, where fifty or more Indians worked and lived. Yet the Monarch workers patronized downtown St. Johns to shop, drink, socialize, or to catch the streetcar into Portland. After a quick ferry ride and walk up the hill, so too did Indians working across the Willamette River in Linnton. Targeting downtown

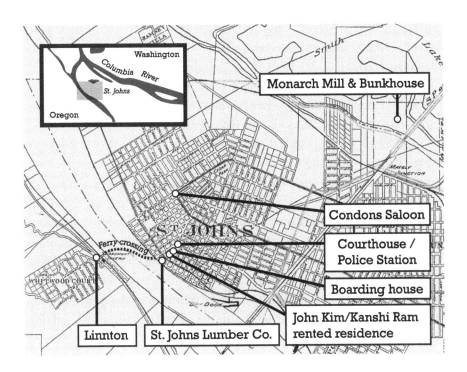

was a pointed message to this broader Indian community, perpetrated for differing reasons by whites of differing social strata.

Local businessmen, city officials, and the *Review* were financially and politically invested in the benefits of St. Johns' "destiny of glorious growth" that flowed overwhelmingly to whites by means of the racial proscriptions on professional licensure, bank loans, and property ownership. Backing, if not plotting, the riot was their means of protecting and ensuring St. Johns' future against racial interlopers, aka a "Hindu city."[86] Several city officials and employees, though not convicted, were indicted and otherwise implicated for condoning or participating in the night's violence. Mayor Hendricks and city attorney Collier essentially made the defense of rioters a plank for reelection. The city council, meeting the day after the riot, did not call for an investigation of the night's events, but instead ensured both city and private legal representation for arrested volunteer firefighters, police, and other residents.

Peter Autzen, owner of Portland Manufacturing Company, allegedly burned down by an Indian, was listed as a potential character witness for Dickey at trial.[87] Prominent citizens like Dr. Joseph McChesney, "physician and surgeon," and real estate agent J. S. McKinney paid Dickey's $3,000 bail and attorney's fees (equivalent to approximately $85,000 in 2021). J. H. Walker of Oregon City, a "timber superintendent," and Thomas G. Farnell, a Portland "merchant," also posted $2000. [88] These men's involvement underscores that Dickey had notable upper-class backing. Who else in the community had the means and the motivation to support the rioters, perhaps contributing to Dickey's attorney fees or posting bail for other men?

Careful review of the night's details also suggests that the riot was, at least in part, premeditated. The *Review* signaled that, on the night of March 21, the crowd met "either by accident *or design* [emphasis added]."[89] One report stated that Dickey dismissed his crew at 3:30 on the afternoon of the incident (a power reflecting his lower-management role), and took a readied petition to demand that Condon's stop serving Indians.[90] While other accounts make no mention of the petition, they do describe that, after Dickey and others spilled into the street outside of Condon's Saloon, a crowd of two to three hundred quickly converged and took up Dickey's directives. Perhaps circulating the petition was enough to notify the men to gather. DDA Garland, however, charged that the town's fire alarm had been sounded as a signal to gather the crowd, and several volunteer firefighters were indicted coconspirators. The *Review* dismissed Garland's claim, saying the alarm was merely the means for firefighters to assemble for their regular meeting. It was, however, enough of a question that the newspaper felt compelled to dispute it. Riot organizers certainly could have utilized a known event—like the firefighters' alarm—for their own purposes.[91]

The crowd might also have been confident they would have the run of the town, as Dickey reportedly paid off police officer Dunbar to not interfere.[92] There was testimony that the mayor did not interfere, even while hearing an Indian man plead for the mayor's protection as he was dragged away and loaded onto the Portland-bound streetcar. Instead, the mayor reportedly told the lingering crowd, "Now boys, if you just quit it now, we will see that they are all run out by Wednesday."[93] Was there a second phase to the night's plan that did not play itself out, because of the Indians' demand for the immediate intervention of the Multnomah County district attorney's office and British consul?

While the riot demonstrated both convergence and collusion among different social strata of whites in St. Johns, the ramifications of men's involvement was far from equivalent. Of the many participants, laborers were the majority of those arrested and charged. Of the two convicted, one was a laborer, the other a low-level manager. Wealthy or influential members of St. Johns desired a white St. Johns, but laborers were objectively the plan's on-the-ground enforcers and bore the brunt of the night's consequences. Small-town life enabled mill managers, owners, and foremen to know, or find, the like-minded or vulnerable to do their bidding. Foreman Dickey was an invaluable intermediary in this respect: trusted by elites and supervising and working with mill laborers.

Mill manager Ayers contradicted the dominant logic of race and labor management in St. Johns. He continued to employ Indians while simultaneously blaming white workers for his need to do so. Using language nearly identical to that of Bellingham mill owners in 1907, Ayers voiced the common bromide that white workers were lazy, not available or reliable, and only worked for "whiskey money."[94] Industrialists and their managers like Ayers commonly pitted workers against one another to reduce wages and foster workplace compliance. What Mr. Ayers and others left self-servingly unsaid was that Indians' reliability and hard work was, in part, a product of the very competition that he and his mill fostered. Indians' tenuous economic and social position necessitated they be model workers to secure and maintain employment in the reputedly free labor market. Ayer's stance was at odds with prominent local community voices—the mayor, Judge Olson, *Review* reporters—who believed Indians' visible presence blighted the town's reputation, threatening citizen safety and white employment.

Class power differential in St. Johns did not preclude white laborers' independent agency. They were, however, animated by fears and anxieties distinct from city officials, industry owners, foremen, or middle-class professionals and business owners. If laborers were, effectively, ground troops for broader efforts to expel Indians, they also acted as "free white workers" who construed Indians as social and economic threats outside the bonds of class solidarity. Their downtown interventions were about the preservation of status, not businesses. Sharing leisure time in Condon's Saloon symbolized a troubling equivalence between Indian and white workers' standing; the rhetoric of "invasion" more social than economic. Author Isabel Wilkerson describes the psychology of white status as "an inherited, unspoken superiority, a natural deservedness over subordinated castes. They had relied on this illusion, perhaps beyond the realm of consciousness, . . . in a forbiddingly competitive society 'in which downward social mobility was a constant fear,' the historian David Roediger wrote. 'One might lose everything, but not whiteness.'"[95] Expressions of white anxiety and entitlement were carried across multiple platforms before and after 1910.

Across the North American west, exclusionist organizations and activists were instrumental in promoting anti-Asian beliefs and hostilities. True to form, they exploited the riot and, similar to the *St. Johns Review*, invoked the fear of "Hindus" dominating the town. The *White Man*, an openly white supremacist newspaper published outside of Oregon, also employed the well-worn trope of nonwhite men's threat to white womanhood, reporting that the "300–400 Hindus in St Johns"

form half the visible population at all times. They were grouped on the walks and entrances of stores and would stare at and frighten the women and children and pass insulting remarks in pigeon English at the young women. The Hindus are accustomed in their country to use any language they see fit to women, and they keep up the practice in the United States. . . . The newspapers state the cause of the riot was a squabble in a saloon between a white man and a Hindu. They fail to state, however, that the cause of the saloon fight was the fact that a Hindu had made an insulting and suggestive gesture to a young white woman, and he had actually put his hands on her and frightened her into a hysterical condition.[96]

In St. Johns, however, no local or contemporaneous evidence of the AEL or other explicitly exclusionist labor organizations remains, and perhaps never existed. In a sense it was unnecessary. Mainstream labor organizations and overt exclusionist movements dovetailed in both strategy and philosophy, and labor newspapers of the day framed a pervasive anti-Asian message. On both accounts, Portland was no exception. Well before March 1910, an explicit exclusionist message ran in the pages of the *Portland Labor Press* (*PLP*), the city's leading labor newspaper and the mouthpiece of the Portland Federated Trades Council.

In the years preceding the St. Johns unrest, the pages of the *PLP* were peppered with anti-Asian rhetoric against the Chinese and Japanese that soon enveloped Indians. The *PLP* ran numerous reprints of exclusionist missives and demands to maintain the 1882 Chinese Exclusion Act. There were calls to prevent the admission of "coolie labor" and enjoinders to "join a labor union and protect yourself against the Japanese invasion." The paper argued that the solution to crime was to target immigrants. It carried numerous aspirational reports on the white settler colonies of New Zealand and Australian labor organizations' efforts to restrict Chinese immigration.[97] In March 1907, the *PLP* supported the launch of a local Labor Party, which supported Asian exclusion.

The paper did not simply express competitive fears but constructed Asian laborers as morally deficient if not depraved. Its pages carried obscene notes, such as "Three bad Chinamen have been turned into good ones by electrocution [at] the Massachusetts state prison for killing four others in a tong war. Total of seven reformed Chinese for the state."[98] In February 1910, in the supposed service of labor, the *PLP* wrote, "It is said no one ever sees a Jap funeral and that the 10-cent Jap restaurant makes use of the cadavers to save butcher bills. This is a little strong, but it is passing from hand to hand among some of the union labor men as a means of encouraging patronage of white cooks."[99] Such dehumanizing articles fed white supremacist views and actions and delineated the *PLP*'s position on the racial boundary of laborers to be organized and defended. Over the years, the *PLP* also ran numerous articles and calls from the AEL in its pages. In February 1910, it openly trumpeted the AEL's shrill claims: "There recently arrived in one day 191 Hindoo laborers at the port of San Francisco. Many people consider them worse than the Chinese coolie." [100]

As would be expected, the *PLP* also reported on strikes, documented the state of various trades, and opined on civic elections. Preceding the riot, the newspaper's overall view of the state of labor in Portland was positive. In the summer of 1907, it reported that the council represented five thousand men and women and more than forty unions.[101] By February 1910, the paper declared that "every union

YOUR POWER LIES IN ORGANIZATION

BUILD MILITANT UNIONISM

Industrial Workers of the World
222 SW Main
Portland..........Oregon

Poster from Portland IWW Chapter,
date unknown, Oregon Hist. Soc.
Research Lib., Orhi77728

in Portland" reported an increase in membership and "slow but steady improvement in hours and wages."[102]

There is little evidence that differential wages were an issue. The *PLP* generally charged that Asian laborers undercut white wages but offered nothing more detailed regarding Indians in St. Johns. The *Review* reported few specifics about Indians' wages in St. Johns; its one mention stated that Indians made $1.80 per day while whites earned $2.00. A 10 percent wage disparity, and no indication by the *PLP* or others of a shortage of jobs, does not square with the level of animosity exhibited against Indians, suggesting that more was at stake.

Intersecting with its consistent anti-Asian politics was the *PLP*'s hostility toward the newly formed Industrial Workers of the World (IWW), the only labor organization that thoroughly rejected the PLP's and others' racial boundaries of solidarity. The *PLP* condemned the IWW for two reasons. First, the IWW opposed the American Federation of Labor (AFL) with which the *PLP* and the Trades Council were associated. Unlike the IWW, the AFL under the leadership of Samuel Gompers was a "craft" union of trades. It organized the better-paid, more stably employed, and overwhelmingly white workers and was an avid proponent of Chinese exclusion. Second, the *PLP* attacked the IWW for its recruitment of Chinese, Japanese, and Indian workers—all overrepresented in less-rewarded and less respected positions, and often termed unskilled—into its organization, fighting for all laborers rights. Punjab-born and soon-to-be Ghadar leader Sohan Singh Bhakna, of St. Johns, was one such Portland member.[103]

Unfortunately, it is impossible to report the IWW's exact position on St. Johns. The March 1910 troubles were not covered in the pages of the *Industrial Worker*, then a four-page weekly IWW newspaper for the Northwest. The omission is plausibly explained by the newspaper's focus on the Spokane Free Speech Fight, a major, national, yearlong battle for the IWW that was resolved almost simultaneously with the riot. The reporting gap does not mean, however, that the IWW was not a forceful local presence; it had multiple chapters in and around Portland that led a number of strikes between 1907 and 1916.[104] Further, while the PLP and other labor papers wrote with a racially poisoned pen, the IWW and its press was committed to interracial, anticapitalist unionism. It called on white workers to "do away with racial prejudice and imaginary boundary lines, recognize that all workers belong to the international nation of wealth producers, and clearly see that our only enemy is the capitalist class and the only boundary line is between exploiter and exploited."[105] Beyond just words, the group actively recruited laborers of all ethnicities, publishing and organizing in multiple languages.

The IWW was not without flaws. They ran some articles that repeated racist clichés, an unsurprising fact given the ubiquity of racial supremacist action and thinking.[106] Less obviously problematic was the IWW's casting of Indians as "manly unionists deserving of class inclusion."[107] On one level, this countered the depiction of Indians by British colonizers and many North American labor leaders as "servile and unmanly." (Ghadris also cast themselves and the struggle in gendered terms.[108]) The IWW critiqued the AFL's "manhood" for bowing to industry's divide-and-conquer tactics and promoted the grit of Asian workers through numerous accounts of global labor struggles.[109] However, as historian Kornel Chang and others argue, manhood and whiteness were overlapping outlooks of control.[110] Meaning that, besides sidelining women, "manhood" did not escape the racial confines of the day.

Despite their shortcomings, Indians in Portland and across the global West had capable, committed allies. The IWW's internationalist, anticapitalist stance was, as Chang writes, "remarkable by any standard."[111] For IWW organizers, radical Indian nationalists, along with Mexicans and others, concretized their vision of a global struggle against capitalism.[112] Together the groups forged a dynamic fusion between the struggles against national subjugation and class exploitation, worrisome to US, Canadian, and British authorities alike.[113]

As these brief snapshots of labor organizations suggest, across the US west, laborers banded together in organizations with diverse outlooks and aims to confront the massive changes and threats to their lives and livelihoods. The post–Civil War industrialism that transformed the region had dramatically transformed people's lives and dreams. Workers had a host of reasons to be restless about their lives, marked as they were by instability, transience, and danger.

Laborers of all ethnicities were locked in struggle with industrialists over their conditions. Western work was dangerous, and laborers lopsidedly bore the dangers of the mining and timber industries fueling the economy.[114] Private industrial police beat, murdered, and blackballed them for daring to demand safety in the mines, adequate food in logging camps, and an eight-hour day. Employment was frequently erratic. In 1914, the average duration of a lumber camp job was fifteen to thirty days, a cannery was a month, and a mining operation was two months.[115] The boom-and-bust cycles of speculative and market-driven economies were compounded by the magnitude of the industrial engine being brought on line in the North American west. As it bumped and jostled with world markets, it upended people's lives as the labor deck reshuffled to account for too many workers in a place or time, adding to laborers' insecurities.

As industrialists upgraded technologies, the demand for unskilled work increased, as did the racialized gulf between skilled and unskilled labor.[116] The implications of these divides flowed well beyond money. One held the promise of stability, family life, personal accumulation, and self-worth. Home ownership, churches, and schools followed steady workers, as did mainline labor organizations. The unskilled faced migrancy, rough and impermanent living conditions, and tenuous social standing.[117] These differences were even more pronounced in the Pacific Northwest, where craft laborers generally earned higher wages, owned more homes, and married more than their counterparts in the east.[118] Such markers of stability were culturally loaded in settler colonial countries, where the domination of land and Indigenous peoples was a reflection of racial superiority. Society was encoded as being made by and for the stable and upstanding, not the racially imbued shiftless and undesirable "other"; the organization of work and civil society forming an ugly feedback loop regarding racial standing.

Tragically, across the world and across the North American west, white laborers' opposition to their exploitation by industrialists commonly became fused and, arguably, diffused by a hatred of "the other." Even when whites worked side by side with Chinese, Japanese, and Indian workers, they were largely unable to act in common against labor exploitation. Instead, among millions displaced from and deprived in their home countries and in a milieu of different languages and cultures, white supremacy reared its ugly head. Unlike the precious radicals in the IWW or a few socialist circles, many laborers and their organizations were unwilling to stand for parity as the most effective weapon in their fight for economic equality and social power. [119] Instead, on March 21 in St. Johns, as in so many times and towns before, numerous laborers attempted to expel and dominate their Indian coworkers in an effort to preserve their (often marginally) privileged status as free, white workers.

After the riot, G. L. Perrine, a self-described socialist, wrote a letter to the *Review* that, on first blush, could be construed (as I first did) as confused but sympathetic to Indians. Read through the politics of the mainstream global labor movement, however, it succinctly expresses its entrenched supremacist views. Perrine, citing the Republican Party platforms of the 1880s as his authority, and employing well-worn dog-whistle terms, voiced opposition to all forms of slave and contract labor on US shores. Like the Republicans, he argued that "cheap labor 'degrades' the laborers by lowering the standard of their living," and he critiqued the "capitalist class" for promoting such debased conditions. While declaring that "Hindus" are not the working man's enemy, Perrine's solution is nonetheless telling. "We feel we would lift the Hindu up; but we are opposed to having him drag us down. This we can do by *excluding him and all others of his class from our shores* [emphasis added]."[120]

Perrine, the self-identified socialist, did not call for workers of the world to unite, or to fight for the equality of all those laboring in America. Instead, he argued for the exclusion of the racially defined slave and contract worker to defend American—read white—workers. Perrine's letter expresses the "white labourism"—class struggle fused with racism—that dominated the global organized labor movement.[121] The global pervasiveness of such politics works to explain how the themes of white right and the Hindu peril seemingly emerged overnight in the streets of St. Johns and Portland's labor press.

Justice in St. Johns was woefully inadequate, but that trials even occurred was noteworthy. The much larger 1907 anti-Asian riots in Bellingham and Vancouver, BC, received no such prosecutorial attention. In Washington, the British consulate in Seattle performed the formality of a complaint to the US government but pressed no further. Bellingham authorities threatened action, but those arrested were never prosecuted, reportedly due to their inability to secure witnesses.[122] In Vancouver, the government took no action against the rioters. Instead, the local and provincial governments, in league with British colonial authorities, banned further Indian immigration and intensively surveilled the extant community.[123]

In response to a smaller riot, Oregon authorities aided by the British and US governments indicted multiple assailants and convicted two. Malarkey's reports make clear that, had it not been for state intervention, witness testimony would not have been secured in St. Johns.[124] With the exception of Boring, the St. Johns legal and political battle was unprecedented for Indians in the North American west. Its ambivalent outcome was emblematic of the Portland area's specific racial strategy in the service of white supremacy and securing a labor force.[125]

The failure to secure numerous convictions, impose jail time, or definitively incriminate city officials is indicative of its political limits. Whites—laborers, foremen, and officials alike—were publicly disciplined (indictments and a trial) but not penalized (no jail time or fines). Yet by prosecuting the St. Johns rioters, Portland authorities made an object lesson about mob violence in small-town Oregon and the businessmen, city officials, and common people who refused to toe the line. Importantly, authorities' actions enabled Indians to return to their jobs, a process that did not occur in Everett or Bellingham, but was the very purpose of Portland's no-violence policy.[126] What Portland and British authorities did not anticipate is that after the trials, aimed at ensuring a workforce and burnishing the "protector" image of British authorities, Indians would draw their own independent political conclusions regarding justice and colonial politics.

British consul Laidlaw, as a Portland resident and member of the city's elite, likely respected the local racial ethos and was intimately engaged with the St. Johns' prosecution.[127] His involvement also infuriated the *Review*, and for months the newspaper railed at the overreach of the "British lion," furious it did not support a "white-man's" St. Johns as it had in British Columbia after 1907.[128] Blinded by its parochial racism, the *Review* could not conceive of Indians as having any importance to the British Empire, let alone that Indians globally were driving the transformations in British tactics pursued by Consul Laidlaw and his superiors.

In 1910, Consul Laidlaw advocated on behalf of Indians because he viewed mollifying his subjects as best serving British interests. The British Crown and its consulates had been closely monitoring and were deeply concerned about the unrest and radical organizing among Indians in North America, especially in Vancouver, BC, and San Francisco. By intervening in St. Johns, Consul Laidlaw attempted to blunt Indians' roiling discontent and foster the belief that British and US authorities could be trusted to protect Indians' lives and dignity. Having gained some credibility and commendation for his role in investigating the 1907 Washington state anti-Indian violence and prosecution of the Boring, Oregon, murderers, Laidlaw was entrusted with handling the 1910 St. Johns imbroglio in the best interests of his government.[129]

That Laidlaw was attending to his government's, and not Indians', welfare is illustrated by a seemingly minor housekeeping detail. Once it was decided that no further prosecutions would be pursued, particularly of the mayor or police, Laidlaw sought approval for attorney Malarkey's substantial legal bill ($850, or roughly $25,000 a century later).[130] There were also other bills to attend to. Nine men who were attacked the night of March 21 submitted affidavits prepared by Malarkey (for which he likely charged), listing their losses to the consulate. Harnam Singh detailed lost days of work and stolen articles of clothing and cash totaling $29.75 ($850 in 2021 value). The itemizations of

G. Frank, Sunder Singh, Dulla, Inder [Indar] Singh, Khem Chand, B. Singh, Maharaj, and Dalip Singh were of a similar sort and value, the nine men's combined totals amounting to half of Malarkey's invoice.[131] Malarkey was paid, the injured Indians were not.

Because there was no conviction of any government official in St. Johns, British officials from Portland to London reasoned there were no grounds for submitting Indians' damages to the US government.[132] (That the British government should compensate them was not mentioned.) The British had sought a political verdict, and, by the metrics of Malarkey's report, it was achieved, and he was paid handsomely for delivering it. Assisting Indians in seeking remuneration for their losses simply did not figure into their geopolitical calculations.

Securing a political verdict, however, sent British authorities down a slippery political slope, one that encouraged a measure of Indian civic power. Indians became plaintiffs who brought a white mayor, policemen, and others up on charges, and they were heard in the local papers. They challenged entrenched white power and tasted what it meant to have some of the very rights denied to them under British rule, however tenuous and incomplete it proved to be in St. Johns. After Dickey's conviction, neither Consul Laidlaw nor police agent Hopkinson detected anything of political concern among area laborers in late 1911 or early 1912, only their supposed distrust of radical Taraknath Das.[133] Both Laidlaw and Hopkinson, like their superiors, stayed focused on the threat of West Coast students and radical intellectuals. But as St. Johns' resident Sohan Singh Bhakna later wrote, in laborers' eyes, Laidlaw "did not do anything meaningful" with respect to the riot.[134] With the close of the trials, they embarked on their own independent path toward justice and liberation.

On the night of March 21, 1910, men armed with a sense of entitlement, economic fear, and ethnic belligerence robbed, beat, and temporarily expelled dozens of "Hindu" men. The attorneys, consuls, judges, and press reported on and prosecuted what appeared to be a maddening local incident. It proved to be far from just another white riot in another small, upstart western town. St. Johns had global ramifications.

Through the course of the St. Johns fight, Indians grew and transformed. If Oregon had been the last hope for carving out a more peaceful or fruitful life, that notion was shattered for many in March 1910.

In response, Indians acted. They pushed the district attorney, British consulate, and the other officials to intercede. They raised money, gained and discussed press coverage and how to respond, and debated legal strategies and the implications of courtroom decisions. In this, they had the support of Indians throughout the region, which in turn strengthened regional networks and ties. Maybe some were emboldened by their success, if others were sobered by its limits. But they no doubt discussed and argued about what the riot and the ensuing two-year fight meant—for their future and for their life plans.

Events in small-town St. Johns fused with the string of broken promises, poverty, and dispossession, and came to threaten the British Empire. The rising restive tide of the community, the product of injustices suffered in India and across the global diaspora, conditioned and formed their response. Not content with minor momentary justice against local attackers, Indians in St. Johns focused on transforming their global subjugated status. Timing, personalities, experience, and simple chance sparked an unforeseeable synergy in St. Johns. With the dismissal of the final cases in 1912, Indians in St. Johns initiated meetings and alliances that culminated in Ghadar one short year later.

4
From St. Johns to Astoria: From Riots to Anticolonial Organizing

The St. Johns' attack was, in the words of Sohan Singh Bhakna, "a wakeup call and a game changer for Indians working in Oregon and Washington State." They were not simply angry, they were changed. Bhakna tells of "habitual drinkers [who] totally became sober and stopped visiting bars altogether. Where they would bribe to get ahead of each other to get jobs, now they would help out a coworker who was unjustly treated or thrown out of job. They would even give him free food until he found employment. This coworker sympathy now went beyond Indians. If a worker from another country was unfairly treated or forced to accept lower wages, Indians would help him too."[1]

Just as Indians had been invisible and underestimated in St. Johns, so too was the rich community of radicalized global people they worked and lived among. Bhakna recalled that, as Indians transformed their own habits and interactions, "other foreign workers began to sympathize with them. . . . Workers from . . . Japan, China, Turkey, Russia, and Ireland . . . were all working together and there were freedom struggles going on in these countries also. Whenever the mill stopped, even for 5 minutes, they would share the news collected from newspapers and letters from home with each other and exchange opinions." After 1910, there was no other attack against Indian workers, which Bhakna attributed to "the new awakening among Indians to fight back and winning the sympathy of other co-workers from other countries who began to help them in the just struggle."[2]

By early spring of 1912, as the riot trials came to a close, a group of Indians gathered in St. Johns to study and debate the causes of their suffering and the means for ending it.[3] They called themselves the Pacific Coast Hindi Association (sometimes translated as Hindustan

Association of the Pacific Coast) and elected laborer Sohan Singh Bhakna president, labor contractor Kanshi Ram/John Kim treasurer, and G. D. Kumar, a radical colleague of Taraknath Das, general secretary. They began with actions common for the times—importing papers from India to stay abreast of news and sponsoring Indian students to train in the United States.[4] (Training students in the West in technical skills and nationalist thought outside of British interference was a common go-to for organizers preparing for Indian self-rule.) Within six months, the group grew to some seventy members, including a second chapter in Astoria headed by Kesar Singh, Munshi Karim Bakhsh, and Munshi Ram.[5]

The men had plenty to talk about. They had organized immediately after that dark March 1910 night, yet in the end justice remained elusive and their fundamental status unchanged. Why were they so hated when, like millions of others, they had migrated to work? Why, despite the queen's promise, did subjugation shadow them everywhere? Their discussions and debates animated bunkhouses and work breaks, enriched by the experiences and insights of other global workers and Indian activists like Pandurang Khankhoje, an Oregon Agricultural College student.[6] It was a dangerous line of questioning. Within a year, the Hindi Association became the organizing core for Ghadar, and the clearest confirmation of Sohan Singh Bhakna's assessment that the riot and its aftermath had led them to take "the slavery curse to their hearts for the first time."[7] Events large and small had brought them to this juncture.

Everyday life supplied endless reminders of Indians' second-class status. As Bhakna recounted, "Many times kids will follow us in streets . . . shouting 'Hindoo Slaves!' We were made to feel too ashamed to look back."[8] Men were often barred from or assigned special seats in theaters and saloons. It was reminiscent of home, where railcars were segregated between British and Indians, and signs in public places read, "Dogs and Indians not allowed." Professor Teja Singh, then of Vancouver, BC, visited Bhakna in Portland. Hungry after touring city sites, they were turned away from lunch in what he described as an "American" hotel, finally taking their meal instead at a Japanese restaurant.[9] All around them, as Bhakna recalled, they witnessed America's relative freedoms—to vote (men and women), to carry a gun, to develop one's own country. It provided an illuminating contrast to their colonial lives in India. Given Indians' exclusion from such rights in India and North America, it was also a gnawing taunt.[10]

Important as these day-to-day encounters and gestures were, events beyond the ordinary and the local fueled their ruminations. With startling reach, speed, and detail, news traveled the globe through letters, telegrams, newspapers, religious services, and by word of mouth from those traveling by ship, rail, and on their own two feet. Indians in St. Johns were wired into the global migrant community networks growing increasingly restive against British colonial rule and contributing news from St. Johns.[11]

The Oregon men considered their experiences—both the riot and its aftermath—from the broader lens of the diasporic community, especially in evaluating British intentions. British consul Laidlaw and the Crown may have hoped to quiet the rising restive tide by intervening on Indians' behalf in St. Johns. But it proved too little, too late. After all they had endured, Indians in Oregon and elsewhere were not easily disabused of their mounting mistrust of the British, which flourished particularly in the political aftermath of the 1907 violence and authorities' overt and covert attacks on overseas Indians. As Bhakna later reflected,

It was not that the foreign workers were all Indians, nor was it that they were the only ones accepting lower wages than others. In fact Japanese and Chinese would accept lower wages than Indians to get work. Still the American worker was madder at Indians. The respective governments of other workers were always there to back them up. Only Indian workers were slaves and orphan-like and that was the reason for their humiliation and insults. Now the Indian worker had not any doubt left in their mind that the real reason for their unrelenting humiliation was their being slaves in their country India.[12]

Indians were coming to, as radical theorist Antonio Gramsci expressed it, "the consciousness of what one really is."[13] Ghadar historians commonly tag that awareness to an unprecedented union of Indian intellectuals, students, veterans, and laborers, a first in Indian overseas organizations.[14] Long after-the-fact memoirs blur precise accounts of time, place, and people, further complicated by competing claims to being Ghadar founders.[15] Yet Indians in Oregon were undoubtedly aided in their emergent political consciousness by a small army of peripatetic radical Indian intellectuals in the West: G. D. Kumar, Taraknath Das, Ram Nath Puri, Pandurang Khankhoje, Thakur Das, and Har Dayal, with their many experiences, alliances, presses, and fleeting organizations. Self-exiled or expelled by Indian colonial authorities because of their politics, these nationalists engaged in what was impossible in India or the expatriate centers of Europe: learning from, agitating among, and organizing with laborers.

Indians in St. Johns were likewise moved by the winds of change blowing south from British Columbia, where roughly half of the community comprised veterans of British colonial forces.[16] Infuriated by the 1908 Continuous Journey provision and the proposed removal of Indians to British Honduras, the Vancouver gurdwara became a community organizing center. Lingering faith in British promises frayed as Indians' multiple petitions and delegations requesting concessions fell on deaf governmental ears, even for those who had loyally served. By 1910, the community raged against deportations and proscriptions against familial migrations.[17] Capturing the political stakes of these battles, Chagan Kairaj Varma, aka Hussain Rahim, whose targeted deportation was defeated by community action, vowed that "if you drive us Hindus out of Canada we will drive every white man out of India."[18] By 1912, the visit of Duke Connaught, the governor general of Canada, Queen Victoria's son and England's highest ranking officer in Canada, was publicly boycotted by prominent Sikh military veterans.[19] A growing distrust and humiliation led many toward an increasingly militant turn, with multiple programs and people vying over the path forward. In other words, it was not just anti-Hindu rumblings that made landfall in St. Johns, but the rising tide of Indian radicalism.

The shift was more than the result of a generalized anger but arose from a very particular politics. As historian Maia Ramnath writes, Ghadar connected "the history of race and class in the United States, and of colonization in what we would now call the global south."[20] Ramnath describes not an abstraction, but the thoughts and actions of flesh-and-blood people. One seemingly apocryphal story that has survived and is often cited in Ghadar literature captures this turn. It recounts an interaction between Sohan Singh Bhakna and a friend, who were seeking a job from a local mill foreman.

> The manager of the mill offered them chairs respectfully:
> When they asked about a job he replied: "There is enough work but not for you."
> "Why not for us?" they asked meekly.
> "You ask for work. I want that both of you should be shot," the factory manager said excitedly.
> "Why? What have we done?"
> "How large is your population?"
> "Three hundred million."
> "Three hundred million men or sheep?"
> "Men."
> "Men? Had you been men you could not have been slaves until now," he said contemptuously and added "Go, I shall give you a gun each. First liberate your country. When you would come as liberated people to America, I would be in the forefront to welcome you."[21]

A similarly inclined letter to the editor appeared in the *Morning Oregonian,* reading in part, "Isn't it about time those Hindus got wise to themselves and followed the example of China? It's up to the Hindus themselves. . . . Why don't our friend Kenchu Kun try to be a second Sun Yat-sen?"[22] The letter signals both a limited (and garbled) recognition of Kanshi Ram/Jon Kim's leadership and that Indians' future direction was a question in Portland.

It seems improbable, though not impossible, that a mill foreman offered Bhakna and his friend guns to fight for their liberty in India. But read as a parable, the story arguably situates Ramnath's point precisely where, as she writes, "the politics of labor, race and imperialism converge."[23] It draws the links between the threats of economic and bodily violence Indians faced in North America. It suggests that their submission (or not) was a choice. It proffers the need to return to India, guns in hand, to make themselves free as a condition for their (highly gendered) respect and to take part in the liberties (however flawed) Indians observed daily in America, including the right to be free

American wage laborers, to vote, to own land, and to fully participate in civic life. Bhakna expressed these connections in the everyday language and familiar setting in which Indians lived as racialized laborers and colonized people.

Bhakna's story also sheds a bright light on why Ghadris did not stay and fight for equal rights in America but instead returned to transform India as the source of their global disrespect. They now understood Queen Victoria's promise of an equal, colorblind imperial status for the whites-first reality stalking Indians everywhere. In Bhakna's story, overthrowing the British was intimately tied to their ability to be considered free laborers and citizens by the mythical mill foreman. In short, it guides us beyond consideration of the injurious curse of racists, to the workings and divides of global labor, which, combined with British crimes in the homeland, politicized and soon motivated thousands to reverse the course of their lives and risk everything to overthrow colonial rule.

Bhakna's account also highlights a surprising intertwining and synergy to the racial targeting and democratic exclusion of Indians and others, which in settler colonies paralleled a historic extension of democratic rights to landless whites. The Indians who founded Ghadar fought those laborers who targeted them for their nonwhiteness. But they also sought the rights and relative freedoms those same white workers exercised, just as British authorities feared they might. Indians explicitly did both in St. Johns. As historian Harish Puri has long argued, it was in their exposure to democratic freedoms, if deeply riven by class and racial oppression, that Indians saw the power of self-rule.[24] Indians came to understand that obtaining the right to rule and be citizens of their own country—rights globally reserved for whites—were crucial. Without such powers, they would always be considered "black thieves everywhere," as a later Ghadar poem expressed it.[25] In the aftermath of the St. Johns riot, Indians demanded and received a taste of such rights and sought them for their country.

At its foundation, Ghadar was a movement of workers, initiated, fueled, and framed by their life experience. In St. Johns, a core of laborers, as if living the scene from Sohan Singh Bhakna's mill-manager tale, joined the essentials of their lives in North America and as colonized peoples in India. Their instincts and experiences were given voice and form by important radicals with whom they worked over the years. In that dynamic process, as historian Puri argues, intellectuals, students, and workers alike were transformed.[26]

By late 1912, the seventy-some members of Oregon's Pacific Coast Hindi Association sought greater political direction. Those who had provided much of their guidance were not available: Taraknath Das was studying at UC Berkeley, and Gurdit Kumar had fallen ill.[27] So, in the fall of 1912, the Hindi Association invited Har Dayal north.[28] He arrived in St. Johns six months later, and the course of radical Indian politics changed.

Har Dayal became, without question, Ghadar's most prominent public figure. But on his fateful trip from the Bay Area to Oregon in the spring of 1913, he was as much convert as catalyst. Like most Indian nationalists—whether in Bengal, Paris, London, New York, or San Francisco—he had long operated without a mass base.[29] In Oregon that fact dramatically changed.

Dayal is described as brilliant by both contemporaries and historians. In 1905, he was awarded a scholarship to Oxford by the government of India with the expectation he would return to India and a position within the colonial apparatus. Shortly before completion of his studies, however, Dayal quit Oxford in protest of British rule, signaling his refusal to serve it. After leaving Oxford, Dayal worked among the Indian émigré nationalist circles of London and Paris, where he interacted with Russian, Egyptian, Irish, and other revolutionists for several years. He got critical, hands-on experience writing speeches and articles and preparing newspapers for global distribution, including for smuggling into India. [30]

After leaving Europe, he traveled to several West Indian islands in deep consideration of his own philosophy and life's work. By early 1911, he had made his way to America with the intention of enrolling in Harvard graduate school. Dayal's plans changed, reportedly at the urging of Teja Singh. From his organizing in British Columbia against the British Honduras relocation plan, Teja Singh was acutely aware of the important stirrings among laborers in the West and urged Har Dayal to join them. After drifting geographically and philosophically a bit longer, Dayal had become entrenched in San Francisco and its broad, international, radical scene by the late summer of 1911.[31]

Dayal biographer Emily Brown writes that, by "the end of 1912, Har Dayal was a figure to be reckoned with, as well known in Washington [DC] as he had been in official circles in London, Delhi, Calcutta and Simla. His literary production had made him one of the most 'avidly' read young Indians of his time. . . . Wherever Hay Dayal went, he was excitement."[32] It was for good reason that in the fall of 1912 Thakur Das, then of St. Johns but reportedly sent to organize in Oregon by leaders within Parisian Indian émigré circles, recommended the laborers invite Har Dayal to help determine their next steps. It is conceivable that Dayal delayed travel through Oregon's southern mountain range until after winter, and because friend Bhai Parmanand could not accompany him until spring. Many researchers, however, believe Dayal simply underestimated the seriousness of the Oregon laborers and prioritized his speaking and publishing commitments in California. It was six-plus months before he arrived in St. Johns.[33]

Dayal's life had been defined by the oppositional politics espoused principally by the more privileged classes. In the summer of 1912, Dayal worked with the prosperous potato farmer Jawala Singh to spon-sor students from India to attend UC Berkeley.[34] He also spoke at a San Francisco IWW conference. (His speeches before the IWW formed perhaps his most notable associations with laborers before the rise of Ghadar.) By the fall, he was embroiled in a controversy regarding his support for anarchism and free love, which contributed to his resigna-tion of a Stanford University lectureship. He helped found the Radical Club, a group of prominent professors, attorneys, and intellectuals who met once a month over dinner to discuss topics of interest to members. By October, a month after leaving Stanford, he attempted to form a new organization, the Fraternity of the Red Flag. A kind of "monastic order for 'radical comrades'" meant to foster an ascetic lifestyle and radical political work, the group never found expression outside Dayal's scripted rules and principles.[35] In December 1912 in Berkeley, Dayal hailed an assassination attempt in Delhi against British viceroy Charles Hardinge, which was both revelatory of his political inclinations and earned him Canadian police agent Hopkinson's pointed attention.[36]

Further obliging Dayal were three articles in the *Modern Review*, an important forum for Indian nationalist intellectuals. His initial piece discussed the elements of "latent vitality" in India, the first of which he argued was embodied in Western-educated Indian princes, who could be forces for a modern India.[37] India's other vital elements were the old religious orders, the rising Indian middle class, and Muslims, who Dayal believed when equipped with Western education would also provide leaders and minimize Hindu-Muslim strife. His second article, "India and the World Movement," encouraged Indians to study German, French, and Western thought and advocated middle-class "pilgrimages" to Europe (but not England) to model social life. The third article in Dayal's series focused on the Indian peasant's centrality to change in India. During this time Dayal also took up shoemaking as means of gaining an understanding of the "psychology of toil."[38]

Important as theoretical pursuits and alliance-building are to a successful movement, it is hard not to infer from Dayal's priorities that leading politically emboldened laborers was not something he was attuned to or adept at. His activist training had been in Europe, where, unlike in North America, there were no Indian laborers. Biographer Brown concludes that despite Dayal reportedly moving to California to assist his countrymen, he did little more than proclaim himself the mouthpiece of the virtuous, disinherited millions.[39] On finally meeting the animated and organized group of laborers in Oregon, Dayal's trajectory changed dramatically. As historian Puri writes, "When Har Dayal came in their [laborers] midst, his encounters with them aroused . . . visions of organizing a mass revolutionary movement. It transformed him as much as it did his audiences, giving a new sense of destiny to the hopeless Indian farmers and labourers in North America."[40] Dayal was instrumental in Ghadar's crystallization, and transformed by it, however briefly, into a leader of a vibrant workers' anticolonial movement.

In early May 1913, Kanshi Ram/John Kim got the call he had anticipated for months: Dayal had arrived. Ram quickly called his countrymen and set a meeting in his home, a structure off the back of a machine shop in St. Johns.[41] Sohan Singh Bhakna alerted those in local bunkhouses and shacks without phones. Harnam Singh caught the first train in from Bridal Veil, thirty miles upriver on the Columbia. Men in Linnton grabbed the nearby ferry and walked the short distance up from the river to Ram's rented house near St. Johns Lumber. Little, if any, persuasion was needed for the men to assemble. The renowned Har Dayal had finally come to meet them.

Kanshi Ram/John Kim was a foreman at St. Johns Lumber (A) and resided in the back of a
nearby machine shop formerly at the corner of Burlingame and Charleston (B). Ram's residence
and the boarding house across the street were targeted during the 1910 riot. In 1912, the historic
meeting between Har Dayal and local laborers occurred in Kanshi Ram's home. Photo courtesy
of the St. Johns Heritage Association.

The topic for this auspicious May night was "how they could serve
their country." [42] The gathering likely began with formalities—introduc-
tions by those in the room, agreement on an agenda, and the like. The
smaller details have melted into time. But what is remembered is that
the gathering proved a crossroads for the Indian anticolonial movement, and those present became revered independence fighters of
twentieth-century India.

Bhai Parmanand, a well-known radical intellectual who had traveled north with his friend Dayal, made the first proposal: that the mill
men sponsor Indian students to the United States. The assembled
locals and Har Dayal had adopted the idea the year before.[43] But on
this night, as Sohan Singh Bhakna and Harnam Singh later recounted,
several mill men raised serious doubts about Parmanand's proposal.
They pressed the issue, arguing that students simply used their training
for personal ends, not for India's independence.[44] Through the course
of the evening's back-and-forth, an alternative emerged: the need for

direct propaganda among the thousands of Indian laborers of the North American west, many of whom, the men argued, were prosperous and brave. Intensely aware of the rising discontent within their own ranks, the mill men recognized the opportunity to actively and directly agitate for radical change, especially if done in workers' native languages.[45] They did not seek to petition British authorities for better treatment, as some were then doing in British Columbia.[46] In short, the men in St. Johns advocated for their own political existence and power.

Despite all of his past practice, and up to the moment of his apparent accord with Bhai Parmanand that night, Har Dayal changed course.[47] He heard the men. He heard what was so strikingly new and had been until then only a vague hope for radicals like himself. Those gathered were vowing to carry the message and fight for independence. That night Dayal, together with the men assembled in St. Johns, crafted a groundbreaking resolution calling on Indian workers to "gird their loins to liberate India and work on revolutionary lines."[48]

They identified the British as the cause of all suffering of Indians. They asserted the need for an organization to end colonial rule in India through armed revolution against the colonial regime. Dayal had long maintained British colonialism's ruin of India. On this night, he articulated its links to the oppression and disrespect the men faced at home and in North America.[49] Sohan Singh Bhakna and Harnam Singh recollected that those gathered envisioned their new, future government as democratic and based on liberty and equality. They wanted an organization that was secular and political in character. Religion—whether Sikh, Hindu, or Muslim, as those gathered—would be a matter of private belief. As Bhakna put it, they were Hindustanees—"Our religion was patriotism."[50] The political turn toward mutiny and revolt—toward "ghadar," as their movement came to be known—had been made.[51]

Bhai Parmanand, unconvinced of the new direction, left Oregon shortly after the meeting.[52] But the others, like Kanshi Ram/John Kim, Sohan Singh Bhakna, and Harnam Singh, armed with the resolutions from their meeting, set about forming the new organization. Confident they were not alone in their sentiments, they trekked up and down the Columbia River by boat, train, and car in hopes of winning their countrymen to the cause. Within two weeks, they had arranged assemblies in mill towns along the Columbia River. Twenty local men,

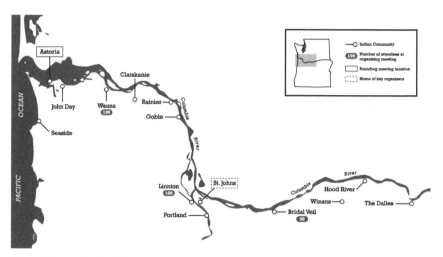

Map of Ghadar Meeting Sites

joined by several from Portland and St. Johns, gathered in Bridal Veil; one hundred in Linnton; and another one hundred near Cathlamet and the Wauna mill site. Across the river, in Woodland, Washington, 150 reportedly attended an organizing meeting and raised $1,200 for the cause.[53] A group of Muslim laborers in Seaside, just west of Astoria, soon affiliated.[54] Those in Astoria were tasked with the practical preparations for the crowning gathering—arranging the hall, meals, and beds for the expected delegates; planning the numerous events and needed security; notifying the press; and crafting the banners and signs proclaiming their cause. By late May, all was ready.

Dayal had waited months to make what proved to be a historic trip to Oregon. He was not alone, however, in underestimating developments there—so too had political police agent Hopkinson. The very political situation in British Columbia that helped stir the St. Johns community demanded Hopkinson's and his informants' concerted attention. In 1910, as the St. Johns prosecution was proceeding, Hopkinson assessed Vancouver as a center of seditious organizing and surveilled and reported on an influential core of militants to national and international government agencies.[55] In response to the policing pressure, a number of prominent BC Indian activists strategically relocated to Seattle and San Francisco, complicating the legal and practical reach of surveilling authorities.

Hopkinson tacked. By 1911, he was working closely with US national officials and San Francisco immigration authorities to build deportation cases against Taraknath Das, Har Dayal, and others, making full use of American laws against suspect immigrants. ("Anarchism" was a favored charge, especially after the 1901 assassination of US president McKinley, by self-avowed anarchist Czolgosz, that brought a legal and public crackdown on anarchism and equating it with so-called foreigners.)[56] On October 19, 1911, as part of a West Coast intelligence tour, Hopkinson visited the Portland Cordage Company and the St. Johns Monarch Mill, evidently believing they were "the only two places in this city where Hindus work."[57] He found nothing of political interest at the Cordage Company.

At the Monarch Mill, he reported only that Das and Bose had "paid a couple of visits . . . and collected money," the latter of which had left some ill feelings. He left town by the afternoon, concluding "that Berkeley, San Francisco, and Seattle are the principal points having Hindu students connected with agitation," and that Das should be prevented from securing citizenship.[58] As historian Seema Sohi documents, by the spring of 1913, Hopkinson had composed a confidential memo to the India Office of London based on consultations with the San Francisco British consul general. In it he argued that the anticolonial movement was now "centered more or less in Berkeley," and his responsibilities should—and did—shift accordingly.[59]

Unlike Berkeley, Oregon was not a radical intellectual center. Authorities likely discounted Oregon because its Indian population was small and without presses, boisterous public meetings, or an evident organizational structure to support a movement, given the absence of a temple.[60] Maybe it also was because, as Harnam Singh felt, there was no strong anti-British sentiment among Indians in the United States at all until 1911 or 1912, dates that track with the transformations wrought in the wake of St. Johns events.[61] More certainly, it marked an underestimation of laborers and labor centers such as St. Johns and Astoria, as some Indian nationalists did.

Hopkinson's unit was also small, and focused its attention and efforts on centers of overt, public radicalism led by students and intellectuals in British Columbia, Seattle, and San Francisco, a strategy calculated for maximum effect. Hopkinson's forces relied heavily on

the immigration administrative apparatus in those same major port cities to carry out their surveillance and counterinsurgency tactics.[62] By
comparison, few Indians traveled through Portland or Astoria's immigration portals, entering the state by other modes of travel. Decades
earlier, policy rifts between Oregon and federal immigration authorities over Chinese exclusion had left cooperative and communication
voids that further hampered Hopkinson's effectiveness.

Other British monitoring authorities, likely because of Hopkinson's
reporting, similarly overlooked or undervalued the new shoot developing
among Oregon laborers. J. C. Ker, the personal assistant to the director
of the Department of Criminal Intelligence in India, wrote a December
1912 report about the state of anti-British activities in North America.
He noted there were "undoubtedly a number of dangerous characters,"
but, as of yet, no "actively seditious or revolutionary association on the
Pacific Coast."[63] While perhaps technically correct in December, in less
than six months' time his report would prove dangerously out of date.

Altogether, the various lapses left Hopkinson and his forces underestimating or unaware of the organizing in St. Johns and elsewhere
along the river. Given the havoc he and his agents wreaked, especially
in Vancouver, BC, it proved a consequential policing gap.[64] Only by
training his crow's vision on the bright shiny thing that was Har Dayal
did Hopkinson's view finally shift to Astoria in June of 1913.[65]

In 1913, Astoria was a rain-drenched town of ten thousand-some
residents perched on the forested banks of the Columbia River near its
furious, four-mile-wide convergence with the Pacific Ocean.[66] It was
Oregon's third largest city and tied into a global commercial and labor
network. Whites built Astoria on Clatsop lands, whose settlements had
long dotted the ocean beaches and river estuary of what is now known
as Clatsop County. Clatsop and other Chinook-speakers' homelands
along the mouth of the Columbia were contested earlier than most
in the Pacific Northwest, largely because of wildly lucrative Chinese
markets. Sea otter, beaver, and other fur species were the foundation of
a sprawling global trade dependent on Native hunting and Chinookan
trading networks intermediated by British and US companies.

In 1811 in Astoria, US businessman Jacob Astor's fur traders built
the first non-Native, land-based settlement in the Northwest, which was
soon challenged and occupied by British mercantilists.[67] The United

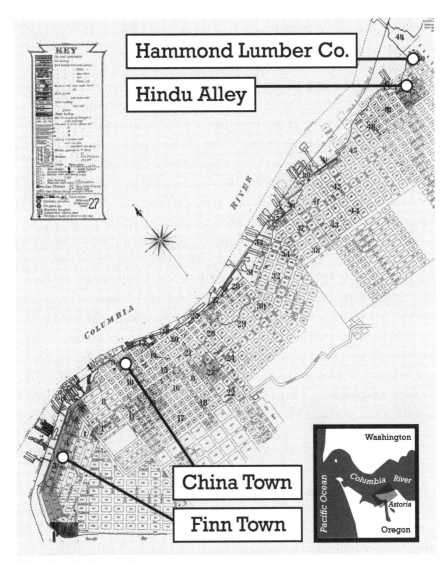

Map of Astoria Communities

States secured its claim to the lower Columbia River from the British with the Oregon Treaty of 1846, while leaving tribal land treaties to languish.[68] Born in the contestation with native peoples and British mercantilists, Astoria manifested Thomas Jefferson's vision of a sea-to-shining-sea America, where white settlers persisted at the edge of promise.

By the late 1800s, fur trading had given way to new industries, as timber rafts and tens of thousands of cans of salmon crossed the Astoria

river bar, bound for San Francisco, Europe, and Asia. Beyond the production of commodities, area industrialists anchored a community
of global peoples who left their mark on the times and on this small,
surprisingly cosmopolitan town. Finnish fishermen supplied the catch,
Chinese crews processed it, and Indian laborers and others worked
the lumber mills that built the boxes for the worldwide shipment of
salmon and other commodities.[69] Each group indelibly shaped Astoria,
and town residents developed a sense of economic interdependence
and relative ethnic tolerance. Indians' settlement and Ghadar's launch
in Astoria can be appreciated as a legacy of, and sequel to, the town's
history, shaped by the many peoples who made it home.

On Halloween 1906, a small article appeared in the back pages of
the *Astoria Daily Budget*. It reported that "Sunday Sing" had died in the
local hospital after having been found two weeks earlier on city streets
mortally ill with tuberculosis. The few lines about his death were placed
among news about the price of eggs and a boat sale, and ended with
"very little if anything is known of him altho there are some Hindoos
working at the Hume mill who visited him when he was first taken to
the hospital."[70] Perhaps more interesting than these scant details is the
paper's reportage on "Sing's" death, which seemingly reveals a reporter,
if not a town, that unlike St. Johns was willing to recognize a new community in its midst.

Besides the explicit admission that "little if anything is known of
him," other aspects of the article suggest that the reporter, and likely
others, had been unaware of the Indians in town. But the reporter wrote
what they understood. Sing was a familiar Chinese name to many,
given their prominence in Astoria's life and recent history. But "Sunday
Sing" was not Chinese, and in its reporting over the next few days, the
paper changed "Sing" to "Singh," a name taken by many Sikhs, and the
crude "Hindoo" became "Hindu." Whether this reporter understood
that Singh was from Hindustan, but not a Hindu, is unclear. But within
a few days, "Hindoo Sunday Sing" was transformed into Rauma Singh,
a local Hindu mill worker. His passing was no longer consigned to the
newspaper's back pages but became a story of some social note and the
first substantive appearance of local Indians in the Astoria press.[71]

Over the next several days, the *Daily Budget* reported that several
Indians had enlisted Astoria's British vice consul Cherry to petition

the coroner and the court on their behalf. They wanted to cremate Rauma Singh, as was their custom; the coroner had planned on burying Rauma, as was the city's dominant custom. Rauma's countrymen prevailed. On November 2, his sheet-wrapped body was carried in a horse-drawn carriage and accompanied by a procession that included the deputy coroner, the city physician, and other prominent Astorians. On arrival at an agreed-on riverside site, they formally turned Rauma Singh's body over to his compatriots.[72] There, the millworkers had built a funeral pyre, where they laid Rauma's body. Chanting, they dipped from twelve pounds of melted butter and ladled it onto the fire to stoke and purify the flame, the last rite taking the better part of the day.[73] Two attending Christian reverends, revealing their skepticism if not prejudices, reported that, far from a grisly affair, the cremation had been conducted with reverence and dignity.[74] A few days later, and with some outrage, the paper reported that while most citizens had been respectful, some locals had desecrated the cremation site.[75]

While the reporting on Rauma Singh's death indicates that the presence of Indians in town was news to many Astorians, the cultural negotiations surrounding his passing were not. Euro-Americans and their customs dominated, but the town was a mix of peoples, and the streets buzzed with their many languages. While largely inhabiting ethnic enclaves, lives nonetheless overlapped. Clatsops, Chinese, Finns, Swedes, Greeks, Turks, and others lived in the town's many boardinghouses, attended church, published newspapers, grew gardens, drank and gambled in local saloons, frequented pool halls and wrestling matches, bought groceries and staples, sold wares, rode busses and trains, and walked the town's lanes. Special cultural events like Finnish midsummer and Chinese New Year touched the whole town. Nestled in the narrow space between the river and the hills, Astoria's physical contours almost required crossovers and interactions.[76] People carried out their lives according to their accustomed social observances, if adapted to this new world.

For some residents this cheek-to-jowl living generated disdain. But for others—as seen with Rauma Singh's passing and the response of Astoria's governing figures—it fostered a different response, and one different than in St. Johns or Bellingham. Astoria became a place where Chinese, Finns, and Indians, in different ways and times, found the means to resist domination and create cultural countercurrents in work, sport, and politics.

Rauma Singh's employers, the Humes, were some of the early entrepreneurs responsible for Astoria's burgeoning industry and diverse crews. In 1903, they built a lumber mill in Astoria to construct boxes to service their national and international shipments of canned salmon, their first and wildly successful enterprise in Astoria. Brothers William and George Hume, with friend Andrew Hapgood, had established the first Pacific salmon canning operation in Sacramento and relocated to the lower Columbia River after the depletion and degradation of local runs.[77] As rival enterprises sought to cash in on what seemed like an endless supply of fish, the canning industry quickly dominated the river. In twenty years, fifty-five canneries sprang up along the north and south shores of the river, packing two-thirds of the entire Pacific Coast salmon production by 1894.[78] By the late 1880s, the Humes employed several thousand Chinese in Astoria alone.[79]

Chinese laborers made Astoria's canning industry—then the largest in the world—both possible and profitable; in turn, the industry was the catalyst for the complex Chinese community aggregating at the mouth of the river.[80] Astoria's Chinatown was the center of the Columbia River Chinese population, and later its commercial and social heart. Underscoring their centrality, Astoria's mayor, facing a critical World War I labor shortage, fundraised among the local Chinese community for a trip to Washington, DC, to lobby for the repeal of the Chinese Exclusion Act.[81] Due to the impact of Chinese exclusion, the peak of Astoria's Chinese community had ebbed by the time Indians arrived. By then, however, the Chinese had shaped the town's landscape and character.[82]

Astoria's importance to the Chinese community had consequences beyond employment. Much like the later Indian settlers, Astoria offered shelter from the time's economic and political storms.[83] In the mid-1880s, Chinese workers faced waves of vigilantism, particularly in California, home to the majority of Chinese in the US west.[84] Western Oregon's racial policy against ethnic violence made the state attractive, despite futures sharply constrained by Oregon's explicit structural racism.[85] As the *Daily Astorian* accurately reported in 1886, three thousand-some Chinese sought Astoria's safer ground and the economic security of its canning industry. This did not equate to believing in racial and civic equality; the next day the morning newspaper ran a lengthy editorial acknowledging the centrality of the Chinese to Astoria's economic well-being, while strongly supporting their formal, national exclusion. [86]

Simultaneously segregated, yet integral to the town's life, the Chinese presence could be seen and felt in Astoria. Overwhelmingly men, they lived in barracks behind the waterfront canneries and cooked, cleaned, and created domestic life together. Behind their quarters could be found the Chinese grocers, barkeeps, doctors, inventors, and other entrepreneurs who serviced the community. A number of these merchants also engaged in a lively business with Portland's Chinatown upriver. A handful of Chinese men worked as boat helpers or knit nets in the offseason, but were otherwise banned from fishing by white, and often Finnish, boatmen.[87]

The Chinese interacted in a variety of ways with the wider Astoria community. Some labored in the town's wealthy homes, others ran restaurants.[88] Chinese gardeners supplied not just the bunkhouses but also many other town residents with fresh produce. In 1903, Chinese businessmen contributed to and workmen participated in the regatta, Astoria's biggest social event, established to lionize the canneries. There were Chinese-run opium and gambling spots, and judging from police records, these were utilized by an array of Astorians. Chinese New Year was celebrated and, in at least one year, attended by Astoria's mayor and chief of police. During the height of the annual fish runs, live opera ran every night for two weeks in a rented hall, later replaced by a dedicated, community-constructed venue.[89]

Astoria's Chinese community also formed a variety of fraternal organizations, some linked to securing and negotiating labor contracts, some cultural, others managing the business of vice, and still others concerned with the politics of home. Their political organizations were rooted in China's social upheavals, including against the ruling emperors, and Chinese Astorians influenced and played out these larger alignments. [90] Chinese labor contractors often used their power to enforce political conservatism on the bunkhouse.[91] Despite contractors' efforts, Chinese nationalist reformer Sun Yat Sen snuck into Astoria and addressed residents during a US fundraising tour.[92] By 1913, in an interesting coincidence with Indian organizing in Astoria, the only remaining Chinese political organization in town supported Sun Yat Sen's new republican government.[93]

Chinese immigrants faced a highly racialized world both in and out of the canneries. "Chinatown" is, after all, a more palatable way of saying the Chinese lived in a segregated commercial and social world. This built environment reflected the prejudice of many of the town's Euro-American residents. As historian Chris Friday writes, "In 1879, the editor of the *Weekly Astorian* declared that 'we cannot possibly colonize the Chinese in any one place in the city, but it should be done if possible.'"[94] Astoria's segregation, or de facto colonization, of Chinese residents reflected the social and cultural limits of the town, while providing a reserve labor force from which area-wide owners drew.[95]

For more than forty years, speeches, press articles, and individual acts of violence were aimed at the Chinese.[96] They were discriminated against in the very industry they enabled. Canneries marketed sanitation efforts in part to assuage the broader public's fear of a pilloried people handling their foodstuffs.[97] Operators depended on the skill and speed of numerous Chinese butchers and can testers, yet these were the lower-paid positions.[98] The better-paid, more specialized laborers were Euro-American, and primarily domestic-born, reflecting the highly racialized, two-tiered labor force schema employed by canneries and other industries. Counterintuitively, this stratification worked in favor of continued Chinese employment, in that they did not threaten, but instead provided whites access to better-paid cannery positions.[99]

Yet, in Astoria there were no anti-Chinese riots or other extralegal forms of communal violence or expulsions.[100] Instead, at the height of some of the US west's worst anti-Chinese violence, the *Weekly Astorian* reasoned, in 1886, "they [the Chinese] congregate here in the same fashion [as San Francisco] because they are driven off elsewhere and have no place else to go." The paper reasoned that "*many Astorians refrained from anti-Chinese activities because they believed the laborers might abandon the canneries, thereby causing the collapse of the local economy* [emphasis added]."[101]

Astorians' belief that they were beholden to Chinese residents was well founded. Chinese workers expanded opportunities for skilled white laborers, generated tremendous wealth for the cannery owners

Hammond Lumber Mill Work Crew with a number of Indian workmen, CCHS Image 05.001.007

and community at large, contributed needed community skills and services, and composed a significant, enduring, and enriching presence in the city. On some level, the townspeople of Astoria understood that their prosperity was reliant on their Chinese neighbors. Astorians' attitudes shifted with the times and new migrations, and primed Indians' arrival, motivated at least in part by regional violence and their need for employment.

Near the turn of the century, successful Montana businessman A. B. Hammond passed through Portland frequently, recognized it was becoming a Northwest hub, and began investing in the region. After building Astoria's railroad, a critical infrastructure for the town's industry and tourism, he purchased and renamed the Hume lumber mill in 1908.[102] By 1910, Astoria mills had a payroll of $20 million (in today's dollars); ten years later, the Astoria area was Oregon's leading lumber producer.[103] Hammond's new investments represented a ratcheting up of the industrial focus and infrastructure in the Columbia River town and more thoroughly tied its fortunes and people into global networks including, as time would tell, the Indian nationalist cause.[104]

Hammond's enterprises were, however, dwarfed by other Northwest mill towns such as nearby Grays Harbor, Washington. Those mill towns existed largely to serve the industry that fueled the state's

A circa 1910 photograph of Astoria's Hammond Lumber Mill with mill housing known as "Hindu Alley" in the foreground. CCHS Image 3957.625

economy and spawned hostile physical and cultural landscapes that dominated residents' lives. Grays Harbor mill owners, government officials, and newspapermen waged war on its international laborers and radical activists (considered one and the same). Their polarized encounters affected the town's city council fights and campaigns, newspaper advertising policies, and shopping patterns. Beatings and jailings were a routine part of community life.[105] Albert Johnson, a committed, nativist newspaperman, honed his anti-immigrant and antiradical activism amid these strikes. In 1913 he began a twenty-year, hate-filled national congressional career directly responsible for marginalizing Indians for decades.[106] Astoria, by contrast, was relatively stable, more diverse in its economic pursuits, and a boon to Indian organizing.

Hammond was a driven, ambitious, and wealthy man, whose approximately six hundred Astoria mill employees came from Sweden, Italy, Greece, Turkey, Japan, and the Middle East, and included at least a hundred Indians.[107] Accounts differ as to whether Hammond agents traveled to India to recruit workers, a practice regularly utilized for European laborers.[108] However, active recruitment of Indians was not needed for long, as Indians arrived by their own volition, especially following ethnic violence in 1907. Known for his virulent opposition to labor organizing, Hammond's recruitment of any and all in the purpose of profit nonetheless created conditions for a broad sharing of experience among global workers.

By 1913, several constellations of Indians were living in and around Astoria, as well as around other nearby lumber operations along the Columbia, numbering upward of one hundred men. The largest and most well-known community was along the waterfront near the Hammond mill in Alderbrook, where "Singhs" and "Khans" lived in company bunkhouses and a few stand-alone cabins. From about 1906 until the mill burned down, that area of Birch Street between Fifty-First and Fifty-Second Streets was known as Astoria's Hindu Alley.[109] About six men lived together on Duane Street in downtown Astoria. Farther east, roughly halfway between St. Johns and Astoria, about thirty Indians lived and worked in the scattered river communities of Goble, Cathlamet, Rainier, and Wauna, an organizing site described in Ghadri memoirs and confirmed in census records.[110] Seaside, just west of Astoria, was home to several young Afghan Muslim men.[111]

Life was not without conflict for Indians in Astoria. Reporters, laborers, and other townspeople used racist and anti-immigrant justifications to argue for their expulsion from the mill, for cuts in their wages, or to justify individual acts of violence.[112] It was far from perfect, but nowhere else in Oregon were Indians such seemingly visible

Bakhshish Singh and Rattan Kaur Dhillon with their four children Kartar, Karm, Budh, and Kapur. Courtesy of Erika Surat Andersen/SAADA. The family lived in Alderbrook near the mill from 1916 to 1922, much of that time in a home built by Bakhshish.

members of a town's work and cultural life. Astorians never mounted the kind of anti-Hindu violence that many had witnessed from California to British Columbia or in nearby St. Johns, and a stable community of Indians endured and organized there. Ultimately, it was a 1922 fire that ended Hammond Mill and the town's Indian community.[113]

Indians made full use of the town's possibilities, finding and creating allies and room to breathe in their organizing to free their homeland. Some in the Chinese community contributed with their nationalist inclinations and undertakings. Finnish Astorians added a different history and sensibility that molded the town's character, including its radical leanings, epitomized by their socialist hall. Finns, like Chinese and Indians, were part of a larger tide escaping a home in economic and political turmoil.[114] From a country with a large fishing culture, many began emigrating to Astoria in the 1850s, their numbers growing through the end of the century. By 1905 they constituted almost 20 percent of the watery hamlet's population.[115]

Finnish farmers, shopkeepers, and fishermen largely did not compete with the Chinese or Indians for work. Fishermen had effectively excluded Chinese from Astoria's fishing fleet in the late 1800s, but were also dependent on skilled Chinese cannery workers to turn their catch into cash.[116] Finnish laborers were primarily lower-paid millworkers, and thus outside the mainstream labor movement that focused on upper-tier workmen, shunned radical politics, and promoted white supremacy.[117] Finns were also at odds with some of the anti-Asian campaigns circulating in the US west, given that many welcomed Japan's 1905 military defeat of Russia, the country that had long occupied and devastated their homeland.[118]

In both popular culture and eugenicist intellectual circles, Finns were the butt of ethnic slurs, caricatured as knife-fighting, binge-drinking, violence-prone revolutionaries.[119] An ethnic group's—whether Jewish, Italian or Indian—inclination toward radical politics also led to negative racialization in these times.[120] Though one of the United States' smaller European immigrant groups, Finns were massively overrepresented nationally in the ranks of radical organizations, making up, for example, the largest bloc of ethnic socialists in the nation.[121] This was both a carryover from politics in Finland and a complicated reaction to their new lives, including their exclusion from conventional

English-speaking labor organizations. The common moniker of "Red Finn" reflected this affinity for socialism's red flag, and delineated them from those conservative Finns, nicknamed Church or White Finns, who were staunch supporters of the political, social, and moral order of the day.

Much like the Chinese, Finns had a tangible presence in town. They lived in Uniontown in bachelor boardinghouses and family homes, and maintained a flourishing commercial center, all at the west end of Astoria. Called the Helsinki of the West, it was the largest Finnish community west of the Mississippi River. Despite divisions between radicals and conservatives, Finns joined together in community projects combating alcoholism, forming co-ops, and sponsoring cultural and educational events to promote and maintain Finnish ways.[122] The Church Finns were numerically dominant, but the radical Finns had an influence well beyond their numbers. The peak of their activity and influence tightly coincided with the presence of the Indian laborers in Astoria, roughly from 1904 through World War I.

In 1904, a handful of radicals formed the Astoria Finnish Socialist Club (Astoria SSK). By 1918, it had grown to some four hundred paid members. Women made up a third of its membership as full partners, not relegated to a woman's auxiliary. The balance of the club's recruits was mainly drawn from the bachelor fishermen of town. The Astoria SSK reportedly became "the most active Finnish-American organization in Astoria" and was one of the largest and most influential locals within the national Finnish Socialist Federation. In Astoria, the group's politics were an amalgam of the internationalism and labor focus of socialist politics, expressed with an ardent Finnish educational and cultural emphasis.[123] The Finnish socialists shaped Astoria's public culture, including Indians', in two very concrete ways: with their press and with their hall.[124]

To promote their socialist views and educate a wider audience, they produced two weekly Finnish papers in Astoria.[125] The papers speak to the vigor of the socialists, and spread the Astoria SSK's influence in the town, region, and country. Launched in 1907, the *Toveri* (*Comrade*) was the most circulated Finnish newspaper in Astoria, often the main source of news from and about Finland for the broader Finnish community, and extended socialists' influence beyond its committed circles.[126] It was also the regional paper for Finnish social-ists, read throughout the US west.[127] The *Toveritar* (*Woman Comrade*), initiated by women in 1911, produced by and for women, was the official women's press of the national Finnish Socialist Federation, with a readership of 8,540 by 1918.[128]

The prestige of these newspapers drew some of the most capable editors and writers from around the country to Astoria. These women and men were talented organizers and propagandists, schooled and experienced in the broader socialist politics of the United States, and a critical counter, if still controversial, to the parochialism that often infects small towns. Providing a backhanded measure of the newspa-pers' importance, attacks on the editors or on the advertising sources for these presses were often at the heart of attempts to silence the socialists' voice, organized by competing businesses, local officials, Church Finns, and other Astorians.[129]

In 1911, the Finnish radicals unveiled their second major achieve-ment: a four-story Socialist Hall, complete with an 825-seat theater, a billiard and card room, storefront, bowling alley, gym, library, meet-ing rooms, and a ballroom with "the finest dance floor in Oregon." As historian Paul G. Hummasti writes, it was "the grandest building in Uniontown and the second largest of its type in Astoria."[130] The impor-tance of this hall is hard to overstate. It was a hub of cultural pride and continuity, and a symbol in the landscape confirming socialists' pres-ence and commitment to community. It was also a public intellectual center where organizers could address large audiences. The hall, with others like it throughout the country, fostered collective and mindful engagement with the issues facing ethnic and laboring communities.[131]

These were times of great debates about the source of laborers' dif-ficult lives, the denial of full civic participation to women and those judged nonwhite, and the violence meted out to people seeking to change these conditions. These issues were amplified by world war and the struggles for national autonomy. Voting advocates vied with syndi-calists or anarchists, while armed-struggle advocates debated go-slow believers. These issues took form in people and organizations, and the halls and newspapers gave them voice and reach.

The impact and importance of these radical organizations can be seen in the spring of 1912, during a bitterly fought labor struggle in

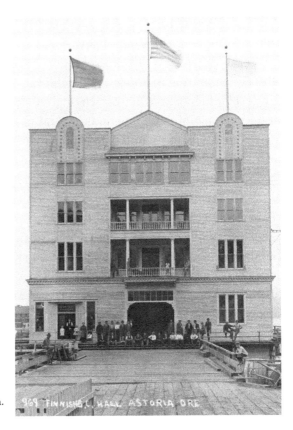

Finnish Socialist Hall of Astoria.
CCHS 21041.540

Grays Harbor, Washington, eighty miles north of Astoria. The strike was initiated and led largely by unorganized Greek and Finnish millwork-ers, joined by dockworkers and loggers, with organizational backing from the IWW. Ultimately, some three thousand lumber and shingle mill workers and five thousand loggers struck, forcing the shutdown of the largest lumber-producing region in the world.

Too numerous for the IWW's modest hall, workers streamed into Grays Harbor's Croat or Finnish socialist halls to plan and organize. Finnish and other socialists on the local city council were often the only opposition to the local government's aggressive and violent strike-breakers. Reports on the struggle were carried well beyond the US west, including through the pages of the *Toveri* and *Toveritar*, and detailed women's roles and the multiethnic and cross-skill unity, including Indians' refusal to scab, which altogether made the strike successful. Besides strike updates, the newspapers reflected and amplified the debates over structural causes, and laborers' strategies and tactics that animated organizations nationally.[132]

These debates also took expression in Astoria proper as socialist editors, committed members, and public audiences argued over political developments and issues, stirring passions and shifting alliances. In the rich mix of newspaper editors and writers, merchants and labor contractors, visiting scholars, literate laborers, and laboring students, people found the linguistic means to express these affinities across communities.

Thus, for Indians, the Finnish Socialist Hall was not simply a convenient rental, but an invigorating and welcoming milieu for their radical dreams. Likewise, their choice of Astoria as the place to establish Ghadar was no accident. Indian activists skillfully used their knowledge of local conditions and navigated the differing racial and radical tolerances across the North American west and within Oregon to their advantage. First and foremost, organizing outside of Canada put them beyond the most direct reach of British authorities and Hopkinson's police. Further, while the Indian communities in Astoria and St. Johns were roughly equivalent in size, Astorians never perpetrated mass violence as happened in St. Johns. Moreover, Astoria was a town with broad radical sympathies and a measure of ethnic tolerance. Sharp-eyed Indian leaders recognized Astoria's openings, harnessed them to outmaneuver the worst intrusions of Hopkinson's hostile, and often murderous, political police, and publicly launched their historic challenge to the British Empire.

On the morning of June 1, 1913, delegates from workers' groups along the Columbia River and beyond, some forty strong, streamed into Astoria, joining forces with the town's one hundred or more Indian residents. Word of the organizing had spread north and south, drawing Hindus, Muslims, laborers, students, and intellectuals. Activist and soon-to-be Ghadar leader Pandurang Khankhoje was present.[133] Veteran Bhai Bhag Singh, who had torched his military medals in protest at the Vancouver gurdwara, joined students from prestigious California universities.[134] Most numerous were Punjabi Sikh laborers from across the Northwest. Reflecting the everyday constraints yet lofty intentions shaping their lives, they convened on a Sunday, a day many had free from the mills, to forge their revolutionary program. Among those gathered were Sohan Singh Bhakna, Uttam Singh Kassel, and Kanshi Ram/John Kim.[135] Young Kartar Singh Sarabha poetically captured the unifying moment and diversity of those present, writing, "Our profession is to launch revolution, This is our *namaz*, This is our *Sandhya*, Our *puja*, our worship, This is our religion, Our work."[136]

Har Dayal arrived by train from Portland and was met at the station with chants of "Bande Mataram" (Hail or Praise the Motherland). People who had been beaten, robbed, or cursed as coolie slaves boldly paraded through Astoria announcing and celebrating their revolutionary aims. Two electric train cars and two motor cars, apt icons of thriving, modern denizens, were decorated with placards declaring "India" and "Freedom" and wound through town to its east end.[137] The assemblage shared a bond of excitement and strength as the haze of indecision fell away and people and plans came together.

A town newspaper reported that following the parade Har Dayal was to "deliver lectures at a big meeting of Hindus."[138] Where they convened is hazy. Punjabi police reports on Ghadar insurgents claim that, "After taking food at the Hindu Hotel, a public meeting was held at which proceedings were opened by Ram Chand. He was followed by Hardayal."[139] Extant records show no such "Hindu Hotel." Likely more accurate is the next day's local newspaper account, which wrote that at the end of the parade Indians convened in "the east end of the city," which most townspeople knew as Hindu Alley.[140] There, Dayal addressed his kinsmen, and perhaps slept and ate in their bunkhouses and cabins.

Delegates also found time and place for the closed or clandestine meetings that would be a necessary part of any revolutionary organizing. The area's thick forests and noisy river might have served them well in this. But what is perhaps most surprising is the extent to which organizers desired Astorians learn of their dreams, challenges, and plans. They contacted newspaper editors, and on Friday, May 30, 1913, the *Morning Astorian* published a press announcement from Munshi Ram, secretary of the Hindu Association of Astoria, which appeared on a page with other community notices about theater productions and the summer train schedule to Portland. Yet this was no routine community affair. In Astoria, Indians' historic desire and efforts for radical change were delivered substantially in their own voice and widely reported. Over the years of researching Indians' lives in Oregon, I have located perhaps five articles—whether about sports, riots, or just daily life—that quote Indians. This one article announcing Ghadar contains more of Indian laborers' own words than all the rest combined, a fact that feels profoundly appropriate given its purpose.

Hindu Scholar Coming; Noted Professor Lectures Here Sunday"
Morning Astorian, May 30, 1913

On behalf of the Hindu residents of Astoria, I wish to inform you that Mr. Har Dyal, M.A., formerly scholar of St. John's College Oxford, and professor in Stanford University, will visit Astoria on Sunday and deliver lectures at a big meeting of Hindus.

Mr. Dyal is noted as a philosopher and revolutionist in India, and his speeches in this country have been reported in "The Bulletin" of San Francisco on several occasions. He will be accompanied by Mr. R. Chandra, a well known Hindu journalist and author, who is at present a political refugee in this country.

Both gentlemen will arrive from Portland on Sunday morning. The local Hindu community will accord them a splendid reception at the railroad station.

I hope you will kindly report this incident in your columns. Mr. Dyal and Mr. Chandra have expressed to see you and I trust you will be able to arrange an interview with them. You will find that they will tell you many interesting things about India past and present. They also intend to deliver a lecture on India for the American residents of Astoria.

With best compliments, yours faithfully,
MUNSHI RAM,
Secretary Hindu Association
Astoria, Oregon[141]

Munshi Ram's notice, in both language and tone, was addressed to the Astoria community at large. He wrote with impeccable English and clarity of thought, likely the result of a collective effort, as activist work often is. Ram assumed the reader's knowledge of Hindus in Astoria, and of their organization, the Hindu Association. The announcement openly promoted a revolutionist and immigrant political refugee, at a time when the politicians and authorities of many burgs had viciously attacked immigrants as threatening, radical intruders. Yet Ram betrays no fear of Astorians. He informs them of Dayal's and Chandra's place and time of arrival and of Indians' plans to gather and celebrate with a "splendid reception" and invites one and all to join them at the rail station and lecture. Ram's notice signals a comfort in and openness with the community in which he lived, even while promoting immigrant revolutionists.

Local papers promoted and reported the events, especially Har Dayal's talk at the Finnish Socialist Hall. Its capacious auditorium was well-suited for the gathering, as was its reputation as a center for radical labor politics. The *Astoria Daily Budget* described Dayal as a "noted Hindu lecturer" who would speak on "The Anti-British Revolutionary Movement in India."[142] On June 7, the *Morning Astorian* penned a one-paragraph review of Dayal's lecture on its editorial page, stating there is "no good reason to doubt from his viewpoint, most of what he said is true." It went on to add, however, that "yet there is still another side to the coin of history," and that is "what the British have done for the civilization of India [and] what she has paid for the graceless task of governing there, in blood and treasure and sacrifice generally."[143]

By contrast, the *Weekly Astorian* advertised the talk, and then devoted two full columns, of a six-page paper, to an apparent verbatim excerpt of Dayal's speech. The article ended with Har Dayal's analysis that "within ten years a great upheaval of the downtrodden led by the educated classes of the country may be confidently predicted. Foreign capital should therefore fight shy of India as there is going to be trouble in the region very soon. Greece bled under Turkey and Italy groaned under Austria. These two mother races of the Aryan civilization have been rescued from bondage in the 19th century. Now India should be helped to realize her destiny and she is struggling to be free."[144]

At a time of openly violent ethnic attacks throughout the North American west, often endorsed by town police and mayors, in Astoria militants made the press, invited local residents to hear about their cause, and safely convened the public and covert meetings necessary to launch their global movement. In Astoria they celebrated together, chose officers, raised money, and planned next steps. They breathed new life into themselves and their hopes for self-respect and a self-governed homeland. In the spring of 1913, Indians launched a movement to challenge the British Empire and transform the future of their country.

Ghadar was a leap in Indians' North American organizing against global subjugation, a momentous first step born of a profound shift in personal and collective aspirations. It was also just that—a first step. Organizers would soon face both predictable and unimaginable challenges, delivered by the greatest colonial power on earth and its many allies. In less than two years' time—not the ten predicted by Har Dayal in the Finnish Hall—Ghadar and its program would be put to the test.

5

The Movement, the Leaving, and Diverging Paths

Astoria delegates formalized the official program of the Pacific Coast Hindi Association in late spring 1913. They endorsed immediate, direct, and radical political propaganda among the thousands of working men who had gained political consciousness, and funds, to advance a movement. Armed revolution was ratified as the means to end British rule in India, to be followed with the establishment of a caste-free, secular, democratic and independent Indian nation, a so-called United States of India. Appointing a leadership committee composed of Sikhs, Hindus, and Muslims, members declared religion an individual matter, not a membership principle or organizational point of debate. Delegates voted to establish a public office in San Francisco to function as an organizing center and publishing site.[1] To finance the movement, the Astoria gathering of chiefly laborers contributed $10,000— nearly a quarter million in 2020 US dollars—in addition to contractor Kanshi Ram/John Kim's donation of a sizable piece of land.[2]

In the immediate wake of the Astoria gathering, Ghadar's organizational progress stalled. Delegates had tasked Har Dayal with securing the printing press and office space, yet by October no discernible progress had been made. Sohan Singh Bhakna wrote to Dayal and expressed his, and others', frustration about the lack of headway and possible squandering of laborers' monies.[3] Dayal complained of ill health and suggested someone else be found for the tasks. Making it clear that for laboring members Ghadar was no idle commitment, Bhakna rebuked Dayal as, "the first to complain of complacency regarding workers' patriotism," and asked, "Are you afraid of working for the country?"[4] Dayal rallied.

On November 1, 1913, the unapologetically revolutionary organization was announced to the world. Indians lifted the Pacific Coast Hindi

San Francisco Ghadar Ashram

Association's flag—red, yellow, and green, symbolizing the unity of Hindustan's religious traditions—over the Yugantar Ashram at 436 Hill Street, San Francisco. The inauguration of their global headquarters was accompanied by the release of the first issue of *Ghadr*. Published weekly at the ashram, the newspaper quickly became the global movement's moniker. In its own words, *Ghadr* existed to convey, "the message of a rebellion to the nation once a week. It is brave, outspoken, unbridled, soft footed, and given to use strong language. It is lightning, a storm and a flame of fire. . . . We are the harbinger of freedom." Its masthead declared itself "Enemy of the English Raj," and in the words of its lead article, "Our Name and Our Work," were one and the same: mutiny.[5]

Har Dayal, the group's chief spokesperson, oversaw the ashram and staff and *Ghadr*'s publication. Khem Chand Gujerati, Harnam Singh, Munshi Ram, Raghvier Dyal Gupta, Hari Singh Usman, Kartar Singh Sarabha, Behari Lal, and Ram Chandra were among the staff. As Sohan Singh Bhakna and others stumped across the US west, *Ghadr* spread news of the organization, publicizing meetings, hailing new chapters, and investing members in its growth. Within weeks of the first issue,

Ghadr had been smuggled into India. Within six months it was spotted in thirty-five countries. Newspapers were passed around, read aloud, excerpted or enclosed in letters, in these and other ways extending the reach of the five thousand weekly subscribed copies across the diaspora.[6] Seventy-two North American chapters sprang up, including in Berkeley, Portland, Astoria, St. Johns, Sacramento, Stockton, and Bridal Veil, with followers in Shanghai, Hong Kong, Manila, Siam, and Panama. Activists were weaving thousands across the globe into a movement for power.[7]

With the movement's printing press and office located in San Francisco, Oregon was supplanted in public importance and repute, but remained a critical rear area. Many of the ashram's initial volunteers came from Oregon. When staff or funds were needed for the headquarters, more often than not letters or cables were sent to Portland.[8] As threats escalated against Dayal, Harnam Singh of Bridal Veil was summoned to act as his personal bodyguard. At different times, Bhagat Singh Thind assisted the ashram staff, strained by surveillance, arrests, and men departing in droves for India.[9] In these ways, Ghadar organizers continued to draw on its deep Oregon roots, especially in a movement operating as much from personal trust and familiarity as formal structure.

From its start, Ghadris actively drew on San Francisco's many activists from the world's revolutionary movements.[10] Pandurang Khankhoje, a member of Ghadar's covert action committee, allied with the Sun Yat Sen forces that had raised a strike force in San Francisco against the Chinese regime, much as Ghadar imagined doing for India. Khankhoje also partnered with Mexican insurgents in California and considered launching an Indian regiment across the border to gain needed military experience. Numerous Irish revolutionaries in the Bay Area, kin in their shared oppressors and mutinous aims, lent their resources and voice to the cause of Indian liberation. Dayal worked with the Industrial Workers of the World and area socialists.[11] *Ghadr* regularly reported on the lessons and state of world struggles, training its followers to recognize the Indian struggle as one part of an international fight against colonial domination.[12]

Situating Ghadar operations in San Francisco also put the group in close proximity to the state's Central Valley and the largest Indian population in the United States. Stockton, eighty miles east and home to North America's second gurdwara, lent important cultural weight and practical support to the new group.[13] Most Indians in California were farmland owners, aspiring owners, and agricultural laborers tending fruit trees, rice, celery, or other crops. Many were enraged by the May 1913 passage of California's Alien Land Law. While principally intended to undercut Japanese farmers and landholders by pegging land ownership to citizenship, the law also threatened Indians' dreams of owning farms and primed their enthusiastic reception to *Ghadr*.[14] Highlighting the varied paths to politicization across the North American west, a second organizational Ghadar conference was held in Sacramento, California, in December 1913. Recruits and funds poured in.[15]

Ghadr was the unifying spirit and bond of the nascent global movement, and Har Dayal stressed the importance of members gaining "an accurate understanding of the politics and science of political economy."[16] A "Balance Sheet of English Rule," was a regular front-page feature, chronicling the Raj's myriad means of bleeding and insulting India and providing readers facts and figures to argue for their cause. Dayal tied their movement to earlier Indian revolutionaries, including articles about India's first troop ghadar in 1857. There were pieces on current events in India, whether rebel acts or British acts of tyranny and abuse. Behari Lal, a close associate of Dayal, wrote that "for the first time readers received the kind of information which they had never before been given—a revelation that shook them to their very depths."[17] Beyond its content, *Ghadr*'s kindling and unifying role can be tied to its use of vernacular languages as urged by Sohan Singh Bhakna and Harnam Singh, among others. Editions were published first in Urdu (the Hindustani native to India and Pakistan), then Gurmukhi (the Sikh and Punjabi script) and Hindi, along with special articles in English.[18]

The newspaper signified far more than information. In the pages of *Ghadr*, people ignored or reviled by the communities and countries in which they lived saw their life experiences writ large. In *Ghadr*, Indian history and their real-time lives in Natal, Australia, Hong Kong, or North America became one, and the truth of their existence appeared in black and white for all to know. Colonialism's

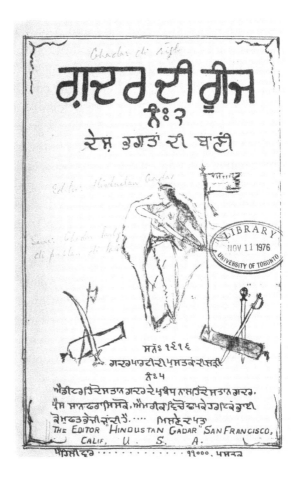

Ghadr–di-Gunj (Echoes of Mutiny)—Poetry Collection 1914. Image courtesy of SAADA

racial logic had relegated Indians to nonsubjects, incapable of being citizens with a country and a self-made future. In *Ghadr* they voiced and demonstrated their ability and desire to be and do just that. It was a manifestation of their dreams, their resolve, and their humanity. It was electric. It was transformative.

Much of Ghadar's vision was imparted through poetry, a deeply held tradition among India's many peoples, regions, and religions. A familiar, heartfelt, and oral practice, verse carried the aims and views of the new organization to the many marginally or nonliterate members and subscribers. This populist poetry, unlike *Ghadr's* weekly analytical articles or reports, was often the work of laborers expressing the experiences and attitudes of the organization's core members.[19] The first collected volume, *Echoes of Mutiny (Ghadr-di-Gunj)*, published in the spring of

1914 with a run of twelve thousand copies, followed by at least three more editions with runs of upward of ten thousand each, hints at the works' popularity.[20] More telling than print statistics is where the lyric calls could be heard. Recitations of the pain of subjugation and visions of insurrection echoed from the fields of California to the stockades of Hong Kong, and buoyed returning recruits on homebound ships.[21] Calls to join the rebel cause sounded in the temples, docks, and streets of Shanghai, Panama City, San Francisco, and beyond.[22]

In their movement to change the world, Indians were changing themselves, and poetry reflected and shaped that transformation. Ghadar verse, while drawing on a deep tradition, captured the experiences not just of the Indian subcontinent, but also of the diasporic community. As historian Jan-Paul Shason writes, "The poetry is full of [Punjabi-ized] words reflecting their daily experiences: union, port, machine, West, golden, tax, jail, deputation . . . Africa . . . mister . . . duty . . . scientist . . . dirty."[23] Stanzas described migrants' pain, dishonor, and humiliation, with "coolie" a common, shameful theme. Poems linked their dishonor abroad to their subjugation at home.[24]

> Scattered from China to Africa, we are hurt, and have gone
>   down over the years
> What have we earned in coming to America? Having left our
>   country for years now
> Everywhere they hate us calling Coolie! Coolie we are not
>   ashamed enough.

****

> Had not our country been slave, how dare people would laugh
>   at us?
> They would not have told us off, nor would they call us coolie,
>   thief or black?[25]

The verse did not simply document their overseas tribulations, but voiced a strident patriotism and urgent need to free their country, repurposing a shared cultural language and history for radical aims.[26] First among these was the call to act as "Indians" and to put aside regional, religious, and caste identities.

Hindus, Sikhs and Muslims and Bengalis, et al, we are all sons
   of Hindustan
Let us keep religion and doctrinaires aside, we will deal with
   them later, first is the task of war.[27]

****

Together with Hindus and Muslim Pathans
Let's destroy the Englishmen Oh Sikhs
There is absolutely no difference among us
We are all the children of the same mother Oh Sikhs[28]

****

Going after faith
You are more worried about spirituality and meditation
You keep fighting against each other
Over Islam and Hinduism
They have ruined the glory of India
By creating a wedge of Quran and Vedas
Beef or pork cause you pain
Whites eat all of them without shame[29]

****

Oh brothers let's unite to defeat oppressors
Untouchability has resulted in destruction
If you wish to rule
Bury these conflicts for the sake of the nation.[30]

****

Despite being born in the same country
We have been divided in factions
By practicing Untouchability
We have proven to be sectarians.[31]

The poetry pointedly drew on Sikh history, the background of the
majority of members. The Sikh martial tradition traces to seventeenth-
century battles to repel Mughal domination over Punjab, led by the faith's
tenth and last guru, Guru Gobind Singh. During the 1857 mutiny—the

first *ghadar*—many Sikh troops fought to defend British rule, their loyalty and bravery rewarded with promotions and status within the British military forces at home and abroad. Ghadar poets recast this legacy toward a revolutionary purpose. "Outsiders" now meant the British, not the Mughals, and fighting to end colonial domination was the opportunity to reclaim Sikh honor from the shame of defending the British in 1857.[32] That England declared war against Germany in 1914, fifty-seven years after that earlier ghadar, was an auspicious sign, a recurrent theme, and a pointed call to action.

> The Guru [Gobind Singh] established the Panth for selfless
>   service, He fought a marvelous battle
> To remove tyranny from India, battles on many fronts
> And for the protection of this Hind, he sacrificed his dear sons
> Who fought like warriors and set the pace of a true Singh.[33]

****

> Come, venture into the battle front, as Singhs, why bring shame
>   to the proud name of Gobind Singh?
> Guru's name shines through, we the cowards have brought
>   disrepute to that name?
> Just citing the wonderful, the wonderful guru, have we not
>   actually forgotten the political know-how?
> He had vowed to destroy injustice and tyranny, and gave his
>   own life for the cause!
> In the cause, young sons he sacrificed, have you forgotten guru's
>   command?
> Read again his indicts, the glorious deeds, and the commands
>   of our great guru
> And come to the battlefield, let us dedicate life and drink the
>   nectar of Ghadar—the rebellion![34]

****

> Our land would have enjoyed freedom today
> Had we then embraced 'gadar,' O Singhs!
> Mother India's children would not have been for sale today,
> Had we nurtured that 'gadar,' O Singhs![35]

****

You go and fight for the white man; why don't you think, simple
    Singhs?
You regularly attack others' nations; why don't you guard your
    own?
Why would you conquer Tibet, China and Africa to hand over
    to the Enemy?
Soaking your hands in blood, why don't you understand
    Firengi's [foreigner's] treachery?
Arise, glimpse freedom! Why don't you unite to play with the
    colours of holi?[36]

More than anything, the poems fervently declared the time was ripe
for sacrifice and heroism, with perhaps the most iconic piece appearing
on the front page of *Ghadr*'s inaugural issue:

Wanted—Brave soldiers to stir up Ghadar in India.
Pay—Death.
Prize—Martyrdom.
Pension—Liberty.
Field of Battle—India.[37]

The ashram staff aimed to model the precepts of the desired new
India. Worker and student, Hindu, Sikh, and Muslim staff cooked, ate,
slept, and worked together as Hindustanees. Historian Ramnath writes
of the collective ethos in the early office and press, their shared "roman-
ticist emotional intensity [that] was militant, insurrectionist, patriotic,
internationalist, modernist, secularist and antisectarian, and egalitarian, favoring politically federated democratic republicanism, while
leaning ever more toward expressions of their two beloved guiding
principles, liberty and equality." That emotive element initially carried
them and generated the largely informal organization, with tasks and
responsibilities divided spontaneously and the newspaper providing
their most consistent, tangible link.[38] Still, long-standing divisions do
not simply dissolve overnight, and the hairline cracks that would widen
in the taxing days ahead could be detected in these early times. Other

than poetry, students and intellectuals such as Dayal and, later, Ram Chandra shouldered the bulk of the propaganda work. Students often assumed only they, and not the many laborers organizing across the North American west, were Dayal's equal in revolutionary vision and leadership.[39]

Predictably, global authorities did not greet Ghadar's global launch with equal enthusiasm, but sought to stifle its influence and silence its leaders. British authorities had long pressured the US government to take more stringent action against Indians, and Ghadar's growth hardly allayed their fears, especially as war with Germany loomed ever closer. Apart from British efforts, US authorities were involved in their own discrete war on radicals and immigrants.[40] American opinion leaders tagged anarchism and Bolshevism as "foreign ideologies," and enacted laws that barred and deported immigrant proponents.[41] Exactly how, why, and where the two empires' counterinsurgent strands converged with respect to Indians is debated.[42] But on March 25, 1914, mere months after the San Francisco ashram's unveiling, and with obvious benefit to England, US Immigration officials in San Francisco arrested Har Dayal as an anarchist. Har Dayal condemned the "despicable pro-British subservience of the United States Government . . . responsible for my arrest."[43] Poets captured the moment, writing that, when Dayal "told us about the warrants for his arrest, . . . it lit fire in our hearts. . . . The authorities had expected to cower us with the warrants; we only applauded and celebrated. . . . Later the Ghadar council resolved to start the revolution as soon as possible. . . . We sent telegrams everywhere of the news of the imminence of the Ghadar."[44]

Ghadar activists and their allies quickly raised Dayal's bail; the *Morning Oregonian* condescendingly reported, "Ragged, dark-skinned men trickled into town with plenty of money and thousands of dollars were offered by them."[45] With considerable fanfare, supporters escorted Dayal back to the ashram from his Angel Island detention. Dayal and his comrades knew that he faced certain deportation leading to imprisonment or death in India. In April 1914, he jumped bail and fled the United States for Europe, effectively ending his political involvement in North America, but vowing to lead the fight from afar.[46] British authorities hoped Dayal's seizure would decapitate the growing movement. Instead, Punjabi police agents reported Dayal's arrest gave "fresh incentive" to it.[47] Ram Chandra, Bhagwan Singh, Mohammed Bara-katullah, and others stepped forward to manage the office and press, and laborers' committees continued to direct activities on the ground.[48]

As significant as Dayal's arrest was, the organization's most critical challenge lay close ahead. In Astoria, Dayal had predicted a revolutionary confrontation in India in ten years' time, with imperial war its midwife. England's engagement with Germany would divert troops and resources away from India and necessitate British dependency on Indian recruits in European and other military theaters. Ghadris aimed to convince India's armed forces, particularly its many Sikh troops, to mutiny and trigger an Indian uprising against their overextended colonizers.[49] Ghadar's moment of truth, however, arrived far more quickly than Dayal anticipated. On August 4, 1914, just fourteen months after its founding and nine since opening its office, England declared war on Germany.[50] Despite this rapid turn and its daunting challenges, many members committed to not missing the once-in-a-lifetime opportunity.[51]

What to do in the face of interimperial war presented a crossroads for the world's people, just as it did for Indians. Governments viciously attacked those who opposed the unprecedented carnage of World War I and its colonial aims. Additionally, England, Germany, France, the United States, and Japan each propagandized that they alone were the upholder of civilization and the humane defender of colonized peoples, while actively and self-servingly attempting to instigate colonial unrest in one another's backyards.[52] Organizations and comrades across the globe ruptured over whether the future lay in supporting their political leaders' conflicts or in fighting for an independent path, as Ghadris and other leaders and movements strategized. While millions died in empires' trenches, socialists and nationalists led uprisings from Russia to Ireland, Turkey, and Egypt, and popular revolts rocked Germany, Italy, and Hungary. Kingdoms fractured, battered not just by colonial rivals but also by their "own" people.

In India, the British war effort garnered widespread support.[53] Ultimately, more than 1.2 million Indians served overseas in British units, with Punjab supplying more than any region, nearly half the wartime recruits.[54] Abroad, 75,000 Indians were killed and almost as many wounded. Mohandas Gandhi called on Indians to back England's war effort, writing, "If we would improve our status through the help and cooperation of the British, it was our duty to win their help by standing by them in their hour of need," and formed a wartime ambulance unit.[55] Much as they had relied on British prewar promises, Indian National Congress leaders like Motilal Nehru believed Indians' enlistment would be rewarded with home rule.[56] Lajpat Rai, a committed nationalist, founded India Home Rule and its newspaper, *Young India*, in the United States in the fall of 1917. Rai argued that, by enlisting in the US military, Indians would counter British lies about Indians and prove their fitness for self-rule, a position he reassessed after the war.[57] Besides imperial rhetoric, men across the world faced significant government compulsion to enlist.

Oregon, a place so formative to Ghadar, was hardly immune to this profound political juncture, and its bunkhouses and workplaces buzzed with debate. Indians left the state in droves in support of Ghadar aims, while Bhagat Singh Thind of Astoria worked closely with Ghadar, but also became one of America's most famous US Army Indian enlistees.[58]

Programmatically, Ghadar had established its stance toward war at its Astoria convocation, and its newspaper maintained that orientation in the months after. There remained, however, the enormously pressing reality of *how* to accomplish its aims, especially with such a callow organization and with Har Dayal removed from its midst. Complicating matters further still, within months of Dayal's departure, a global referendum on Indian equality unfolded at sea: the Canadian government refused to allow the *Komagata Maru*, carrying almost four hundred Indian and mostly Sikh passengers—one of whom was Bhagat Singh Thind's brother, Jagat—to land in Vancouver. The ensuing political battle embodied many of the whys of Ghadar's existence and became its wartime prelude and crucible, an urgent call for the organization to step forward and seize the moment.[59]

On May 23, 1914, roughly two months after Dayal's arrest and departure, the *Komagata Maru* entered the Vancouver, BC, harbor and challenged Canada's Continuous Journey provision.[60] Enacted in 1908, the provision required Indians to travel directly from, and with a ticket purchased in, their country of birth. Even if migrants met those exacting criteria, authorities knew emigration was a practical impossibility, given the lack of direct transport lines between India and Canada. But this attempt by colonizers to globally sequester Indians set the stage for a new crisis a few short years later. Gurdit Singh chartered the *Komagata Maru*, sailed directly from India to Vancouver, BC, and brought the long-standing fight over Indian immigration to the world stage.[61] Canadian authorities prohibited the ship from docking and, buttressed by white mobs on shore, held it hostage in the Vancouver harbor for two months while depriving passengers of food and water. News of the legal and social battle over the *Komagata Maru*, and the attitudes and policies toward Indians it exposed, exploded across the world and the pages of *Ghadr*.[62]

The British Columbian government convulsed over how to handle the crisis and the competing interests unleashed among itself, the Canadian central government in Ottawa, and the British colonial authorities in India and London.[63] The Indian-led Vancouver Shore Committee and its supporters feverishly hired attorneys, coordinated legal battles, held numerous rallies and meetings, raised money (roughly $620,000 in present-day value), bought and ferried food and water, and purchased the ship's charter in an attempt to keep it in Vancouver. Despite these herculean efforts, authorities forced the *Komagata Maru* to leave Canada, escorted out of the Vancouver harbor by the *Rainbow*—one-half of the Royal Canadian Navy—its only prior mission having been the suppression of a labor strike in Prince Rupert, BC.[64]

Indian outrage over the callous disregard of their countrymen by Canadian and British colonial authorities surged. Gurdit Singh, who led the voyage, aptly framed the stakes: "What is done with this shipload of my people will determine whether we shall have peace in all parts of the British Empire."[65] The passengers were prevented from even touching Canadian shores, and their plight put the lie to the queen's claim that all her subjects enjoyed equal protection of British law and welcome throughout her empire.[66] With the ship's return to India, so went the hopes of many for petitioning governments for fair treatment or change.[67] As Sohan Singh Bhakna offered, "this inhuman and insulting treatment of their fellow countrymen put an end to their endurance." Thousands of Indians came to believe, as did Sohan Singh Bhakna, that "a government which made the *Komagata Maru* incident possible had no moral right to exist."[68] *Ghadr* fanned the global outrage, putting out a special issue devoted to the fight.[69] In multiple ports and armed with newspapers and sometimes weapons, Ghadar organizers like Bhagwan

Singh, Barakatullah, Balwant Singh, and Sohan Singh Bhakna urged the *Komagata Maru*'s passengers to join the fight to end British rule.[70]

The volatile situation intensified further still when, between the *Komagata Maru*'s forced departure from Canada and its return to India, the governments of England and Germany declared war.[71] Facing a formidable European enemy, British colonial authorities could ill afford sedition to infect Indian troops or allow a long-standing colony to become a rear battlefront. They feared, however, that the treatment of the ship's passengers threatened exactly that, especially given Ghadar's active interventions.

Days before the *Komagata Maru*'s arrival, the Indian government pointedly enacted the Ingress into India Ordinance. It empowered the colonial government to restrict, however they saw fit, the reentry into India of those deemed "prejudicial to its safety, interests or tranquility."[72] The law also awarded special powers to regional authorities—expanded and heavily employed in Punjab over the next years—ranging from detention in home villages to jailing and execution. The underlying panic of the legislation was bluntly expressed by an officer in the Central Intelligence Office in Delhi: "*Prima facie*, every Indian returning from America or Canada, whether labourer, artisan or student, must be regarded with the greatest suspicion as a probable active revolutionary, or at any rate as a sympathizer with the revolutionary party."[73] In other words, every North American returnee was suspect.

At the end of September 1914, with the majority of its original passengers on board, the *Komagata Maru* docked upriver from Calcutta in Budge Budge some five months after it had set out. All aboard were now considered lawbreakers and dangerous agitators, and colonial authorities met the ship with guns, put the ship under guard, and moved to arrest Gurdit Singh and others. Passengers shielded Gurdit Singh as British troops opened fire, killing nineteen. People fled into the night, including Gurdit Singh, while dozens less fortunate were captured, and jailed or quarantined in their home villages.[74]

Panicked by the political response surrounding the *Komagata Maru*, colonial authorities also believed it represented the tip of an insurgent tide. In late summer of 1914, troubling reports had trickled into British officials about a rash of sales of Indian-held property in California and British Columbia. An estate broker was approached by a Sikh in Victoria, BC, to liquidate two of his lots at half their value in order to quickly raise money to send Indians home, hinting it was for purposes "unfriendly to the British Government." In Stockton, California, the Khalsa Diwan Society received so many requests for assistance in selling off land it arranged for a company to handle the task.[75] Staking everything they owned, Indians were financing Ghadar's call to return.

In August 1914, as the *Komagata Maru* sailed back to India and European powers declared war, *Ghadr*'s pages called Indians to battle. "O, Warriors, the opportunity you have been looking for has arrived. . . . The war had now started between Germany and England; all the white troops in India would have to leave for battle fronts. Therefore, Hindustanees should proceed to India forthwith."[76] Organizers held meetings in Stockton, Portland, Fresno, and Sacramento, with the larger gatherings publicized by *Ghadr*. Thousands attended and contributed tens of thousands of dollars for weapons and ship passages.[77] *Ghadr* called on its many followers to "make haste for India . . . and 'join all the enemies of the empire' to overthrow the existing government and found a republic."[78]

Mainstream American newspapers also picked up on the story. The *Astoria Daily Budget* in its "Local News of the Lower Columbia District" section, reported,

> The Hindus employed at the Hammond Lumber company's mill are planning to return to India in the immediate future for the purpose of joining in the revolution that is expected to ensue, while England is involved in the war with Germany. The plan as outlined is to go from here to San Francisco and join the Hindus there who are negotiating for the charter of a Japanese vessel to carry them to India.[79]

The news from Astoria ran in Portland papers, including one that reported "every train and boat for the south carries . . . Hindus," and unwittingly prophesied that "if the exodus keeps up much longer Astoria will be entirely deserted by the East Indians."[80] In September, the *Fresno Republican* noted that 350 Hindus had gathered in a local town theater and "for six hours listened to speeches," raising $2,000 for literature supporting a revolt, with many pledging to depart on ships in San Francisco shortly.[81]

In an absurd turnabout highlighted by historian Seema Sohi, the very government agents and political police who had so desperately sought to prevent Indians' entry into North America now scrambled to prevent their return to India. Police agent Hopkinson traveled to Oregon to meet with informants, who reported that hundreds were leaving for India. He gathered names and details. He sent his chief BC informant, Bela Singh, who would soon be killed in revenge for murdering Ghadri Bhai Bhag Singh, to the docks of Vancouver and Victoria to gather intelligence. Wherever he could, Hopkinson alerted Indian authorities about seditious elements entering Indian ports.[82] Still, Punjabi police reports, drawn from ship manifests, estimated that in just the last months of 1914, some eight hundred had landed directly in India. More arrived by indirect routes via Rangoon, Burma, Penang, Malaysia, or Sri Lanka. Over the next two years and from across the globe, some eight thousand heeded Ghadar's call to return to India to wage war against the colonizers.[83]

It is worth pausing to consider the meaning of the thousands of acts behind this movement of people: people's liquidation of property, cashing of paychecks and emptying of bank accounts, giving notice to foremen at mills and farms and bidding friends goodbye; their packing up of basic belongings and walking away from houses and boarding ships back to their natal land. This was nothing less than a grand shift in conviction and aspiration. In belief and in deed, they traded their plans and hope of personal prosperity for the collective hope of a nation and people. In less than ten years' time, their dreams and actions took an about-face, and they staked everything they had, sacrificing their North American future for an Indian one.[84] Through their own resolve, they transformed their migratory, laboring tide into a revolutionary one. Theirs were not simply fervently penned newspaper columns or speeches before thousands. People upended their lives. They were not asking, as the *Komagata Maru*'s Gurdit Singh put it, to join "the hollowness of the equality-cult of the Western world," but instead acting to create their own independent future, and willingly made the sacrifices required.[85] They manifested their poetic dreams.

With the outbreak of hostilities, prewar Ghadar transfigured into three organizational constellations. The groups did not represent a conscious split. Historian Maia Ramnath instead describes this as "less a question of Ghadar than Ghadarites . . . less a party than a movement and a set of commitments."[86] They were, however, indicative of the differing strategies and class dispositions within Ghadar. First, there were the thousands of former peasants, farmers, and military men who made up, as British ambassador Spring-Rice put it, "the long list of returned emigrants of the coolie class."[87] A second grouping, the intellectuals in and of the Berlin India Committee (BIC), coordinated strategies and practical assistance with the German government for an Indian uprising.[88] Lastly, the San Francisco Ghadar organization and its press, abided, staffed, and operated by students and intellectuals, with Ram Chandra often at its lead, communicated with Berlin.[89]

Each band forged practical and political alliances with a spectrum of organizations, individuals, and political movements representing the fault lines of the times and empires: pan-Islamists; revolutionary Hindu nationalists; Marxists; Irish, Chinese, and Mexican revolutionaries; and radical labor and socialist organizations. Ghadar was plagued by the lack of a plan and coordination between those in India and those in Berlin and San Francisco. But collectively, their wide-ranging geographical and political dreams, networks, and practical efforts, if at times quixotic, shaped Ghadar's impact and stoked global authorities' fright.[90]

Har Dayal's whereabouts are relevant. After his March 1914 arrest, he pledged to immediately join his comrades in Germany and lead the uprising from afar. He did not arrive in Berlin until late January of 1915. As historian Harish Puri writes, there is little "evidence . . . to suggest that when the War broke out and his men . . . decided to leave for their country to launch an armed struggle, Har Dayal ever thought of giving them any practical direction or advice." Tellingly, after leaving the United States, Dayal wrote to a friend saying he had come to enjoy his "quiet and regular life" away from the demands of Yugantar Ashram and the growing movement.[91] As Puri argues, there is no telling whether, had Dayal and others in San Francisco, Berlin, and elsewhere focused on a concrete plan and program for insurrection, they might have gotten further. The demands of the times arrived much more quickly than expected and delivered monumental challenges to an organization filled with desire but largely unprepared.

Activists in Berlin, before and after Dayal joined them, focused on securing the support of the German government, especially for the procurement and delivery of weapons for the hoped-for Indian

uprising. German officials had no genuine interest in a free and democratic India. They aimed to use Indians' quest for independence (and
pan-Islamists across Africa and the Middle East) to Germany's military
advantage by saddling England with disloyal troops and social unrest
in a key colony amid inter-imperial war. Toward that end, in early 1915
German authorities gathered a number of significant Indian radicals
then in Europe, soon joined by Har Dayal, and formed the BIC.[92]

Allying with Germany was in keeping with the prevailing realpolitik
of many popular movements operating within the war-torn world. As
historian Ramnath writes, the BIC, "while still oriented toward armed
revolt, was . . . anchored in the military and diplomatic logic of inter-
state power relations." Their tactics presumed "nation-state units as
actors" (versus independent peoples movements) and internationalism
as a physical range of work, not a thoroughgoing political and ideological stance.[93] Hitching India's independence to Germany left BIC organizers struggling to carve out and maintain independence. Prominent
nationalist Lajpat Rai opposed the alliance with Germany, arguing that
"what we want is self-government and not the change of masters." [94]

Still, they were not without achievements. The Berlin activists leveraged Germany's stance to gain the stature and recognition of, as Ghadri
Behari Lal wrote, "the concept of an Indian government in exile."[95] Further, for their own imperial interests, Germany provided the BIC with
a global platform that connected and allied Indians with a diverse range
of anticolonial groups and individuals. While not yielding any regime
change, its real-world possibilities fueled British nightmares.[96]

The German government and the BIC proposed three means by
which to export revolution to India: (1) across the Afghan frontier, (2)
through Siam/Thailand to the Burmese frontier, and (3), by sea from
the Dutch Indies. All were to be coordinated through and with German
consulates and staff. The Siam/Burmese plan was to be the work of the
San Francisco ashram under the direction of Germany via the BIC.[97]
Despite the earnest intentions and efforts of many involved, the plans
yielded few practical results besides a series of missed weapons deliver-
ies, with few to no promised weapons materializing in India, and fed
the US government's pretext for prosecuting Ghadar activists in San
Francisco for collaborating with a wartime enemy.[98]

For its part, the ashram staff continued publishing *Ghadr* and other vital communications. In the heady days of late 1914, they gave embarking recruits what minimal directions were to be had. On the San Francisco docks, Ram Chandra assured them their "duty was clear," and bade them to, "Go to India. Stir up rebellion in every corner of the country. Rob the wealthy and show mercy to the poor. In this way gain universal sympathy. Arms will be provided you on arrival in India. Failing this, you must ransack the police stations for rifles."[99] After the rush of departures, San Francisco Ghadris were largely out of touch with members in India. Chandra and other ashram members fundraised, coordinated support with US allies, and engaged legal defense work. Additionally, as a critical link in Berlin's arms shipment schemes, the ashram channeled large sums of German money, and weathered the escalated surveillance and policing incursions of British and US authorities.[100] Competing loyalties, petty vanities, and brutal real-world challenges soon brought old and new rifts to crisis proportions.

Ghadar was stamped as a worldly reality and not simply a notable political voice by those who returned to India.[101] They did so with few meaningful political ties in India, and little way of knowing how their countrymen felt or viewed the world. They lacked an in-country organization that could support them or withstand the predictable assault of the state and its many spies. Still, with England's declaration of war, thousands from North America and across the diaspora departed for India. They did so at great personal cost and with varied levels of commitment and preparedness.

Many acted with the fire of revolutionary conviction but with little grasp of what would be required. When faced with India's wartime realities, historian Puri estimates that 60 percent of the returnees melted into their families and villages, posing little immediate risk to the regime.[102] Others understood they were unlikely to succeed, but convinced of the larger loss if the moment went unanswered.[103] Despite the odds and obstacles, these determined bands worked to make Ghadar's plans an actuality, preaching to troops and villagers, and were rewarded with the avenging power of the colonial state.

Beyond these three wings of Ghadar stands another under-accounted-for political constellation: Indians who remained in North America. With Ghadris departure for India, the ground cleared for a very different program in the United States. Those who sought land, wives, education, and careers tagged their futures to a different territory, and political belonging had always been present. With radicals' departure for India, their outlook came to the fore. As historian Ramnath writes,

> The difference was between moderates and radicals; between aspiration to the values of the American mainstream as actually practiced—even unto adopting its racialist categories and markers of socioeconomic success—or in their idealized form, venerating in principle the libertarian texts . . . such as the Declaration of Independence. One aimed to acquire land in America; the other to liberate land in India. *In short, there were two different expressions of nationalism*, depending on whether the focus of identification, as well as the chosen vehicle of *the desire for individual and/or collective freedom, was American or Hindustani.*[104] (emphasis added)

Choosing to fashion an American life—especially as wartime President Wilson duplicitously pledged America as a liberating force for the world's oppressed—instead of attempting to unseat the most powerful empire in the world had its obvious motivations.[105] Yet remaining in the United States proved no painless path. Indians were subjected to the US labyrinth of white structural power and racial entrenchment, and to wartime's broad and often brutal antipathies against radicals and immigrants.

Just as Indians in Berlin, San Francisco, or Punjab displayed differences in commitment, awareness, and strategy, those who remained similarly confounded neat divides. Many in the United States donated funds, read and circulated *Ghadr*, and otherwise supported and advocated for Indian independence while also crafting a life in the North American west. Others were unconvinced of the possibility of change, too burdened by their circumstances, or simply frightened by Ghadar's daring plans. Undoubtedly some had no patience with the group, preferring instead to persevere with their own designs on financial or personal success. No matter their choices, few escaped the intractability or the vengeance of empire with respect to Indian belonging.

Sohan Singh Bhakna, undated photo.
Shared by Pashuara Singh Dhillon

Oregon figured large within Indian nationalism's divides, where, as across the US west, personal biography joined historical moment and shaped individuals' actions. Oregon was mostly emptied of Indians as men like Sohan Singh Bhakna rallied recruits in response to Ghadar's call to arms, and he emerged an icon of Indian radical history. Of those who stayed behind, Bhagat Singh Thind was doubtless Oregon's, and the country's, most famous, given his military enlistment and bitter US Supreme Court citizenship case. Bhakna and Thind are avatars of Indians' profound global agency and divergences, with legacies similarly erased by the small, northwestern state where they lived, worked, and organized.

Leaving behind his beloved wife in Punjab, Sohan Singh Bhakna arrived in Seattle, Washington, in 1909. At the recommendation of his friend Harnam Singh, then studying in Seattle, Bhakna quickly made his way to St. Johns, Oregon. He worked in area mills until his departure to help lead the Indian revolution during World War I. Older than many migrants, at thirty-nine, Bhakna was an only son from a relatively well-off landowning family in the village of Bhakna, in the Amritsar district of Punjab. His formal education was limited to the fifth grade, the highest possible in his village, despite his obvious intelligence. Raised a devout Sikh by a loving and long-widowed mother, Sohan Singh Bhakna grew up in an atmosphere of acceptance regardless of caste or religious background.[106]

Bhakna migrated to the United States to pay off debts incurred during youthful missteps. Before leaving, and having put his drinking days behind him, he became interested in Punjab's politically infused religious movements against ritual and caste and in favor of building collective identity across religious divides. He supported the boycott movements against foreign goods and government schools and followed the opposition to the 1906 Colony Bill, which would have made peasants mere tenants of absent British landowners. Alarmed by the widespread cross-religious resistance, the British jailed and deported leaders like Lajpat Rai and Ajit Singh to Burma and, ultimately, rescinded the bill.

As biographer Sohan Singh Josh writes, "It will not be wrong to conclude that he [Bhakna] had started taking interest in political and social affairs before he left for the United States of America."[107] This interest fully flowered in Oregon. Bhakna reportedly joined, attended meetings, and "spoke regularly" at the Portland chapter of the Industrial Workers of the World. In this Bhakna kept company with Har Dayal, Ghadar's most famous public spokesperson. [108] Bhakna also kept the company of other important Indian radicals in North America, including Teja Singh, and circulated among the multiethnic socialist circles and many nationalists from China (reportedly attending lectures by nationalist Sun Yat Sen), Ireland, and Mexico.[109]

Bhakna was in the United States for only five short years before returning to India. A year after arriving, he was in the midst of the St. Johns riot and, soon after, the beginnings of Ghadar. With Ghadar, he forged a lifelong political calling and, with thousands of others, returned to India with hopes of actualizing their collective dreams. Despite decades of imprisonment and personal losses, Bhakna remained actively committed to an inclusive, egalitarian, radical Indian democracy until his 1968 death in India at the age of ninety-eight.[110] His revolutionary stature is such that he has been described as being "an institution by himself."[111] Few share his prominence, but thousands were of his mind. As he said of himself, "I wasn't a poet—I never put together couplets or stanzas. Yes, I could sing the compositions of others."[112] Across the globe and the decades, voicing Ghadar's heart-felt, poetic lines of communal new beginnings, Bhakna sang the radical cause of Indian freedom and equality.

Living or working for a time in the company of Bhakna and his crew was twenty-year-old Bhagat Singh Thind. Like Bhakna, he hailed from Punjab and was also likely familiar with Lajpat Rai's and other nationalists' protests there.[113] Thind's family writes that he was dedicated to the teachings of his Sikh faith, and hoped to become a US citizen, spiritual teacher, and attorney. He was also long inspired by American writers Ralph Waldo Emerson and Henry David Thoreau, part of the religious crosscurrents of the times.[114] Buffeted by his times yet true to his friends and his desire for an independent India, Thind's US life arc is ultimately better conveyed by Emerson's notions of individual will, progress, and self-reliance—"Seek not yourself from outside your-self"—than by Ghadar's collectivist revolutionary aspirations.[115]

A graduate of Khalsa College in Amritsar, Punjab, Thind arrived in Seattle on July 4, 1913.[116] He briefly worked in Washington state lumber mills but soon headed south to Astoria. Hired by the Hammond Lumber Mill, Thind sent money home to his family and saved for his hoped-for American university studies while living at 2564½ Birch Street, in Hindu Alley.[117] Astoria was well-known for having work and a thriving Indian community in 1913. Whether Thind deliberately moved to Ghadar's epicenter mere months after its founding is unknown, but it was a decision that decisively shaped the course of his young life.

Bhagat was the oldest son of Boota Singh Thind, a military veteran jailed and stripped of his pension for opposing British policies.[118] Boota blessed Bhagat's, and younger son Jagat's, pursuit of new lives in America. Yet his sons' new beginnings in North America proved more challenging than the family could have imagined. Bhagat worked for nine months in the Philippines to both finance the costly trip and to outmaneuver the immigration proscriptions against Indians landing in the United States. [119] Nine months after Bhagat's successful landing, Jagat booked a ticket on the *Komagata Maru*. After many worried letters, Bhagat confirmed that Jagat had arrived home safely, but would never attempt the dangerous journey again.[120]

Roughly a year after Bhagat Thind's arrival in Astoria, and amid his concern about his brother's safety, Ghadar issued its call to return. Thind, with a handful of others, remained in Oregon and continued working at Hammond. There are no records to tell us exactly why he made the decision he did.[121] His options as a college-educated young man in India were limited, and, given his father's baleful experience, an Indian military career was a nonstarter. He had also witnessed Jagat and others risk their lives for simply attempting to migrate. Having successfully entered the United States, Bhagat Singh Thind seemingly committed to staying, then and throughout the years.

Watching Oregon empty of friends, while likely difficult, proved the least of Thind's many challenges. In a new land and at a young age, he faced the crosshairs of interimperial war and radical change. He struggled to balance partisan loyalties, friendships, and personal goals amid a tsunami of change. Thind made many seemingly individual choices—to join the US military, gain citizenship, and marry—yet his trajectory was unequivocally tied to Ghadar and the larger arc of Indian belonging. His allegiances and actions in support of Ghadar placed him squarely within the British counterinsurgency campaign that rolled out from India and onto US soil. Joined by US authorities, it swept up Indians daring to advocate for Indian self-rule or simply trying to become citizens. The greater dangers lay in India, but as the years rolled on, the noose tightened around Indians in the United States. Thind's experience is a window into the political landscape for Indians who remained behind.[122]

Sohan Singh Bhakna and Bhagat Singh Thind of Oregon personify the contrasting and shifting frames of Indian independence. With the outbreak of world war, Ghadar leader Sohan Singh Bhakna rallied Indians to overthrow British domination and collectively construct a new future. Thind supported and advocated for Ghadar, but chose to fight for a more individual and American acceptance. In many ways, Thind pursued what Ghadar cast aside, but he did so on political ground it fostered—activism, agency, and radical absence. Thind and Bhakna are of a piece, products and exemplars of their time and conditions. Taken together, their disparate efforts complicate our consideration of the meaning of, paths to, and brutality against Indians' struggle for democratic belonging across the nodes of empire.

6

The Global Punishment of Ghadar

Ghadar's beginnings sprang from the interplay of global and local colonial politics, and so too did its outcomes. In less than two years, Ghadar galvanized Indians across the diaspora and spurred the vengeance of empires. If arrogant and swaggering, the reactions of England and America also stank of fear—of loss of control, of power, of right. Their future governance was in the balance and not only from interimperial war. Revolts, rebellions, and revolutions threatened their existence across the globe. India was one gritty particular; the country stocked England's ill-gotten wealth and Indo-Americans signified the threat of radical, racial interlopers. If not tactically identical or fully coordinated, the ruling powers aligned on one particular: Indian self-rule and citizenship would not be.

Ghadris stepped onto the world stage with boldness and daring and embraced the challenge of their times. In British global cantonments, ports, and villages across Punjab, authorities sprang into high alert against Ghadar's possibility and actuality, hunting for returnees and homegrown recruits alike. The ghost of 1857 had haunted British colonial ranks for decades. With World War I, that nightmare, now insinuated with real-time revolutionaries and German colonial meddling, bloated them with rage.

The British hit the rebels with roundups, secret trials, hangings, and decades of incarceration, often in remote island prisons through a practice called "transportation." British vengeance did not confine itself to Ghadar or to India. Painstakingly detailed by historian Seema Sohi and others, Britain's wide-ranging campaign of retribution spanned decades, targeted protesting civilians and other nationalists, and crossed the seas punishing its subjects in courtrooms from San Francisco to the US Supreme Court. Names of Oregon activists like Kanshi

Ram/John Kim, Sohan Singh Bhakna, Vishnu Pingley, Harnam Singh, Munshi Ram, and Bhagat Singh Thind littered the global suppressive roster.[1] High-level US authorities and institutions proved complicit in hunting down Indians, if periodically engaged in a spitting war with British authorities over the optics, tactics, and timing of doing so. Empire, to paraphrase James Baldwin, embraced violence over change.

Punjab Lieutenant Governor Michael O'Dwyer named Ghadar the most serious wartime threat to British rule in India.[2] Punjab was critical to British troop recruitment and loyalty, the home of most Ghadar returnees and recruits, and O'Dwyer stood at the center of the regime's repressive efforts.[3] Utilizing a global surveillance ring, including Hopkinson and his agents in North America, O'Dwyer worked with central authorities to bolster India's suppressive tools to pursue the rebels. In September of 1914, on the cusp of the *Komagata Maru*'s docking, the Indian government arrogated broad powers with its Ingress into India Act. This conferred the right to screen, confine, and restrict returnees to India and other British colonies and deport them to home districts, usually Punjab, for detainment. [4] Draconian as it was, the act proved inadequate to containing the real-world challenges or authorities' fears.

In the last months of 1914, thousands of mostly laborers and veterans from across the world slipped back into India and other British colonies, preaching revolution in barracks and temples wherever they landed.[5] They had little to no on-the-ground organization or leadership, relying instead on their wits and commitment amid a difficult political landscape.

Ghadris had underestimated the degree to which they had changed in a few short years and assumed their countrymen would instinctively feel as they did. [6] But their fellow Indians had not lived abroad, where they could more freely debate the conditions of their lives. They had not experienced firsthand the lies behind the pledge of equal British status and its links to colonial immiseration. They had not lived among other peoples who were clamoring for change in the mills of the Pacific Northwest, the mountains of Mexico, and the bogs of Ireland. All these experiences had transformed those who heeded Ghadar's call.[7]

Returning insurgents presumed, as an older former sergeant in the British Indian Army in a Wauna, Oregon, organizing meeting preached,

Why waste time in publishing a paper from America? Let some of us go and impress upon the Indians working in Canada and America that they should leave the work and proceed to India in jathas (squads). They should tell the whole things to their fellow brothers in the army and with their help throw the British out. What is after all the strength of the English-men in India? One Englishman comes to the share of five hundred Hindustanees.[8]

Or, as Sohan Singh Bhakna expressed it, "All that was necessary was to open [the soldiers] eyes to the disgrace of slavery."[9] This proved to be no easy "all."

Ghadris gathered recruits in India. But the larger reality was that, unlike the radical returnees, India was awash in political and practical support for England and its war efforts. The Sikh hierarchy in Punjab, long dependent on the largesse of British rulers, denounced Ghadris as spiritual and national turncoats. The Chief Khalsa Diwan, a Sikh religious organization based in Punjab, continued to look to the British as Sikh benefactors, called for continuous prayers in support of the war effort, and formed committees to help track down the insurgents who, in their eyes, disgraced the community. Members of the Indian National Congress also denounced Ghadar and its aims, and recruited for the war effort.[10] Even with these many political obstacles and organizational deficits, a core of Ghadris fought to seize the moment, a stance that cost lives and drove British vengeance.

A small ad hoc band, including Harnam Singh of Bridal Veil, Oregon; Kanshi Ram/John Kim of St. Johns, Oregon; and young Kartar Singh Sarabha of Berkeley, California, worked to win military men and peasants to their mutinous plan, attacked military caches, and some (controversially) carried out targeted banditry to secure arms and funds.[11] Given the dearth of planning, preparation, and organization, theirs were often impulsive and hasty improvisations, costing them dearly in arrests and deaths.[12] Attempting to resolve their pressing organizational needs, Vishnu Ganesh Pingley, a former Oregon Agricultural College student, facilitated contact between respected Bengali radical Rash Bose and the active Ghadris. In late 1914, Bose traveled to Amritsar, Punjab, took stock of the returnees, and committed to assisting with local resources and planning.[13]

February 1915 proved a crossroads. Ghadris, with Bose, planned coordinated actions in military cantons and villages across Northern India.[14] Dependent on their strongest base of support, the 23rd Cavalry in Lahore, the insurgents hoped that other regiments would join and in turn trigger a general uprising among the people. Their plans, already premised on the optimistic reconnaissance reports of a thin network plagued by spies, were further upended by dramatic events that were unfolding in Singapore.[15]

A largely Muslim infantry unit stationed in Singapore, an important British colonial commercial and policing post, was rumored to be imminently deployed against fellow Muslims in Turkey. The unit was likely alerted to their upcoming mission by letters from other overseas Indian soldiers.[16] In response, seven to eight hundred infantrymen seized the Singaporean fort, freed German war prisoners, and killed forty-some British officers and civilians. After a week of fighting "ditch to ditch, house to house, tree to tree," British forces, with the aid of Japanese, French, and Russian soldiers, and locals, retook the garrison.[17] Panicked British authorities reinstated executions—previously outlawed for two decades—and in March wielded the deadly power against the Singaporean rebels with thousands of civilians on hand to absorb the object lesson.[18] Dozens of mutineers were executed, with dozens more imprisoned or transported, many for life.

"Ghadar Singapore"

Rise up and get ready to revolt
What is stopping you from acting faster?
When the macho Muslims have done their part
By raising the flag of Ghadar[19]

With British authorities already unnerved by Ghadar agitation in Punjab, the Singaporean events heightened their sense of dread. As O'Dwyer later wrote of the planned mutiny, "The idea was not fantastic, for it had penetrated as far down as Bengal and . . . Dacca."[20] In a vain attempt to outmaneuver the British troops, now on high alert, Ghadris moved the date of the planned 23rd Cavalry revolt up to February 19. Tipped by spies, truckloads of British troops poured into Punjab on the night of February 18. Despite the valiant efforts of Sarabha and others to press ahead, soldiers aligned with Ghadar mutely "pointed at the white soldiers stiffly parading . . . while others wept."[21] Police raided Bose's headquarters, arrested more than two hundred, including Sarabha, and searched numerous houses, seizing names, plans, and other compromising information.[22] As in Singapore, authorities sought enhanced powers to punish the insurrectionists, including as a lesson to the populace.

Just months earlier, in the fall of 1914, Punjab authorities had unsuccessfully petitioned the central Indian government for more sweeping powers to deal with the brewing insurgency. By March of 1915, persuaded by the troubles in Singapore and Punjab, the central government enacted the Defense of India Act and christened its provisions against Ghadris. The act placed India under martial law, severely restricted any suspect's movement, and established special, secreted tribunals for trying revolutionaries' crimes, which verdicts could not be appealed. The Ghadar movement initiated by laborers in small-town Oregon was cited by no less than Viceroy Charles Hardinge, the British monarch's representative in India, as necessitating such drastic measures to preserve colonized India.[23]

Utilizing the new Defense of India Act, the government mounted a series of conspiracy trials in Punjab and Mandalay (Burma). The first of three Lahore trials was staged inside a prison in April of 1915. Hoping to muzzle Ghadar's incendiary message, and per the express terms of the act, neither the press nor the public were allowed to witness the proceedings. The prosecutors relied on testimony from spies, police agents, and a few former Ghadris promised pardons in return for their cooperation, including Amar Singh, once of St. Johns, and Nwab Khan, once of Astoria.[24] Besides incriminating their former comrades, much of their testimony detailed their treatment as denigrated immigrants and their politicization in the mills of the Pacific Northwest.

The unrepentant Ghadris decided that seven of them—Kartar Singh Sarabha (California) and Sohan Singh Bhakna (Oregon) among them— would take full responsibility for the charges and transform the trial into an indictment of British colonialism and promote Ghadar's vision. In November, Kartar Sarabha, Kanshi Ram/John Kim, Vishnu Pingley, and three other comrades were hanged for conspiring to overthrow

British rule in India; Sohan Singh Bhakna was transported for life. (Bhakna, tracked by British intelligence in his travels across the Pacific, was arrested and detained upon arrival in Calcutta and consequently was not part of the armed actions.)[25] In 1916, after the Mandalay trials, six more met the gallows, including Sohan Lal Pathak, another former Oregon student.[26] In multiple trials across British possessions, altogether 291 Ghadris were tried, 42 sentenced to death, 114 transported for life, 93 imprisoned; eighteen soldiers from the 23rd Cavalry were court-martialed.[27] Fully half of those convicted or otherwise punished by the regime were locals. Seemingly secure in the outcomes of the rigged proceedings, and with the swagger of a thug, Punjab Lieutenant Governor O'Dwyer declared Ghadar "crushed," with its activists and leaders awaiting trial or otherwise contained by August 1915, three years before world war's end.[28]

O'Dwyer's and other authorities' conceit belied a more complex reality. While Ghadris were unsuccessful in turning a consequential number of Indian troops against the British, that did not mean the troops—or the broader populace—were a rock of British loyalty. That unnerving knowledge framed British authorities' wartime messaging and policies. On the one hand, imperial planners relied on Indian troops, fully one-third of England's initial fighting force in France and Belgium, with more later deployed to Mesopotamia, Palestine, and Tanganyika. Viceroy Hardinge claimed this service represented the "deep attachment of the Indian people to the King-Emperor and the Throne."[29] Yet, on the other hand as historian Gajendra Singh argues, despite this supposed "deep attachment," "revolutionary conspiracies in India haunted the imagination of British officialdom," and drove their heavy-handed measures both during and after the war.[30]

Dependent on Indian troops yet fearing their disloyalty, British officials monitored and censored soldiers' letters. Authorities hoped to minimize enlistees reading or writing about happenings that would contribute to self-rule sentiments. Besides Ghadris' on-the-ground work in Lahore and other garrisons, Berlin India Committee (BIC) members actively corresponded with Indian troops in Europe. The horrors of trench warfare and its staggering death toll were arguably more effective in broadly undermining soldiers' allegiance than were the activists. By December 1914, the war's first winter, soldiers' correspondence home had increased in both length and frequency and conveyed a pervasive "fatalistic resignation."[31] Calls to defend a supposedly civilized British Empire against a brutish German foe were threatened by soldiers' descriptions of their bitter, hopeless reality: "We are like goats tied to a butcher's stake. We have no idea when he will come, and there is no one who will release us. We have given up all hope of life. It would be a good thing if my soul were to quit my body."[32] Their letters supplied tips on evading duty and spoke of the pain of losing loved ones and friends.[33]

Combatants' letters were also transformed into counterintelligence weapons in British authorities' hands. They commissioned acclaimed journalist and novelist Rudyard Kipling to rewrite them in an appropriately heroic tone. Unlike the originals, Kipling's colonially reimagined pieces praised British wartime masculinity and its indulgence of Indians' supposed immaturity. In May and June of 1917, Kipling published his series not in India or in England, but in a US weekly, the *Saturday Evening Post*.[34] The choice was no accident, but rather part of a strategy to quash Ghadar's US organizing and support base, centered in San Francisco.

Even with the close of World War I, O'Dwyer's declaration of having "crushed" Ghadar, and propaganda about Indians' undying loyalty, British fears of Indian unrest lingered. They sensed the powder keg beneath them and battled the real-world possibilities manifested by Ghadar. British frights fueled a campaign of revenge and retribution against Ghadar and the broader Indian populace, including an indefinite extension of India's draconian wartime measures. Gandhi's and other Congress moderates' hopes for British postwar concessions evaporated, and propelled their conversion into opponents of the postwar clampdown.[35]

On April 13, 1919, several thousand townspeople gathered in the Jallianwalabagh Park in Amritsar to celebrate Vaisakhi, a North Indian harvest festival and Sikh holiday. Many also peacefully protested the recently passed Rowlatt Act, the indeterminate extension of the suppressive wartime Defense of India Act initially used against Ghadar. Authorities nervously appraised the nonviolent Vaisakhi gathering and its potential to rekindle Punjab's radical contagion. Brigadier-General Reginald Dyer ordered his troops to fire on the unarmed crowd trapped in the enclosed park. People desperately tried to escape, the park walls pockmarked by soldiers' bullets to this day. Officials reported almost four hundred killed, another 1,200 wounded, with unofficial numbers higher still. Lieutenant Governor O'Dwyer commended the carnage and credited General Dyer with preventing another rebellion in Punjab.[36]

A decade later, the empire sought another pound of flesh, this time from Lajpat Rai. After the war, Rai had returned to India from his US exile, where he had promoted US military enlistment, advocated for self-rule, and earned one of the largest British counterintelligence dossiers.[37] In 1928 in Lahore, Rai led a nonviolent demonstration of five thousand to protest a breathtakingly arrogant meeting of British officials—one that excluded all Indians—to decide whether Indians were ready for self-rule. Police superintendent James A. Scott ordered demonstrators to clear the path for the converging commissioners; Rai urged the crowd to hold their ground. For his stance that day—and in punishment for his years of steadfastly advocating for Indian independence—Scott savagely beat Rai. He died from his injuries a few weeks later.[38]

Colonial authorities continued to assault and condemn people, protests, and movements across the country—anticaste, Muslim League, industrial workers, farmers—who were demanding societal reform and greater independence. Enraged and disillusioned by England's broken promises of reform, tens of thousands moved from loyalty to active opposition. Increasingly the question was not whether there would be change in India, but on what terms. For the British, suppressing programs for radical and thoroughgoing change was essential to their continued bleeding of India, a campaign they did not confine to India.

In the many trials of Ghadris staged in India, the North American west, particularly California, surfaced as a dangerous seditious locus, and the British government turned, and returned, to uprooting and punishing its proponents and supporters. Directly and indirectly aided by the US government, the British government pursued its counter-revolutionary aims from Punjab to North America.

Their efforts to suppress Indian nationalists coincided with and fed a broader American domestic clampdown. Before entering World War I, US legislators barricaded against a growing radical, and growing nonwhite, public they often correctly perceived as hostile to their rule. With the 1917 Immigration Act, also called the Asiatic Barred Zone,

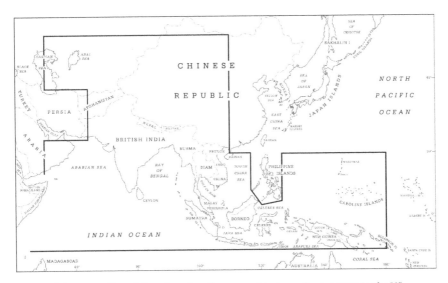

A map of the Asiatic Barred Zone based on the geographical coordinates given in the US Immigration Act of 1917. Source: Les O'Neill, Archaeology Programme, University of Otago, Dunedin, NZ

"polygamists," "anarchists," and most peoples from Asia, including Indians, were banned from entering the United States, and deportation measures were expanded and streamlined.[39] Once the country was officially at war, millions of citizens and noncitizen residents were compelled into military service.[40] With the Espionage and Sedition Acts of 1917–1918, officials usurped broad interpretative and punitive powers to criminalize any form of speech criticizing the war, government, or military.[41] Immigrant and alternative newspapers were silenced; thousands were rounded up, jailed, deported, or victimized by vigilantes fueled by frenzied patriotism and virulent racism.[42] In this domestic war, Indo-Americans were both target and means, as well as a measure of the convergence of anti-Asian racism and antiradicalism.[43]

While collaborating against Indians, the two powers did not proceed in perfect lockstep. England declared war in 1914, three years before the US. British war efforts were directed at Germany, its militarily threatening neighbor and competitor for colonial possessions. England also faced a coterie of global nationalists challenging "their" colonies, insurgencies sometimes funded by Germany. US president Wilson, representing an emergent colonial power removed from the battlefields, cast American wartime aims as furthering a democratic world order and its tutelage as the path to colonial independence.[44] England and the United States moved through these discrete, and often competing, practical and rhetorical necessities across time and place while mutually pursuing colonial power grounded in white supremacy.

World war and the threats of insurrection intensified British concerns about Indians in North America, and they heightened and honed their prewar suppressive strategies: policing, immigration control, and blocking Indo-American citizenship. Policing formed the bedrock of British efforts, its government having openly shared intelligence and personnel with US authorities since the 1907 anti-Asian riots. By 1914, with Britain's declaration of war and Ghadris return to India, US and British joint surveillance efforts intensified, particularly with the San Francisco conspiracy trial (detailed below).

With respect to immigration controls, British authorities welcomed US efforts and stepped up their own curtailment of Indian migration with its risk of contamination from democratic, socialist, and nationalist activists. The British closed down or otherwise complicated ship transport to North America and heavily winnowed those attempting to leave India. They welcomed the influence of nativists within the American immigration apparatus, especially in San Francisco. They annotated Indian travel documents to trigger US laws that excluded and deported immigrants with radical beliefs such as anarchism. In 1917, three years into its war effort, England received a welcome assist in corralling Indians with the US government's passage of the Asiatic Barred Zone.[45]

Yet despite its considerable powers, England's lack of direct legal and political jurisdiction over emigrants residing in the US hampered their control efforts. Indo-American citizenship was particularly vexing. First, it established a dangerous political benchmark for British colonizers vis-à-vis India. Second, it limited British reach against Indian radical organizers. British officials attempted to block Taraknath Das's US citizenship, but proved unsuccessful even when armed with Agent Hopkinson's reports of Das being a "proven" anarchist.[46] With US status, Das was relatively insulated from deportation and persecution in India, and continued to espouse radical causes. With Har Dayal, British intelligence and US laws worked to more satisfying authoritarian effect. Aided by Hopkinson, American authorities arrested noncitizen Dayal as an anarchist in April of 1914, and robbed the San Francisco

Ghadar headquarters of its recognized leadership at a key moment in the struggle.[47]

For their part, leading US federal authorities formally opposed every application of Indian nationals for citizenship.[48] As early as 1907, US attorney general Bonaparte stated, "Under no construction of the law can natives of British India be regarded as white persons."[49] Demonstrating the country's settler colonial roots, American federal policy also reflected an alignment with powerful West Coast nativists and explicit British anti-Indian pressures. [50] Yet federal authorities did not control every local courtroom or other governing authority arbitrating civic status. Some sixty-five to seventy Indians, including Taraknath Das, gained US citizenship before the US Supreme Court's postwar *Thind* decision explicitly outlawed Indian citizenship.[51] US authorities brutally attempted to control the growth of radicalism and the power of nonwhite peoples; whether *Thind* in particular would have transpired without British pressure or involvement remains an intriguing open question, examined in chapter 7.

While war with Germany posed new and pressing necessities, it also provided British authorities with new suppressive opportunities. In particular, with time and active intervention, the British successfully parlayed the German government's insinuation within one strand of Indian nationalists—the Berlin India Committee and its ties to the California ashram—into a strategy for obligating US authorities to prosecute Indians in America. [52] To establish this connection and enlist the US government in its campaign to crush Ghadar, the British established a de facto intelligence center in San Francisco, led by its consul general and comprising agents from the Indian police and a host of British agencies including naval intelligence, the security service (MI5), the secret intelligence service (MI6), and "dozens of informants, double-agents and private detectives."[53] Their machinations effectively interfaced with the US government's growing campaign against radical laborers and immigrants.

In 1915, British ambassador Spring-Rice requested US authorities investigate a German-financed arms shipment for violating US neutrality laws—that is, tolerating (German) activities on US soil against a country (England) with which it was at peace. Ambassador Spring-Rice did not immediately link his complaint to Indians. He knew, however, that the weapons were purchased in New York by German diplomats associated with the BIC. The armaments had been shipped by train to California and loaded onto the steamship *Annie Larsen* in San Diego. The *Annie Larsen* was to rendezvous off the coast of Mexico with the *Maverick*, offload its cache, and the *Maverick* was to then sail to India via Burma and deliver the weapons to awaiting Ghadris.[54]

The *Annie Larsen* was an utter practical failure. It missed its connection with the *Maverick* and ultimately wandered into an Aberdeen, Washington, port to the bafflement of local authorities.[55] The mishap did, however, prove a British counterrevolutionary boon. US authorities believed the *Annie Larsen* was intended to aid the Mexican revolution then underway. British officials, with the aid of their improvised San Francisco intelligence station, convinced them of the Indian intrigue behind the shipment and pressed for and enabled the prosecution of what became known as the German-Hindu conspiracy.[56]

With the rising possibility of the United States formally joining the war, highlighting German activities on US soil appealed to an increasingly edgy US president Wilson and a US public inclined to clamp down on Germans as a putative national threat. Germans in wartime America were threatened for, and prohibited from, speaking their language. Their books were burned. German businesses adopted anglicized names, and frankfurters became hot dogs. Stories of the inherent brutality of Germans were ubiquitous.[57] For the British, connecting radical Indians in the United States to Germany was vital. There were no US laws against Indians returning to India during war, as long as they hadn't explicitly organized a military expedition or been recruited by a foreign army—in this case, Germany.[58] England took the lead in proving that connection.

In February 1916, British ambassador Spring-Rice sent transcripts of the Lahore conspiracy trials, along with military intelligence confirming German cooperation with Ghadar, to his counterpart in the US State Department.[59] Ambassador Spring-Rice claimed that the first Lahore trial proved that California was the epicenter of the insurgency and, per its intelligence including the *Annie Larsen* affair, Germany was aiding their struggle. Ambassador Spring-Rice argued the United States was injuring Britain and its possessions by sheltering Ghadar and its press. The ambassador's complaints were in turn forwarded by the US

State Department to the US Justice Department with instructions for it to take "radical action" on the information, meaning to aggressively prosecute Ghadar and its German confederates. [60] Tellingly, US officials never disputed Britain's rightful claim to India, only the implications and technicalities of possible US criminal charges.

To further push US authorities to make a case, the British sent high-ranking intelligence agents to British Columbia and New York, supplementing those already on British consular payrolls. The agents were tasked with ferreting out both Ghadar activists and German maneuverings among Indians. "Bundles of papers" detailing the "international conspiracy" were soon regularly delivered to the US State Department from Ambassador Spring-Rice, along with his regular and alarmist references to the German-Hindu conspiracy.[61]

The US Justice Department assigned two of its own agents toward the same end. They found no actionable evidence of conspiracy due to the technical provisions of the US law, and likely a different compulsion given India was not a US colony. While the British strategy did not prove immediately successful, the US Justice Department expanded its roster of suspect Indians as a result of British intelligence linking them to Germany. The US list now included anyone connected with the San Francisco Ghadar office, the BIC, or the *Annie Larsen*.[62] In short, they had a broad net aimed at Indians advocating for self-rule, potentially not only those who volunteered in the California office, but also those who subscribed to and spread its publications, donated funds, or spoke on its behalf.

In a separate matter, US officials' arrest and January 1917 conviction of San Francisco German consul Franz Bopp and twenty-nine others for conspiring to stop US supply and munitions ships proved a major turning point in unifying US and British aims. [63] The *Bopp* affair did not immediately pertain to Indians; the months-long trial focused on German interference in US war productions. The British government seized on it, however, as their opportunity to definitively associate Indians with Germans now convicted of engaging in military operations on US soil.[64] Some five years later, the case acquired another direct connection to Indians. The *Bopp* trial judge was a member of the appellate court that forwarded an era-defining Indian citizenship case to the US Supreme Court—*United States v. Bhagat Singh Thind* (detailed in chapter 7).[65]

In March 1917, the chief of British intelligence in the United States bypassed formal diplomatic channels and tipped New York City police about a supposed bomb plot. Police arrested several Indian nationals, including Dr. C. K. Chakravarty, who promptly confessed to having been sent by the BIC to purchase arms and munitions for the US wing of the Indian revolutionary movement.[66] Chakravarty's arrest and confession provided the critical piece to legally bind Indian activists to the German government. Close on the heels of the New York arrests, federal officials raided the San Francisco ashram and seized global mailing lists filled with precious names.[67]

On the morning of April 6, 1917, pledging to make the world "safe for democracy," President Wilson signed the US formal declaration of war on Germany.[68] Later that same day, and one month after the New York City arrests, US assistant attorney general Warren ordered the arrest of Ram Chandra and sixteen other Indians for their roles in the now-named German-Hindu Conspiracy.[69] Guided by British intelligence, US federal agents stormed the Ghadar headquarters and hunted down Ghadris as far south as the Mexican border.[70] The timing is a telling window into how large the threat of Indians loomed in the minds of warring leaders. As historian Joan Jensen writes, in the United States, "the first suspects arrested by the federal government . . . were East Indians. Not until that afternoon did Warren order the arrest of seventy Germans who he considered the most prominent and dangerous agents in the United States."[71]

Tasked with successfully prosecuting the German-Hindu Conspiracy case, US Ninth Circuit district attorney John W. Preston worried about translating the arrests into formal, triable charges, including the evidentiary and legal theories required to link the *Annie Larsen* and German cases to Indians in California. Again, the British did not disappoint. To seal the link between the Germans and Indians, British agents delivered John B. Starr-Hunt, a US crewman for the *Annie Larsen* who had confessed to its gun-running plan. Starr-Hunt testified before the San Francisco grand jury, the body responsible for issuing formal indictments.[72] The strategy seemingly worked. On International Workers Day, May 1, 1917, less than a month after their arrest, Ram Chandra and seven other Indians were officially charged with violating US neutrality laws and organizing a military venture against England, a country with which the US was at peace.[73] National headlines warned of dangerous mutinous insurgents, while the *Saturday Evening Post* ran Kipling's manufactured tales of undying Indian loyalty.[74] By July 1917, 124 more were indicted. Ultimately, as men escaped across borders or turned state's evidence, only thirty-five were tried in San Francisco, seventeen of whom were Indians, the rest German Americans or German nationals.[75]

Besides the conspicuous sharing of policing and evidence, British and US authorities jointly devised the legal strategy for the US conspiracy cases. They decided to test-drive their prosecutorial strategies in a smaller Chicago case focused on Indians and, if successful, proceed with the San Francisco showstopper.[76] The Chicago case produced four convictions. More importantly, the verdicts established legal precedent for the broadest possible definition for a "military expedition or enterprise" that the German-Hindu Conspiracy trials were predicated on. Prosecutors weren't obligated to prove any actual criminal acts. They simply had to prove that two or more of the defendants "conspired" about—as in, simply discussed—a military invasion, and some person made a move, in the broadest of terms, to further it. Rules of evidence were significantly loosened, allowing unproven accusations into the record while prosecutors called on jurors to "hold the line for democracy."[77] Authorities' attempt at legal and political domination did not go unchallenged. Portrayed as conspirators against a lawful government, Indians in and out of the courtroom contested the legitimacy of British rule and the justness of their struggle for independence.[78]

Especially in those early American days of World War I, framing the Indian struggle as a "conspiracy" or "plot" appealed to national fears and cast Indians and their independence movement as outside the pale of US values and not a historical analog.[79] Again, none of the BIC's plans were aimed at the US government or people; Ghadar, in all its iterations, targeted British colonial rule. Conspiracy charges also cast a long shadow across Indians' many alliances with Irish, Mexican, and Chinese nationalists, anarchists, socialists, and other radical laborers and organizations, most of whom were already in the US governments' line of fire. Underscoring the US political climate, and utilizing the Espionage and Draft Acts, US attorney Preston concurrently prosecuted 112 IWW members in Chicago for leading massive wartime strikes. Those proceedings rivaled the size, expense, and notoriety of the German-Hindu Conspiracy case.[80]

On November 20, 1917, the San Francisco German-Hindu Conspiracy trial opened; it formally involved three governments and ran for five long months. Then the largest federal trial in US history, it carried a price tag of nearly $3 million ($66.5 million in present-day value), three-quarters of which was paid by the British government. For two years, more than two hundred British secret agents—over and above those already on their surveillance payroll—labored in California building the case for convictions. US federal prosecutors, fed by multiple policing and intelligence agencies, spirited 150 witnesses and five hundred documents and other exhibits from across the globe to make their case.[81] US agents laundered British intelligence reports for the court record, rewriting them as their own in order to conceal the extent of British involvement.[82] Robert Nathan, a British barrister, retired Indian police agent, and MI5 member, operated as a phantom district attorney under the pseudonym Charles Lamb in the lead-up to the trial. For the entirety of the trial, continuing to conceal his identity, Nathan sat at the prosecutor's table.[83]

Fifteen attorneys represented the German and Indian defendants. A number of the German defendants held official posts in the United States. [84] Among the Indians were men well-known in Oregon, like Munshi Ram (author of the Astoria press announcement of Ghadar's formation), Taraknath Das (publicist and translator in the St. Johns riot trials), and Ram Chandra (who worked, studied, and convalesced among Astoria's laborers and for a time ran the San Francisco ashram).

The *San Francisco Chronicle*, describing the courtroom during the testimony of someone turned state's witness, captured the democratic farce:

The tense scene found its climax when four or five of the Hindoo defendants rose to their feet shouting, "That is not right—it is wrong," when Interpreter Gould translated one of the witness' answers. "Sit down—keep your seats," ordered Judge Van Fleet, "the Court will protect your rights—" "Have justice—this is a farce—give us justice," cried the Hindoos as deputy marshals started toward them. "Your counsel will protect your rights," said

Judge Van Fleet. . . . *"But your honor, replied Bhagwan Singh, one of the alleged chief defendants, "our counsel cannot understand our language."* (emphasis added) [85]

As alleged, the conspiracy involved anti-British revolts between 1914 and 1917, and incriminated all three arms of Ghadar: the Berlin India Committee, the San Francisco ashram, and Ghadris in India. Defendants were charged with having conspired to recruit Indians with previously legal, public propaganda—speeches and *Ghadr*—to leave the United States to fight the British Raj. Prosecutors criminalized Ghadar's global support, arguing that organizers depended on Indian networks from Hawai'i to Bangkok and at least a dozen German consuls.[86] Or, as federal DA Preston's opening statement claimed, the "conspiracy reached the entire world."[87] Much of this was hyperbole and reactionary theater. It is also a window into authorities' fears about an ill-prepared band of Indians and the larger global threat of subjugated peoples plotting mutinies, sometimes with German promises of shiploads of weapons and tactical assistance. The British and US governments spared little in their suppressive efforts.

In addition to delivering an extraordinary spectacle of collaborative global policing and suppression, the San Francisco trial utilized and elevated previous British and US governmental leitmotifs employed against Indians. The prosecution traded in overt racial slurs, and specifically targeted Indian subversion, anarchism, and Indo-American citizenship as threats.[88] Federal DA Preston deployed the "Hindu menace," already an incitement for many white laborers, to more sinister heights, arguing that the trouble all began with the arrival of Har Dayal, a "rank, out-and-out Anarchist" who sought "revolution everywhere."[89] Indians were no longer simply an economic and cultural menace to the United States. They were now dangerous subversives that, given *Ghadr*'s support for self-government throughout the colonial world, threatened "both national security . . . and Anglo-American dominance across Asia and the Pacific."[90] Many of the Indian defendants, like their compatriots in India, used the trial to continue their indictment of British rule and expound their radical vision. For some, like Chakravarty, that included appealing to Wilsonian ideals regarding the rights of colonized peoples, a thoroughly hollow pledge even if only considering Indians' experience.[91]

Prosecutors explicitly linked Indians' ability to threaten, conspire, and organize to their possession of US citizenship. Federal DA Preston specifically called out Taraknath Das, "a figure of 'infamy and treachery,'" who "'drank from the fountains of our learning' and 'cloth[ed] himself with our citizenship'" only to plot and violate US laws. [92] As historian Sohi writes, "Preston's call . . . simultaneously warned of the dangers of allowing the naturalization cases of political radicals to move forward and reinforced the racial boundaries of citizenship."[93]

On April 23, 1918, 155 days after the trial began and after mere hours of jury deliberation, twenty-nine defendants were found guilty of conspiring against US neutrality laws and organizing a military expedition against a country (England) with which the United States was at peace. The German defendants received prison sentences varying from six months to two years, along with fines from $1,000 to $10,000. Of the fourteen Indians convicted, Taraknath Das received the heaviest penalty, of twenty-two months, served at McNeil Island Penitentiary in Washington, with others receiving lesser times and fines. None of the defendants were deported to India, given British fears about radical contagion, a contingency that would be rescinded, however, if they resumed nationalist agitation on release.[94]

Ram Chandra was ultimately sentenced not by the state, but by fellow defendant Ram Singh, who was enraged by widespread accusations and likely personal knowledge of Chandra's bilking of large sums of organizational money. A *New York Times* front-page article described the dramatic courtroom scene as follows:

> Ram Chandra arose and started across the room. Ram Singh also arose. He raised his revolver and began firing. Ram Chandra staggered forward and fell dead before the witness chair, with a bullet in his heart and two others in his body. At the same moment, Ram Singh fell. [US marshal] Holohan, a man of great stature, had shot once with his arm high over his head, so that the bullet should clear nearby counsel. The shot broke Ram Singh's neck.[95]

The murders were symptomatic of the pressures within the San Francisco ashram, where members were subjected to global spies, raids, recanting comrades, military setbacks, and Indian secret tribunals, executions, and jailings aggravated by bags of German-funneled money.

The convictions were the product of extensive and high-level collaboration between the two governments. Yet both had reason to conceal that very fact, and effectively did so for decades. That the British used US courts in its war against Indian nationalists would sully the reputation of US democracy, a key banner of US war efforts and puffery for the colonial world. Additionally, it endangered other hyphenated Americans' loyalty if the US government became known for aiding a foreign power against former subjects as the British did. For the British, drawing attention to their US efforts to suppress Ghadar furthered the radicals' reputation in India, and did so when the British sought to crush or channel the foment toward less radical resolutions.[96]

Still, the US and British governments had not quite completed their global pursuit of Indians and their brutal denial of their political equality. Just a few short years after the San Francisco conspiracy verdicts, and in keeping with DA Preston's warnings in the trial, the US Supreme Court decision in *U.S. v. Bhagat Singh Thind* locked Indians out of citizenship, with all of its attendant rights and possibilities, for decades.

7

Bhagat Singh Thind and the Whiteness of Empire

In the years during and around World War I, the United States became an even more dangerous place for Indians. Simply "living while Indian" was suspect; espousing independence brought a special hell. Ashram staff, Ghadar supporters, and other prominent nationalists like Lajpat Rai confronted the combined fire of the US government's domestic crackdown on immigrants and radicals, and the specific US-British offensive against Indians.[1] Hundreds who stayed behind faced questions of how to survive let alone build some semblance of a future—farms, businesses, education, professions, and marriages—their choices strewn with pitfalls and dangers. During this time, Bhagat Singh Thind continued to openly promote Ghadar, served in the US military, and twice sought citizenship as protection and pathway to a future. He became a lightning rod and symbol of Indians' subjugated status and foreclosed opportunities.

After the great leaving of 1914, Thind periodically assisted the San Francisco ashram staff who were intensely organizing, publishing, and fundraising while severely taxed by the departure of hundreds of Ghadris and by overt government suppression. When in Oregon, he circulated *Ghadr* and collected money for the organization. His name joined the growing list of surveilled Indians.

In January of 1917, after a fractious San Francisco Ghadar meeting, Thind returned to Oregon. While living in Wauna, a few miles upriver from Astoria, he filed a Declaration of Intention, a mandated step in the citizenship process. While most questions on the form were mundane, others hint at critical US political battle lines, notably the obtuse questions about race and politics crafted to deny certain immigrants entry or to establish grounds for their later expulsion. Thind provided all requested information, including that he was "white" in color and "dark" in complexion, and married to Chint Kaur, still in Punjab. As required by the gatekeepers of the white, Christian nation, Thind swore, "I am not an anarchist; I am not a polygamist nor a believer in the practice of polygamy" before signing and dating the form. [2]

Three weeks later the US government passed the landmark Immigration Act of 1917. The act banned Indians and all peoples from wide swaths of Asia from entering the United States, and became commonly known as the Asiatic Barred Zone. It also specifically barred other so-called undesirables: homosexuals, idiots, feeble-minded persons, criminals, epileptics, insane persons, alcoholics, professional beggars, all persons mentally or physically defective, polygamists, and anarchists.[3] Additionally, it expanded the government's window for deporting immigrants deemed illegal or undesirable.[4]

Thind could have filed his declaration considerably sooner than he did. His family holds that he had always intended to naturalize and remain in the United States.[5] But whatever his dreams were upon arrival in 1913, the political situation had shifted dramatically in four short years. Educated and literate, Thind likely followed newspaper accounts and murmurings before the act's passage and understood it would prevent him from legally reentering the United States if he visited his wife and family in India.[6] It also cast a long political shadow over building a life in the United States. Just three years earlier, and well-known to Thind, US Immigration authorities had arrested and readied for deportation Ghadar leader and noncitizen Dayal for anarchist associations. With the act's passage, the looming US entry into war (April 1917), his homeland ravaged, and the arrests, jailing, and murder of Ghadris, US citizenship offered Thind some promise of safety and stability. He grabbed for the brass ring while continuing his political commitments.

In 1918, Thind visited Bhagwan Singh Gayanee, Santokh Singh, Gopal Singh, and Taraknath Das, all convicted in the San Francisco trial and sentenced that April to Washington's McNeil Island Penitentiary. The imprisoned men appealed to him to assist the San Francisco office and not let the important work of the organization and its newspaper languish. Despite the risk to his citizenship bid, Thind obliged. According to British intelligence records, entangled in bitter infighting in the ashram, Thind left after a month.[7]

Date	Event
January 1917	Thind files Declaration of Intent to Naturalize
February 1917	Immigration Act passed, aka Asiatic Barred Zone
April 1917	US enters World War I
May 1917	Selective Service Act requires all men register for the US military
June 1917	Espionage Act passed, broadly criminalizing opposition to the war
April 1918	Convictions in German-Hindu Conspiracy trial
May 1918	Noncitizens serving in the US military may naturalize
July 1918	Thind enlists

Returning to Astoria, Thind enlisted in the US Army and, in July 1918, began serving at Fort Lewis, Washington, one of some twenty-seven Singhs and seventeen Khans in the United States who served during World War I.[8] Thind and other Indo-American enlistees were highlighted in Lajpat Rai's *Young India* with editorial encouragements to follow their example.[9] Promoted to acting sergeant, Thind remained at Fort Lewis, never saw conflict, and was one of the first turbaned Sikhs to serve in the US Army. With the end of hostilities and six months of service, he was honorably discharged. [10]

Thind had previously signaled his inclination for the military. Shortly after arriving in 1913, and mirroring his father's career in India, he applied to the US Army Signal Reserve Corps as a commissioned officer. He was rejected for want of citizenship.[11] In the succeeding years, he may have construed little daylight between US military enlistment and promotion of Indian self-rule. Respected nationalist Lajpat Rai advocated both. For some Ghadris, but hardly all, the United States was a democracy to be supported and emulated, beliefs reinforced by President Wilson's wartime rhetoric of making the world "safe for democracy" and cynical advocacy of colonies' right to self-determination.[12]

Although Thind's thoughts about enlistment are inaccessible, a trail of state coercion is quite clear. At a minimum, Thind had to register for military service. The May 1917 Selective Service Act required any male between the age of twenty-one and thirty (amended, in 1918, to eighteen and forty-five) to register, whether a citizen or not. Nationally, some ten million men did so, Indians among them.[13] In Oregon,

INDIAN World War I MILITARY REGISTRATION					
	CA	WA	OR	OTHER	TOTAL
Singh	887	33	78	50	1048
Khan (not all from India)	49	18	13	110	190
INDIAN World War I MILITARY SERVICE (records do not provide accurate state origins)					
Singh					25–27
Khan (not all from India)					17

"All U.S., World War I Draft Registration Cards, 1917–1918," Results Veterans Administration Master Index, 1917–1940, Ancestry for "Singh" and "Khan," Ancestry.com, in World War I Draft Registration Cards, 1917–1918 and US, Veterans Administration Master Index, 1917–1940 all accessed April 26, 2023. Detailed links as follows: https://www.ancestry.com/search/collections/6482/?name=_singh&count=50&residence=_oregon-usa_40; https://www.ancestry.com/search/collections/6482/?name=_khan&count=50&residence=_oregon-usa_40; https://www.ancestry.com/search/collections/6482/?name=_singh&count=50&name_x=_1&residence=_california-usa_7&fh=900&fsk=MDs4OTk7NTA-61-; https://www.ancestry.com/search/collections/6482/?name=_khan&count=50&name_x=_1&residence=_california-usa_7&fh=50&fsk=MDs0OTs1MA-61--61-; https://www.ancestry.com/search/collections/6482/?name=_singh&count=50&name_x=_1&residence=_washington-usa_50; https://www.ancestry.com/search/collections/6482/?name=_khan&count=50&name_x=_1&residence=_washington-usa_50; total registrations: https://www.ancestry.com/search/collections/6482/?name=_singh&count=50&name_x=_1&bsk=MDs2NTA7NTUw&fh=600; SERVED: https://www.ancestry.com/search/collections/61861/?name=_singh&count=50.

seventy-eight Singhs and a dozen Khans registered, together with almost nine hundred primarily from the farmlands of California, figures that provide a rough snapshot of where communities endured in the wake of Ghadris' exodus to India.

Any man who refused to register faced persecution by authorities and quasi-public groups like the American Protective League that surveilled, arrested, and physically attacked supposed subversives of whatever ethnicity.[14] President Wilson condemned war opponents not simply as dissenters, but as "agents and dupes" of the German kaiser.[15] In June 1917 Congress passed the Espionage Act, which defined opposition to the war—mere speech even, let alone protests or work stoppages—punishable by $10,000, twenty years in jail, or both.[16] As historian Adam Hochschild writes, with a broad surveillance program already operating, the Espionage Act provided the government with a "club to smash left wing forces of all kinds."[17] The IWW, then almost 150,000 strong and dubbed "unhung traitors" by former president Theodore Roosevelt, emerged as one of the authorities favored targets.[18]

Still, the entry into the war was unpopular among many in the United States, and the government used the rhetoric of militaristic patriotism and the force of the law to secure servicemen.[19] The Selective Service Act of 1917 instituted a compulsory draft, one that, while opposed by tens of thousands, nonetheless secured close to a half a million men in just the first recruiting round of 1917. About a quarter of those compelled to serve were noncitizens and subject to the draft for having filed a Declaration of Intent to naturalize.[20]

In 1918, Congress updated the act and, among other changes, extended citizenship to enlisted noncitizens.[21] Men needed only to prove they were on active duty and provide two superior officers' attestations to their loyalty. Within a year of its enactment, often through mass ceremonies on military bases, almost two hundred thousand overwhelmingly European immigrants were granted citizenship under the act's provisions.[22] Service was potentially a dear price for civic admission, given the millions who died in wartime trenches. Further, the congressional update carried a sizable stick. Per the law, anyone who had filed a Declaration of Intent but refused to serve was forever barred from citizenship. The Bureau of Naturalization actively monitored compliance, working with local draft boards to ferret out such "slacking foreigners."[23]

"Young India," October 1918, SAADA

In this political atmosphere, for Thind and thousands of other so-called aliens, military service—whether by enlistment or the draft—established loyalty and kept their citizenship bids viable and on an ostensibly reliable path. Thind was briefly successful. In Washington, on December 9, 1918, dressed in his turban and military uniform, Thind was awarded citizenship, stating, "I'm willing and eager to undertake the responsibilities of citizenship, having shown my eagerness by buying Liberty bonds to help carry on America's part in the war and by enlisting in the fighting forces of the country."[24]

Four days later, at the urging of a local Bureau of Naturalization agent, the court revoked Thind's status. As the judge stated in his ruling upholding the federal government's objection, Thind "lacked sufficient proof of his raciality."[25] Much like Indians soldiering for the British, Thind could serve, but was denied political equality. Thind's plight also highlighted the ambiguities within the Selective Service Act and the broader tensions of his times, when loyalty to the nation uneasily (and briefly) vied with race for membership in the US polity.[26]

The US government promoted military enlistment with posters and newspapers articles, and many racially barred from US citizenship seized on the seeming opportunity. The largest enrollment of non-Europeans occurred in Hawai'i, where 40 percent of enlistees were Japanese.[27] But permitting military service to supplant race as a citizenship qualifier remained both politically controversial and technically murky within the Selective Service Act. Regional courtrooms diverged about conferring citizenship on Asian servicemen. In December of 1918, federal district judge Horace Vaughn of Honolulu announced that he would naturalize all Asians who served. Judge Vaughn was no champion of equality; he had recently ruled civilian Japanese American Takao Ozawa as racially unqualified for citizenship, an objection later upheld by the US Supreme Court. Disqualifying servicemen, however, was a bridge too far for the judge. His stance unleashed a storm of controversy.

As reported by the Hawai'i district attorney, the white citizenry of Hawai'i harbored a "grave feeling" that Judge Vaughn's naturalizations would upset the balance of power with large numbers of Japanese voters, legislators, senators, or even a Japanese police force.[28] Attempted voter registrations, marriages, and land deals of Japanese people naturalized in Hawai'i were rejected in California.[29] Leaders within the national Bureau of Naturalization split as to whether race trumped military service, leaving agents in the field confused and court rulings varying from state to state.[30] In Washington state, soldier Thind caught the wrong end of this national debate.[31]

In early 1919, honorably discharged civilian and noncitizen Thind returned to Oregon, a place he knew well, if now emptied of its many activists and their urgent work. On May 6, 1919, five months after his Washington setback but perversely required to reference it in his new paperwork, he again petitioned for citizenship.[32] Thind's

"President Wilson on tour is shocked by an unexpected reception, Seattle, Washington, September 13, 1918." The protest was organized by the IWW. University of Washington Libraries Society and Culture Collection SOC11739

decision to file in Portland was likely the product of moving back to a familiar place, and perhaps a tactical calculation. Historically, area courts had been surprisingly supportive of Chinese merchants during Chinese Exclusion. More recently, and with British backing, they had prosecuted anti-Indian vigilantes, a stance that might carry over to citizenship.[33]

Wartime Oregon, however, was a contentious place. On the one hand, business was booming, with strong wages and jobs aplenty. The region also, as historian Michael Helquist writes, "experienced one of the nation's most vigorous clampdowns on dissent, and the strife hardly skipped a beat for the [1918] armistice."[34] Prewar "preparedness" parades brought fifteen thousand people into the streets of Portland. Portland's mayor declared a ban on "unpatriotic gatherings" in 1917. Wobblies were massacred and rounded up in nearby Washington—in Everett in 1916 and Centralia in 1919. In June of 1917, IWW organizers shut down much of Oregon and the region's critical wartime timber industry, and authorities arrested hundreds of the strikers. Attempting to undermine the IWW's influence, including in Oregon, the government formed the Loyal Legion of Loggers and Lumbermen (LLLL), and mandated membership for workers in Northwest woods and mills.[35] In 1918, the government tried and won two major sedition cases in the very Portland courts deciding Thind's legal future.

Thind lived and worked in Linnton, a mill town a few miles down-river from Portland. The president of Linnton's lumber mill, E. D. King-sley, and another lumberman witnessed Thind's petition.[36] Thind hired local Portland attorney Thomas Mannix, an immigrant Irishman active in the nationalist movement and the broader radical antiwar circles of Portland, to assist him with his case.[37] Attorney Mannix did not peti-tion based on Thind's military service, a strategy that had not gone well in Washington. Further, with the war's close, the nativist movement campaigned against soldier-citizens as part of its "100% Americanism" agenda, and judicial opinion similarly began to turn against naturaliz-ing nonwhite veterans.[38] Mannix argued instead that Thind, an "Aryan" Indian, qualified for citizenship as a white person. The case was heard by Oregon federal district court judge Charles Wolverton (Judge Wolverton, an adherent of the Deady-Scott racial policy, years earlier had been explicitly named by the Immigration Service as integral to Portland becoming a "haven" for Chinese).[39] In 1920, Judge Wolverton granted Thind status.[40]

Judge Wolverton's ruling memorandum in *Thind* summarized many of the hot-button issues of the day with respect to race, citizenship, labor, and loyalty. Unlike in Washington state, Thind's political views were explicitly considered by the Oregon court. The federal govern-ment had alerted the court to Thind's association with Ghadar and to British and US intelligence concerns.[41] Surprisingly, this proved not to be a stumbling block for Judge Wolverton; he accepted Thind's explana-tion that, while he was acquainted with many Ghadris and shared their desire for an independent India, he believed only in nonviolent method. Supporting world war evidently fell outside of the jurist's pacifist cri-teria. The judge's relative unconcern about Thind's political association was notably out of step with federal and regional counterparts.

Thind's 1918 military service and 1913 attempted enlistment estab-lished in Judge Wolverton's eyes that his "deportment had been that of a good citizen."[42] Thind's membership card in the LLLL was also proffered as evidence of his loyalty and upstanding character. Attor-ney Mannix did not, however, include Thind's letters to other Ghadris debating whether to strike in support of some labor organization's opposition to World War I. Similarly, Thind's efforts in Linnton to organize a contingent to carry the flag of Indian independence with

Sinn Fein Irish nationalists in a Seattle march were not submitted for the court's review.[43]

In his written decision, Judge Wolverton cited naturalization cases across the country that had already ruled that a "high class Hindu coming from Punjab"—as Wolverton, Thind, and Mannix referred to him despite being a Sikh—was "ethnologically a white person" and therefore entitled to citizenship. Yet "whiteness" was far from a settled legal standard. Naturalization decisions across the country were split on whether Indians were white and consequently eligible for naturalization. [44] On October 18, 1920, Judge Wolverton, based on his interpretation of the supposed science of race and multiple US court rulings, concluded that Thind was "entitled to his naturalization" and issued Thind's certification one month later.[45]

The ruling was immediately appealed by the US government in the person of Lester Humphreys, a US federal district attorney for Oregon, which Judge Wolverton was required to hear. DA Humphreys posited that Thind was ineligible for citizenship, as were all "Hindus," because he was not "a free white person."[46] His chief witness was naturalization examiner W. H. Tomlinson of Portland. Tomlinson's testimony was in keeping with federal policy and brief and to the point: "Bhagat Singh Thind is a native of Amritsar Punjab, India, and to the best of my information and belief is not a free white person."[47] In late March 1921, Judge Wolverton ruled against the government and again determined that Thind, "as a native of Punjab, India . . . [and] a Hindu is entitled under the laws of the United States to admission to citizenship."[48] DA Humphreys, with the assent of his superiors, refused to drop the matter.

Portland's US district attorney's office, where Humphreys worked, had been involved in a number of contentious, high-profile wartime cases. In 1918, it spearheaded the prosecution, conviction, and ultimate imprisonment for sedition of Dr. Marie Equi, a Portland physician, feminist, abortionist, anarchist, lesbian, IWW supporter, and labor and antiwar activist (attorney Mannix was part of Equi's social circles). Equi had very publicly protested the war and was arrested the same day as hundreds of others across the country, including Socialist Party leader and presidential candidate Eugene Debs.[49]

During Equi's trial, the prosecutor claimed in his closing statement to the jury that, "unless you put this woman in jail, it [the red flag] will float over the world," and recited the "Star Spangled Banner."[50] A year later, reflecting and enforcing the grotesque wave of anti-German hysteria during the war, the Portland DA's office prosecuted prominent, prosperous, Liberty-bond-buying, German-born local businessman Henry Albers for pro-German (and thus treasonous during wartime) statements reportedly made after drinking too much on a train home from San Francisco.[51]

If Judge Wolverton appeared out of step with many federal authorities regarding whiteness and nationalist Indians, DA Humphreys was not. In biography, political proclivities, and organizational affiliation, DA Humphreys was aligned with a national network of fellow veterans from the recent Philippine war who played an outsized role in the government's World War I domestic clampdown against immigrants and radicals. War veteran, white supremacist, and former president Theodore Roosevelt loudly beat the drum for World War I. Major Ralph Van Deman adapted his Philippine war surveillance system, grounded in torture, for the US War Department in 1917. With dozens of branch offices employing Pinkerton's and other private labor spies, it soon surpassed the Justice Department's Bureau of Investigation.[52] National Guardsmen, many having trained in the Philippines, shot down striking Colorado miners.[53] Chicago's American Protective League, led by a Philippine war vet schooled in torture, organized civilians to track thousands of supposed wartime spies and slackers, soon a national vigilante network of twenty-five thousand.[54] Far from outliers, these and other organizations and activities were enabled and approved by high-level officials of the US government.[55]

DA Humphreys, with impressive credentials as a racist and nativist zealot, actively and successfully pursued power and prestige in Portland's social and business circles. A leader in the state's Democratic Party, he, together with his wife Evangeline, frequently appeared in Portland's society pages.[56] He was a prominent member of the American Legion, a patriotic veterans' organization, and lectured to local members and to other business clubs and organizations around Portland.[57] One such speech was credited with clinching the 1919 Oregon American Legion's advocacy for an injunction against all immigration into the United States and the prohibition of all Portland public assemblies protesting the treatment of people suspected of disloyalty, people like Equi or Albers.[58]

Portland Telegram, August 2, 1921. Oregon district attorney Lester Humphreys (fifth from the left directly behind white robe) in a 1921 photo with other Portland notables, including the mayor and chief of police, and the Exalted Cyclops of the newly organized Ku Klux Klan of Oregon. Oregon Historical Society.

In 1921, Humphreys was photographed alongside Portland notables—the mayor and chief of police among them—and the Exalted Cyclops of the newly reorganized Ku Klux Klan of Oregon.[59] While being photographed with the Klan does not prove membership, the KKK's postwar philosophy of "100% pure Americanism," and its dedication to organizing native-born white Protestant gentiles, coincides with the philosophies marking the larger trajectory of Humphrey's life. It also proved no obstacle to his prestige and rocketing career.[60] He was appointed to head the Portland US district attorney's office and commended by US attorney general A. Mitchell Palmer, architect of the notorious Palmer Raids against radicals and immigrants.[61] Humphreys was, in other words, well insinuated with national leaders and the reactionary politics of his times.

Shortly after the 1921 KKK photograph, DA Humphreys appealed Judge Wolverton's *Thind* ruling to the Ninth Circuit Federal Appeals Court.[62] Humphreys was following a national lead. The US attorney general had long opposed Indian citizenship.[63] National Immigration Department Bureau chief Richard K. Campbell's views were that "off-color races not only unfit but as well undesirable additions to the body politic." Campbell advised "U.S. attorneys and through them clerks of courts to deny Indians citizenship as a means of "forc[ing] courts into making decisions one way or the other."[64] With Humphreys and the *Thind* case, national authorities hit their mark.[65]

That *Thind* was not the only Indian citizenship case under consideration nationally punctuates DA Humphrey's pivotal role in pushing it up the legal chain. Though it is difficult to determine their exact status without an exhaustive search of every state court, between 1915 and 1923 some twenty-six "Singh" petitions were in the legal pipeline, ten at or before Thind's May 1919 Oregon petition, and sixteen after.[66] One striking feature of *Thind* is that it centered on a man publicly associated with Ghadar and the state where it began.

The Ninth Circuit appellate court was based in San Francisco, and its judges were well aware of the German-Hindu Conspiracy trial.[67] One of them, Judge Hunt, was temporarily reassigned to the San Francisco district court in order to preside over the 1917 *Bopp* case, a legal precursor to the German-Hindu Conspiracy matter.[68] The Ninth Circuit panel was also acutely aware of the contentious issues surrounding race and citizenship. The court's far-ranging legal authority—covering California, Washington, Idaho, Montana, Nevada, Oregon, and Hawai'i—was home to a markedly diverse population. Its rulings involved and affected millions—Chinese, Japanese, Indians, and others—outside of America's historic black and white legal citizenship binary. In 1917, the Ninth reviewed and forwarded the Hawai'i-based *Takao Ozawa* case for the US Supreme Court's determination on the racial eligibility of Japanese Americans for citizenship. Having recently upheld Dr. Marie Equi's conviction, the court was also quite conscious of Portland radicals. In short, the Ninth Circuit appellate court judges had multiple reasons to appreciate *Thind*'s importance. In October of 1921, they unanimously certified the case for a definitive and nationally binding opinion by the US Supreme Court.

The high court was to apply post–Civil War Section 2169 Revised Statutes regarding the racial determinants of citizenship, its relevant language being "aliens being free white persons and to aliens of African nativity and to persons of African descent."[69] The US Supreme Court could make such a ruling only *if* a matter successfully came up through the lower courts; they were and are formally barred from directly requesting cases. Further, no other court *except* the country's highest court can establish precedent for the country as a whole, and, once set, no lower court can go against precedent without legislative change of the provision at issue. Importantly, the high court is not a neutral institution, as witnessed by its rulings over the decades favoring Chinese exclusion, foreclosing African American citizenship and enfranchisement, limiting women's bodily autonomy, and other onerous decisions. The court's opinions reflect the justices' dispositions and shape the country's bearing.[70]

With *Thind*, the federal Supreme Court could settle the messy field of conflicting court rulings across the country about who was legally white. Beyond that pressing US agenda, it is difficult not to see the fight for Indian global belonging lurking just beneath the case's surface. Moves, both joint and discrete, by the US and British governments against Indo-American citizenship and activists were pointed and long-standing.[71] The San Francisco conspiracy trial involved global heads of state, diplomats, federal prosecutors, judges, staff, and investigators. As scholar Doug Coulson so importantly argues, to imagine that such high-level and massive counterinsurgent collaboration evaporated as the highest US court considered Indo-American citizenship strains credulity.[72] The British concealed their involvement in the San Francisco German-Hindu Conspiracy trial for fear of its impact on the nationalist struggle in India, making it well worth asking whether British authorities were motivated to do the same with *Thind*.[73]

To date, no one has unearthed more definitive British fingerprints on *Thind*. Its objective effect, however, was a political and practical gift to British colonizers. At a minimum, *Thind* was the product of an opportune judicial through-line—a nativist Oregon DA Humphreys and a motivated western appeals court—fully realized by the US Supreme Court. Arising from a perfect storm of political will and structural opportunity, the case advanced both the British and US governments' postwar aims.

On its face, targeting Indo-American citizenship in the 1920s was wildly disproportionate with the few thousand Indians who remained in the United States. It was in line, however, with British postwar fears of Indian nationalist foment and the US agenda of aggressive racism and national fealty. The era-defining 1917 Russian socialist revolution—showcasing the power of a relatively small group of radicals—did little to allay an imperial sense of urgency.[74]

For England, Indo-American citizenship furnished a potent political standard they could ill afford, given their stonewalling of the ongoing struggle in India for independence and self-rule. Further, with the war's conclusion, Ghadar was no longer treasonous and could (and did) legally reconstitute in the United States. As historian Dignan writes, British rulers were concerned that their "prewar difficulties might reappear, especially if/when Ghadr leaders advised resident Indians to apply for American citizenship."[75] Nationalists could again migrate from India and again organize against British rule with the relative protection of citizenship.

As described, the US government was engaged in its own antidemocratic domestic assault, both in and out of the courtroom, grounded in real-world transformations. Historian Mae Ngai argues that World War I both destabilized and enshrined nation-states, leaving massive border and immigration controls in its wake, with much of that apparatus aimed at preventing millions of destitute European refugees from flooding the United States.[76] To US officials, their double threat was the radicalism they had long associated with such migrants, as Indians had also come to symbolize.

Much of the US government and populace were at war with those already ostensibly included within—and who defined the social health of—the US polity. Hundreds of thousands of African Americans had answered President Wilson's wartime call to make the world "safe for democracy." Yet, upon returning home, and largely with impunity, they were assaulted across the country by violent white mobs in an epidemic of public lynching. In the summer of 1919, more African Americans died at the hands of whites than had in decades.[77] In short, like the British in India, the postwar United States was waging a crusade against multiracial democracy.

Underneath this political noise and violence was the reality that US industrialization had created a population increasingly at odds with the country's white settler foundations. Without legal and popular intervention, the price for breakneck development risked the country's racial order. By 1920, the United States no longer needed the same massive infusion of immigrants that had sustained industrialization.[78] In this economic and political postwar climate, many lawmakers and citizens clamored to turn off the migratory spigot, fortify white right, and restrict US citizenship to its enduring criteria of "free white persons."[79]

This impulse, particularly urgent in the US west, contextualizes the Ninth Circuit's certification of both *Ozawa* and *Thind* for the US Supreme Court. Provisions within the Chinese Exclusion Act of 1882 had settled the ineligibility of Chinese immigrants for US citizenship. But, as Ngai writes, "Japanese, Asian Indians, Armenians, Syrians, Mexicans, and other people . . . posed a challenge to the race categories in citizenship law. Where did they stand in relation to the black-white paradigm?"[80] The US Supreme Court actively and decisively shaped that resolution.

Throughout his eight-year legal battle, Thind displayed a keen understanding of the era's operative racial science and its function within US history and jurisprudence. He did not dispute the prevailing racial pseudoscience and its social implications, but argued for its applicability to him and his bid for citizenship.[81]

The legal parameters of the day required that Thind prove his whiteness, a race-based marker of identity. Whiteness is a colonial fiction, a justification and system of power with no basis in the natural world. This is not to say that there are no physical and cultural differences among peoples of the globe. Rather, those differences have absolutely no relationship to their suitability for self-rule and citizenship. Nevertheless, colonizers have used race in the construction and rationalization of empires and its pseudoscientific ranking of peoples as Caucasian, Mongolian, or Negroid. As a political fabrication, "whiteness" is by definition unstable, changing across time and place. Its constant, as scholar Susan Koshy writes, is its institutional power to organize and exclude diverse bodies.[82]

Since 1790, US citizenship was reserved for free white men.[83] In the 1860s, after a bloody civil war, formerly enslaved African American men were formally included by constitutional amendment but effectively denied inclusion in practice. The passage of the Fourteenth Amendment was accompanied by congressional debate over dropping whiteness as criteria for citizenship altogether. Led by an Oregonian, legislators opposed to citizenship for Native and Chinese men defeated the proposal (a role eerily reprised by Oregon DA Humphreys forty years later).[84] While African American citizenship was narrowly defined as those with "African nativity or descent," whites had no such geographic tether, which facilitated the incorporation of diverse Europeans across time and changing political needs.[85]

In the early 1900s, almost no Asian citizenship applicants filed as black, given both the stringent geographical requirement and the bitter social consequence of US blackness.[86] In law and popular opinion, blackness remained conceptually tied to bondage and to peoples who were not self-ruled. America's Black-white citizenship polarity, with entrenched colonial meanings rooted in slavery, set the terms for millions of immigrants seeking civic status. To secure status, "Asians"—a broad legal category of people including Syrians, Japanese, and Indians—were therefore forced to contend in an ugly US game: seeking whiteness legally premised on its distance from blackness.

In 1922, just two months prior to Thind's hearing, the US Supreme Court ruled on the Hawaiian citizenship case of Takao Ozawa. The justices denied Ozawa's bid not based on his skin tone or his lack of social and familial accomplishments; they ruled that Ozawa was categorically not Caucasian but Mongolian, as were all Japanese people per the pseudoscientific categories of the day. The *Ozawa* decision was a cruel and momentous ruling for the Japanese community. However, for Thind and his community it was a hopeful sign. The same specious anthropology used to exclude Ozawa had long classified Indians as Aryans, a subset of Caucasians.[87]

The central issue for the high court's consideration in *Thind* was, "Is a high-caste Hindu of full Indian blood, born at Amrit Sar, Punjab, India, a white person?" As legal historian Haney López writes, "The language betrays entrenched beliefs about the racial significance of class and caste, blood and birthplace, and even religion in establishing racial identity." "Hindu" also conflated race and religion and was used despite Thind and the vast majority of Indian immigrants being Sikhs.[88] Thind's homeland, turban, and pigmentation were the legal and social determinants of a colonially imagined "race."

The government's brief to the court traded in a civilizational reading of race. Citing India's colonizers as its authorities, the US government's attorney argued that British experience proved that Hindus were a "subject race" and "wholly alien to Western civilization and utterly incapable of assimilation to Western habit and customs, mode of life, political and social institutions." Central to their "alien" standing was caste. The attorney clarified that "free" was not simply an opposite to enslaved Africans but also defined a "type of civilization . . . inclusive of only such men . . . as belonged to a civilization known as the white civilization."[89] It was an astoundingly circular and self-serving argument that lionized those who enslaved millions of Africans and pillaged India. The court's ultimate decision doubled down on this logic; it normalized imperial conquest and abetted the British Crown's continuing domination of India.

In court, using the convoluted math of racial pseudoscience, Thind and his attorneys held that the recognized anthropological sources established him as "Aryan," and therefore Caucasian, and therefore white, and therefore qualified for US citizenship.[90] They problematically argued that Hinduism's caste practices ensured Thind's racial purity as an Aryan (and despite his being a Sikh, a religion doctrinally opposed to caste).[91] In a letter presented to the court, Thind stated that being a high-caste Hindu ensured his racial purity.[92] Thind also drew a pointed parallel to US history, favorably noting that Aryans in India drove out Indigenous peoples and took charge of their lands as resolutely as European settlers had done in the United States.

Attorney Mannix further argued that "the high-class Hindu regards the aboriginal Indian Mongoloid in the same manner as the American regards the Negro, speaking from a matrimonial standpoint." In case his point was missed, he repeated it a few pages later, stating that "it would be just as disgraceful for a high-class Hindu to marry a member of one of the lower castes as it would be for an American gentleman to marry a member of the negro race. . . . The offspring is subject to the same social degradation."[93] Little light can be found between Thind's rationales and those of the state.[94] The differences turned primarily on Thind's claim to whiteness.

Penning the court's unanimous opinion, Justice George Sutherland, a naturalized British immigrant, took no issue per se with Thind's being Caucasian, as defined by "science," but discounted its importance. More relevant to the court was that the "average man knows perfectly well that there are unmistakable and profound differences between them [Caucasians] to-day." Arguing that the terms Caucasian and Aryan were newer, "scientific" terms, unknown to the country's founders, the justices reasoned they could only be understood in the context of "familiar speech . . . intended to include only the type of man whom they [the founders] knew as white." Hindus, he continued, unlike the many peoples of Europe, would never assimilate in the United States.[95] Indians, in other words, were altogether different humans from Europeans—a colonizers' logic that justified centuries of barbarism. It was also an argument for citizenship that boiled down to the logic that, as Koshy writes, "whiteness means what white people think it means."[96] And, if not already sufficiently draconian, besides denying Indians citizenship, the court extended its logic to include Koreans, Thai, Vietnamese, and all others from Asia.[97]

The court's ruling was brutish and trite: brown-skinned, turbaned Thind had no place in the white United States.[98] Their three-and-a-half page decision represented a timely move to ensure white structural power in the face of an increasingly diverse country and a politically animated Indian populace. *Thind* and its rippling consequences signify the US nadir of Indians' rights and acceptance with far-reaching ramifications.

Portland's *Morning Oregonian* ran multiple column inches on the verdict, including Thind's response. It also featured a large photo of the bearded and turbaned Thind captioned, "Hindu Contends That He Is White, Despite Decision of United States Supreme Court." The photo could be interpreted as a straightforward portrayal of the protagonist and the case. But given the consistent national vilification of "Hindus," it also had the look of a wanted poster, describing the individual and the crimes for which he is sought, its subtext imagined as "Hindu Wanted for Fraudulently Impersonating Whites." "Fraud" in fact soon became the government's justification for stripping Indians of their citizenship.[99] At a minimum, the photo broadcast a succinct image to the public as to who was, and most especially who was not, white as multiple government bureaus and officials pursued those outside the privileged circle of civic rights and belonging.

The court's ruling cast Indians into a new US legal category. They were now aliens ineligible for citizenship, a highly racialized process

HINDU WILL MAKE CITIZENSHIP FIGHT

U. S. Supreme Court Decision to Be Opposed.

REHEARING TO BE ASKED

Bhagat Sing Thind Says Ruling Regarding His Color Is Insult to Race.

An effort to obtain a rehearing of the case in which the supreme court of the United Sattes recently held that high caste Hindus are not white persons within the meaning of the United States law and are not entitled to naturalization will be made, according to announcement yesterday of Bhagat Singh Thind of Portland.

The case arose out of the efforts of United States naturalization authorities here to cancel the citizenship of Thind. The district court in Oregon refused to cancel the certificate of citizenship and the case was finally carried to the supreme court of the United States.

Court Ruling Adverse.

The supreme court held that the certificate was procured illegally in that Thind was not a white person according to the intent of the American law, and consequently not entitled to citizenship.

Thind, who is now in Portland and who is employed at the West Oregon Lumber company at Linnton, said yesterday that the decision was a surprise to him in that all scientists agree that the Hindus are members of the Aryan race, the great white race from which descended prac-

HINDU CONTENDS THAT HE IS WHITE, DESPITE DECISION OF UNITED STATES SUPREME COURT.

Bhagat Singh Thind, central figure in case which has attracted more than nation-wide attention.

Morning Oregonian, February 24, 1923.

that presented as colorblind law with broad repercussions. Marriages and professions were blocked based on race and civic status. Across the US west, citizenship was enshrined as a prerequisite to land ownership and backed by the power of the US Supreme Court.[100] In California, the many Indians engaged in agriculture were stripped of land titles and barred from future holding, demonstrating afresh that race is both ultimately and immediately about protecting power and property.[101]

While the Supreme Court opined, but did not explicitly rule, on the pertinence of immigration law to citizenship (the second question for consideration in *Thind*), in the wake of *Thind*, governmental agencies made that issue directly relevant. In 1924, the US Congress passed the

Immigration Act, also known as the Johnson-Reed Act, to establish quotas based on the high court's logic. The "Johnson" of this act was none other than Albert Johnson of Grays Harbor, Washington, who near the time of Ghadar's formation in Astoria was shaping a national career relentlessly attacking the IWW, socialists, and immigrants as threatening radical intruders.[102]

Under the Johnson-Reed Act, those commonly considered white persons were allowed entry into the country. [103] Utilizing *Thind*'s newly minted "aliens ineligible for citizenship" category, anyone barred from citizenship was now unable to even enter the United States. [104] While the act technically allowed 2 percent of immigrants to come to the United States from countries other than those in Europe, the controlling citizenship provision meant that only Europeans living in, for example, South Africa or India could qualify. For the British, this had the added benefit of ensuring that no Indian could enter the United States and raise trouble for colonial rule. The underlying logic of *Thind*, echoed in the act, was that only white people had countries and held citizenship.[105] With that diktat, the United States closed its doors to the world.[106]

Several years after the court's ruling, the US government formally withdrew Thind's status.[107] Shockingly, it also embarked on a campaign to strip some sixty-five Indians of their previously conferred standing by utilizing a 1906 law ordering denaturalization in cases of fraud—a law only employed against six individuals since its enactment.[108] Indian citizens were deemed fraudulent whites. The congressional log documenting this rollback is a tragic account of people's loss of faith, property, and, sometimes, lives.[109] A debarred and despairing Vaisho Das Bagai wrote, "But now they come to me and say, I am no longer an American citizen. . . . What have I made of myself and my children? We cannot exercise our rights, we cannot leave this country. Humility and insults, who are responsible for all of this?"[110] Wives of Indo-American citizens, legally bound to their husbands' status, lost their own citizenship irrespective of their country of birth.[111]

These civic annulments were heartless and unprecedented, even for US history. Japanese citizenship had not been similarly rescinded after *Ozawa*, demonstrating again the seminal influence of nation-states and geopolitical power on domestic politics and personal fortunes.[112] As

Ngai writes, "A small minority group with no national government to speak on their behalf, Indians became targets of legal vengeance."[113]

British authorities did not aid Indians, but they were far from inactive. Since at least 1907, and in concert with US and Canadian settler colonial officials, they had attempted to manage the political repercussions of a global labor system grounded in white supremacy. Each side of this equation had differing and at times competing necessities. For the British, India's need for out-migration unleashed white anxieties and violence in the United States and Canada—witness Bellingham and St. Johns—that in turn increased unrest in India. In an effort to control Indians, both physically and aspirationally, the British pursued multiple strategies: the Continuous Journey Provision, immigration controls, the British Honduras scheme, the San Francisco German-Hindu Conspiracy trial, and outright murder and violence in India. They attempted to conceal or rebrand these maneuverings for fear of their impact on the nationalist struggle.[114] Ghadar's emergence was an object lesson in the limits and stakes of British control and fed US fears of a radical immigrant threat.

Thind reinforced and reinvigorated white domination in the United States. It formally enshrined and broadcast Indians' colonized citizenship status across the globe providing, however intentionally, a significant gift to British colonial rule. *Thind*'s practical implications were real and reinforcing. By labelling Indians as unassimilable, the high court decision effectively denied them key means for thriving in the United States.[115] Should they stay and attempt to navigate US vilification and foreclosed opportunities? Or return to the Raj's deprivations and draconian clampdown, where they were considered political threats simply for having lived in the United States? Finally, while *Thind* was a bald assertion of white power, it also carried significant political risks. Indians now witnessed the highest levels of US government, not just white laborers, brazenly assault them. And any hint of British assent to, or role in, *Thind* carried dire repercussions for British rule of India.

Bhagat Singh Thind and Taraknath Das both publicly denounced the verdict as the result of overt British pressure. Tabindranath Tagore, the first Indian and non-European to become a Nobel Prize laureate, denounced *Thind* and the "utter lack of freedom with which the [US] atmosphere is charged," and vowed never to return to the country again, even to see family and friends.[116] The Indian National Congress passed a resolution condemning the decision and the imperial government's failure to protect its overseas residents. In a thinly veiled nod to the United States, the Madras Legislative Council denied membership in port trusts to nationals from countries that discriminated against Indians. Similarly, some Indian princely states attempted to limit the entry of nationals from countries discriminating against Indians. US missionaries feared reprisals in India and in at least one instance were blocked from purchasing property in the wake of *Thind*. In 1926, New Delhi's central legislature proscribed Indian citizenship to people from countries—read the United States—who did not permit Indian naturalization.[117] One hundred years later, the verdict was remembered by the Lahore *Tribune*.[118]

In its moment, *Thind* forged a potent two-fer: a verdict on whiteness and on Indian citizenship. As the stand-in for both, Bhagat Singh Thind brought the added value of being one of the few remaining Indians connected to Oregon, the birthplace of a global insurgent movement. Ghadar and Bhagat Singh Thind had grown up together in the barracks of the Pacific Northwest. By the 1920s, their paths converged in the crosshairs of the world's most powerful empires. From the prisons of Punjab to the cantonments of Singapore and the highest reaches of US law, empire punished Indians and enshrined whiteness as power. Their combined message was clear: India would not be an independent country and Indo-Americans were not citizens. In the decades that followed, it was a verdict Indians refused to abide.

Epilogue

> We are never as steeped in history as when we pretend not to be, but if we stop pretending we may gain in understanding what we lose in false innocence. Naiveté is often an excuse for those who exercise power. For those upon whom that power is exercised, naiveté is always a mistake.
>
> —Michel-Rolph Trouillot, *Silencing the Past*

In 1947, confronted with a determined movement of millions for self-rule, the British oversaw the transition to independence. In British hands, the price of nationhood became the partition of Punjab, the creation of the ethnically defined countries of India and Pakistan, and the unleashing of historic dislocations and gestational, generational violence. With the same callous indifference and hubris with which they had dominated the region for centuries, the British drew a line on a map, in secret, that affected the fate of millions.

Far from a bloodless administrative decision, Sir Cyril Radcliffe's fiat unleashed an horrific cascade of state and communal violence—one to two million dead, some fifteen million displaced as Muslims fled to Pakistan and Hindus and Sikhs to India, and the wounds of each etched into the landscape, consciousness, and culture of the two newly born nations.[1] Partition was not merely the establishment of national borders, but the erection of a political and cultural minefield fueled by beliefs of ossified divisions and differences between historically intertwined and largely cooperative peoples.[2]

Har Dayal, once Ghadar's most prominent name, did not live to see Indian independence or Indo-American citizenship. In 1919, he recanted his Ghadar politics, alliance with Germany and the Berlin India Committee, and became a home-rule proponent. As biographer

Emily Brown writes, he "was almost Gandhian in assuming that Britain would live up to her moral responsibility, especially in her treatment of the non-white races."[3] Politically defanged, Dayal was granted legal reentry into both England and India, but before he could return to his natal land, he died of heart failure in 1939 while on a visit to the United States.[4] Sohan Singh Bhakna, by contrast, remained a revered revolutionary activist, in and out of Indian jail cells for the duration of his nearly century-long life.

In the United States, Bhagat Singh Thind, denied status by the highest legal authority of the land, made himself into what the court said he was incapable of. Just as the state constructed civic status, so too did Thind, his chosen avenues being marriage, a professional career, and the attainment of a middle-class lifestyle. As a New Thought minister, he traversed the country preaching spiritualism by day, while by night advocating for Indian independence under the close surveilling eye of British police agents.[5]

Ever attuned to changes in US law, Thind achieved formal citizenship in 1936 by ducking through a small legal opening enabled by his World War I military service.[6] A decade later, the civic bars formally fell. With India's independence in the wake of World War II, Indo-Americans were no longer feared as a source of radical nationalism and secured the right to naturalize. Indo-American's formal civic inclusion also contributed to the US postwar democratic facelift paraded before the world's people in furtherance of its colonial ambitions.[7]

These are the outcomes—in the broadest of strokes—of Ghadar and Thind. But beyond compelling stories, what are we to make of their legacy, import, and meaning today?

I came to this project as both an activist and a historian, and with a lifelong prejudice toward the politics of Ghadar.[8] While my beliefs have not fundamentally changed, this research—and the world we live in—complicates any easy conclusions about what change strategies might be judged successful, and what might be gleaned from these pasts for our difficult present.

The story of Ghadar is often told as a tale of futility and failure, if impossibly noble and heroic. Conversely, and especially in the United States, legal petitions and courtrooms like those inhabited by Bhagat Singh Thind are lionized as sites of "real" change, if requiring patience and the long view. After much consideration of these entwined stories, the reality feels considerably more complex. Ghadar did in the immediate sense "fail" at revolution, India gained sovereignty in 1947, and, ultimately, Thind and Indo-Americans generally "won" citizenship. And yet . . .

Yet it is also the case that British fears of Ghadar, broadly defined, fueled their post–World War I clampdown and helped convert political moderates into post–World War I opponents and noncompliance agitators. For British authorities, Ghadar exposed a terrifying possibility that they moved to viciously suppress, sending Ghadris to the gallows, massacring peaceful Punjabis in parks, and unleashing a broad, draconian clampdown on political rights and activists. What they wrought was not a pacified populace but the transformation of many formerly loyal nationalists into a stalwart opposition, with Ghadris and those they inspired actively and independently among them.[9] Mohandas Gandhi, the movement's most famous face, moved from advocating change within British law to launching and leading the noncooperation movement.[10] In the United States, Thind lost his citizenship case in 1923 in part because of Ghadar and the larger fears of radical Indian nationalism. But did Indo-Americans perhaps win status in 1947 in part because of Ghadar's complex impact on the Indian independence struggle?

This is all by way of saying that how we parse who and what is successful is no easy bit. And, for any thinking person, the meanings of "success" and "failure," judged by present-day United States or India, should also give one serious pause. Where does either country stand in the lived reality of a promised multiethnic and just democracy? Are murderous Indian Hindu nationalist mobs and prime ministers or murderous US authorities' and vigilantes' war on immigrants, Black people, and Black enfranchisement signifiers of democratic health?[11] Or are they, as it seems to me, indicators of the pervasiveness of racial and ethnic supremacy that continue to stamp the democracy cradled in our collective colonial legacy? Even if seemingly dormant in one moment, they spring back to life in the briefest of political turns. If we are to ever break free of white supremacy's deadening, murderous grip, we must be clear-eyed in our assessments of its long colonial history. If nothing else, the origin stories of Thind and Ghadar folded into present-day

India and the United States form cautionary tales on how seriously these issues must be taken.

For me, these stories also confirm that complex, multifaceted, and messy resistance is part of our social DNA. That resistance often arises among people who are underestimated if not unseen. That "times" can change in a heartbeat, whether after a riot in 1910 St. Johns or after the merciless Minneapolis police murder of George Floyd in 2020. That to grasp the immediate and the local, we must also look to the horizons of our globe, times, and social making—aka history. And that to understand our collective selves we must grasp the underlying roots of both political-social causes and political-social reactions, and embrace them as our collective history.

Researching Thind's and Ghadar's entwined biographies has taught me how much I have not understood about the formative and foundational history of this country and region, despite believing I'd been paying attention these many years. I suspect I'm not alone in these deficits. Diving into Indians' Oregon legacy has been, for the most part, a welcome gift, a guide to deeper self- and social understanding. We cannot, however, embark on historical excavation and understanding cheaply if we want to honor these lives and if we seek genuine change. It is not enough to simply know the stories; we must struggle to grasp their whys. To accept the challenges of Ghadar and Thind means interrogating the connections and implications of empire from the seemingly most isolated Columbia River towns to the seats of power in Delhi, London, and Washington, DC, connections that remain often painfully salient today.

Our world expands with such attention. It allows us to understand that the unexpected and unlikely are infinitely possible. That Oregon's diverse, global peoples, working and living side by side, produced ugly racial crimes but also wildly unexpected alliances and achievements. That people are stunningly creative in devising the means to thrive and resist, from wrestling to politics, from Oregon to Punjab. All this from considering the experience of perhaps five hundred Indians laboring for at most ten years in dirty, dangerous Oregon lumber mills, seemingly without power, but who birthed a global movement, a legacy, and rattled the bars of the most powerful empires on earth.

Silencing such histories robs our imaginary, diming notions of change agents, alliances, and possibilities. It also disarms us as to the long tendrils of racial supremacy and colonized citizenship poisoning our present. Witness just the past twenty years: the aftermath of September 11, 2001, brought widespread government surveillance, legal assaults, and vigilante attacks on Muslims, Sikhs, and others.[12] In 2020 America, the COVID-19 pandemic was exacerbated by an epidemic of anti-Asian rhetoric and violence.[13] In other words, while we may have overlooked Indians' earthshaking Oregon legacy for decades, the complexly sedimented conditions from which it grew endure. Who and what else is hiding in plain sight, histories that we fail to appreciate or understand at our own peril?

The towering intellect, editor, and Nobel Prize–winning novelist Toni Morrison spoke, in *Beloved*, of "rememory," referring to character Sethe's forgetting of "something she had forgotten she knew."[14] Rememory invokes the presence of that which has seemingly disappeared or has been forgotten—in Sethe's case, her enslavement. Morrison's is a call for truth-telling and reckoning about that which collectively haunts us. History is with us, and within us, whether we choose to reckon with it or not.

"Suchness—Memorial to an Unknown Immigrant"

[In my talk I will project a blank slide for the Ghadar memorial
that I believe should be in Astoria, Oregon. —Johanna Ogden
(email, November 2022)]

The white patch framed by dark
  Is the memorial that exists only in the mindscape.
It is the surface too delicate to bear the weight of any colour.
It has no horizon—here the earth and the sky never meet.
It is the still that always moves.
It is the passport to the unknown with the true likeness of the
    alien

                                              Attested in fate's hand
    With the stamp of no return.

It is the timepiece whose hands move backward striking the
    past
  The moment he left home with moist eyes on the future.
It is the prisoners' dream.
It is the mirror spread out, burnt with the light of hope.
In the daylight sky the moon hangs over the shadowless tree.
It is the crescendo of vowels
  The text with no consonants.
It is the last page of the book of life that caused his end.
The void after the film reel snapped.
The peace frozen.
Suchness.

                                              —Amarjit Chandan

Note: *Tathatd*—suchness—is Sanskrit and Paoli; *shunya*—absolute
emptiness—is a key concept in Buddhist philosophy.[15]

October 2013. Dedication of the Ghadar Party Plaque on Astoria's Riverwalk: moving left from plaque: Pashaura Singh Dhillon, Johanna Ogden, Astoria mayor Will Van Dusen and Astoria city councilperson Karen Mellin. In October 2013, more than three hundred people from across California to British Columbia, with an intrepid few from the East Coast, traveled to Astoria to celebrate and commemorate the founding of Ghadar one hundred years earlier. The event was sponsored by the City of Astoria, notably city councilperson Karen Mellin and Mayor Willis Van Dusen, and enabled and enriched by historians, filmmakers, activists, regional gurdwaras, Ghadri descendants, friends, family, and curious individuals. Over two and a half days, receptions, dances, religious services, communal meals, films, museum displays, historical presentations, and walking tours took place in venues across the town. The event's highlight was the dedication by Mayor Van Dusen and the many children present of the now permanently installed plaque dedicated to Ghadar on Astoria's Riverwalk. Astoria was the first city in North America to officially recognize and celebrate Ghadar and its momentous contributions to Indian and US history. The plaque was stolen in October 2017, but reinstalled and then rededicated in April 2018. A second celebration of Ghadar's founding people was attended by some thousand people in July 2018.

CITY OF ASTORIA
Founded 1811 • Incorporated 1856

PROCLAMATION

WHEREAS: Astoria, Oregon is the oldest settlement in America west of the Rocky Mountains, founded in 1811; and

WHEREAS: By 1911 Astoria had a working waterfront that included fishing, canneries, and lumber mills that contributed to the economic vibrancy of the city; and

WHEREAS: Workers in these industries included in large part immigrant laborers from China, India, and Finland; and.

WHEREAS: The Hammond lumber mill in Alderbrook listed about 100 Indians working alongside Finnish immigrants from 1910-1922; and

WHEREAS: The Indians were inspired by the success of the American Revolution against Great Britain, and by Finland's struggle for independence from Russian occupation; and

WHEREAS: The Indians met at the Finnish Socialist Hall in 1913 and formed the Ghadar (mutiny) Party; and

WHEREAS: Supporters of Ghadar, thousands of whom living in the United States and Canada, returned to India, and inspired their countrymen to fight for their independence from Great Britain, which was achieved in 1947; and

WHEREAS: The Ghadarites fought and died not only for the freedom of their home country, but also for the innate rights of the immigrant worker to lead a dignified and discrimination-free life; and

WHEREAS: 2013 is the 100-year anniversary of this historic meeting that recognizes the universal right of sovereign nations to independence and self-rule.

NOW, THEREFORE, I, Willis L. Van Dusen, Mayor of Astoria, do hereby proclaim 2013 as a celebration of the

CENTENARY OF THE FOUNDING OF THE GHADAR PARTY IN ASTORIA, OREGON

IN WITNESS WHEREOF, I have herewith set my hand and caused the Seal of the City of Astoria to be affixed this 18th day of March, 2013.

Mayor

CITY HALL • 1095 DUANE STREET • ASTORIA, OREGON 97103 • WWW.ASTORIA.OR.US

2013 Astoria Proclamation issued by the City of Astoria in honor of Ghadar. A signed copy hangs in the Desh Bhagat Ghadar Memorial Library of Jalandhar, India, and inspired other such declarations from mayors in the central valley of California.

PROCLAMATION

ਘੋਸ਼ਨਾ

ਜਦੋਂ ਕਿ ਉਰੇਗਨ ਸੂਬੇ ਦਾ ਔਸਟੋਰੀਆ ਸ਼ਹਿਰ ਅਮਰੀਕਾ ਦੇ ਪੱਛਮ ਵਿੱਚ ਪਥਰੀਲੇ ਚਟਾਨੀ ਪਹਾੜਾਂ ਦੇ ਨਾਲ 1811 ਵਿੱਚ ਵਸਾਇਆ ਗਿਆ ਸੀ; ਅਤੇ

ਜਦੋਂ ਕਿ 1911 ਤੱਕ ਔਸਟੋਰੀਆ ਸ਼ਹਿਰ ਨਾਲ ਲਗਦੇ ਪਾਣੀ ਕੰਢੇ ਮੱਛੀਆਂ ਫੜਨੀਆਂ, ਮੱਛੀਆਂ ਨੂੰ ਡੱਬੀਆਂ ਵਿੱਚ ਸੰਭਾਲਣਾ, ਅਤੇ ਲੱਕੜ ਦੀਆਂ ਮਿੱਲਾਂ ਵਿੱਚ ਕੰਮ, ਸ਼ਹਿਰ ਲਈ ਆਰਥਿਕਤਾ ਦੇ ਉਭਾਰ ਦਾ ਕਾਰਨ ਸਨ; ਅਤੇ

ਜਦੋਂ ਕਿ ਇਥੇ ਕੰਮ ਕਰਨ ਵਾਲਿਆਂ ਵਿੱਚ ਵੱਡਾ ਹਿੱਸਾ ਚੀਨ, ਇੰਡੀਆ ਅਤੇ ਫਿਨਲੈਂਡ ਤੋਂ ਪਰਵਾਸ ਲੈ ਕੇ ਆਏ ਮਜ਼ਦੂਰ ਸਨ; ਅਤੇ

ਜਦੋਂ ਕਿ ਹੈਮੰਡ ਲੱਕੜ ਮਿੱਲ ਵਿੱਚ ਫਿਨਲੈਂਡ ਦੇ ਕਾਮਿਆਂ ਨਾਲ ਇੱਕ ਸੌ (100) ਪੰਜਾਬੀ ਸਿੱਖ 1910 ਤੋਂ 1922 ਤੱਕ ਕੰਮ ਕਰਦੇ ਹੁੰਦੇ ਸਨ; ਅਤੇ

ਜਦੋਂ ਕਿ ਬ੍ਰਿਟਨ ਵਿਰੁੱਧ ਅਮਰੀਕਾ ਦੇ ਗਦਰ ਦੀ ਸਫਲਤਾ ਅਤੇ ਫਿਨਲੈਂਡ ਦੇ ਲੋਕਾਂ ਦੀ ਰੂਸ ਦੇ ਕਬਜ਼ੇ ਵਿਰੁੱਧ ਆਜ਼ਾਦੀ ਲਈ ਜਦੋ-ਜਹਿਦ ਨੇ ਪੰਜਾਬੀ ਸਿੱਖਾਂ ਨੂੰ ਆਜ਼ਾਦੀ ਲਈ ਉਤਸ਼ਾਹਤ ਕੀਤਾ; ਅਤੇ

ਜਦੋਂ ਕਿ ਪੰਜਾਬੀ ਸਿੱਖਾਂ ਨੇ 1913 ਵਿੱਚ ਫਿਨਲੈਂਡ ਦੇ ਸਮਾਜਵਾਦੀ ਹਾਲ ਵਿੱਚ ਇਕੱਠ ਕਰਕੇ ਗਦਰ ਪਾਰਟੀ ਦੀ ਨੀਂਹ ਰੱਖੀ; ਅਤੇ

ਜਦੋਂ ਕਿ ਅਮਰੀਕਾ ਅਤੇ ਕੈਨੇਡਾ ਵਿੱਚ ਵਸਦੇ ਗਦਰ ਪਾਰਟੀ ਦੇ ਹਜ਼ਾਰਾਂ ਹੀ ਹਮਾਇਤੀ ਇੰਡੀਆ ਪਰਤੇ ਅਤੇ ਆਪਣੇ ਦੇਸ ਵਾਸੀਆਂ ਨੂੰ ਬ੍ਰਿਟਨ ਤੋਂ ਆਜ਼ਾਦੀ ਲੈਣ ਲਈ ਉਤਸ਼ਾਹਤ ਕੀਤਾ ਜੋ ਕਿ 1947 ਵਿੱਚ ਮਿਲੀ; ਅਤੇ

ਜਦੋਂ ਕਿ ਗਦਰੀ ਨਾ ਕੇਵਲ ਆਪਣੇ ਦੇਸ ਦੀ ਆਜ਼ਾਦੀ, ਸਮਾਨਤਾ ਭਰਪੂਰ ਸਨਮਾਨਤ ਜੀਵਨ ਜਿਊਣ ਲਈ ਲੜੇ ਅਤੇ ਮਰੇ, ਸਗੋਂ ਹਰ ਪਰਵਾਸੀ ਵਾਸੀਆਂ ਦੀ ਸਮਾਨਤਾ ਅਤੇ ਨਸਲੀ ਵਿਤਕਰੇ ਤੋਂ ਆਜ਼ਾਦ, ਸਨਮਾਨਤ ਜੀਵਨ ਜਿਊਣ ਦੇ ਹੱਕ ਲਈ ਵੀ ਲੜੇ ਸਨ; ਅਤੇ

ਜਦੋਂ ਕਿ 2013 ਦਾ ਸਾਲ ਉਸ ਗਦਰ ਲਹਿਰ ਦੇ ਸੌ ਸਾਲਾ ਦਿਵਸ ਉੱਤੇ ਇਸ ਇਤਿਹਾਸਿਕ ਇਕੱਤਰਤਾ ਵਿੱਚ ਸਾਰੀਆਂ ਕੌਮਾਂ ਦੀ ਆਜ਼ਾਦੀ ਅਤੇ ਲੋਕ ਰਾਜ ਲਈ ਪ੍ਰੌੜਤਾ ਕਰਦਾ ਹੈ; ਅਤੇ

ਇਸ ਲਈ ਹੁਣ, ਮੈਂ, ਵਿਲਿੱਸ ਔਸ ਵੈਨ ਡੁਸੈੱਨ, ਔਸਟੋਰੀਆ ਦਾ ਮੇਅਰ, 2013 ਦੇ ਸਾਲ ਨੂੰ ਔਸਟੋਰੀਆ, ਉਰੇਗਨ ਸ਼ਹਿਰ ਵਿੱਚ, ਗਦਰ ਲਹਿਰ ਦੀ ਸਥਾਪਨਾ ਦੇ "ਸ਼ਤਾਬਦੀ ਸਾਲ" ਦਿਵਸ ਦੀ ਘੋਸ਼ਨਾ ਕਰਦਾ ਹਾਂ।

ਇਸ ਨਗਰ-ਨਿਗਮ ਪੱਤਰ ਦੀ ਘੋਸ਼ਨ ਕਰਨ ਦੀ **ਗਵਾਹੀ ਵਿੱਚ** ਮੈਂ ਆਪਣੇ ਹਸਤ ਕਮਲਾਂ ਨਾਲ ਔਸਟੋਰੀਆ ਸ਼ਹਿਰ ਦੀ ਮੋਹਰ 18 ਤਾਰੀਖ ਮਾਰਚ 2013 ਵਾਲੇ ਦਿਨ ਲਗਾਈ ਹੈ।

_____
ਮੇਅਰ

Acknowledgments

By all rights, this should be the longest section of this book. These pages are the product of an enormous circle of guidance, help, support, and inspiration including family, friends, close colleagues, community members, researchers, historians, archivists, librarians, and others.

My family—Leslie, Molly, John, and dear Viv—never (openly) questioned my sanity, but helped, read, cheered, and showed up at every conceivable opportunity. Bob was the best research assistant money did not buy. More, he listened, challenged, encouraged, suggested, sympathized, believed, and endured a decade of distraction.

I have the great fortune of being a part of a circle of women historians who inspire, collaborate, and model intellectual engagement, meaningful work, and fun. Katy Barber read, and reread, drafts and taught me how to write a book in her nonexistent free time. Eliza Canty-Jones provided smart editorial advice and access to Oregon Historical Society's speaking and publishing platforms. Jan Dilg provided expert public history aid and, along with Donna Sinclair, read and encouraged and suggested and encouraged and read.

Mark and Manya Wubbold gave me a warm home, companionship, and easy access to a fridge when mine was low. Deb Gasster was there—for events, for healthy distraction, and just for joy. Besides capable cheering, Aparna Rae organized a fundraiser, joined by many, making another few months without paid employment possible. That broader circle was invaluable for so many reasons—encouragement, confidence, laughter, asking/not asking, and just being funny, talented friends: Tamara King, Hossein Rojhantalab, Tami Dean, Carlton Olson, Jeanne Rogers, Kathy Ziegler, Kalka Thangkiew, Bindy Kang, Mary Wheeler, Liz Safran, Stephanie Brown, Dwight Morrill, Gerson Robboy, Randy Chambers, Bruce LaBrack, and Kathryn Stillings.

Marianne Kedding-Lang commented on a terrible (my accurate word choice) early draft. Tamara King, Lori Shinsato, and Helen Ryan got me over the final formatting finish line. Eve Ashkar, Melissa Lang, and Alecia Giombolini checked and tightened my census and site findings. Kambiz Ghanea Bassiri put me on this trail, and Ranjit Arab convinced me to write a book. The Oregon State University Press staff has been helpful, patient, and welcoming, and I am grateful this work has such a fitting home.

Harish Puri's work has been my touchstone. Further, his and Indu Banga's generous invitation to Chandigarh, India, enabled me to vet new research, meet others in the field, and visit relevant sites. I'm indebted to Darshan Tatla for his research, on-the-ground investigation, and translation help, and to Malwinder Waraich for sharing materials and for his helpful translations.

One of the joys of this project has been the many new people I have met. I am indebted to the community, particularly in Oregon and Washington, who advised me and made this history come alive in ways few historians are privileged to experience. Friends Navneet Kaur, Bahadur Singh, Gurpreet Singh, Sameer Sharma, and Jasmit Singh are at the top of that list, as is Pashaura Singh from California, Sohan Pooni of BC, and Amarjit Chandan of London. Astoria City commissioner Karen Mellin was instrumental to the City of Astoria staging the 2013 centennial celebration of Ghadar's founding, as was Willis van Dusen. Anjali Hursh encouraged and promoted this history and related events throughout her extensive network. I am grateful for translation assistance by Navneet Kaur, Roomina Ahmed, and Pashaura Singh, and for Surinder P. Singh's sharing of one of Bhagwan Singh Gayanee's letters. Thanks go to Sarika Mehta, Linda Olson-Osterlund, and Sankar Raman for radio and documentary coverage.

Many historians cited in this book were also generous enough to chat, correspond, and/or share records with me, including Doug Coulson, David C. Atkinson, Sema Sohi, Arijit Sen, Sohan Pooni, Carl Abbott, Aaron Goings, and Nirvikar Singh. Historians and friends Paul Englesberg and Paul Krause provided expertise and invaluable feedback on drafts and sources. David Thind graciously allowed me an interview. Research librarians and archivists guided me, found things, bailed me out, and were otherwise invaluable: Liisa Penner of Clatsop

Co. Historical Society; Scott Daniels and Renato Rodriguez of Oregon Historical Society; Balwinder Bansal of Desh Bhagat; and Samip Mallick of SAADA. Members of the St. Johns Heritage Association, staff in small-town Oregon libraries and city halls, newspaper editors, and community leaders in The Dalles, Linnton, Scappoose, Rainier, Clatskanie, and Astoria helped locate important local evidence of this story.

I look forward to continued collaborations.

Notes

INTRODUCTION

1 "Punjab Rebellion Utterly Crushed," *Morning Oregonian*, November 27, 1916, p. 1.

2 "Punjab Rebellion."

3 Sohi, *Echoes of Mutiny*, 154, 164, 173. See chapter 6 for more details on Lieutenant Governor O'Dwyer.

4 "Punjab Rebellion," 2.

5 "Punjab Rebellion," 2.

6 Sohi, *Echoes of Mutiny*, 184–197.

7 Hochschild, *American Midnight*, 124, 162; Sohi, *Echoes of Mutiny*, 192; Chang, *Pacific Connections*, 173–175.

8 Ogden, "The Telling Case of Dr. Bhagat Singh Thind," 6–19.

9 Harish Puri, Maia Ramnath, Seema Sohi, Ian Haney Lopez, and Doug Coulson are authors I draw on and cite throughout this book.

10 "Hindu Will Make Citizenship Fight," *Morning Oregonian*, February 24, 1923, p. 10.

11 "21 Arrests Made; Hindu Accusers," *Morning Oregonian*, March 23, 1910, p. 5. See also "Big Doings in St. Johns," *St. Johns (OR) Review*, March 25, 1910, p. 1.

12 "O'Connell to Meet Singh," *Morning Oregonian*, September 20, 1910, p. 10; Advertisement, *Oregonian*, June 20, 1910, p. 3; "Hindu Turban Latest Idea in Fashionable Feminine Headgear," *Sunday Oregonian*, May 29, 1910, sec. 5, p. 6.

13 See chapters 2–4 for examples.

14 Heatherton, "University of Radicalism," 559, https://www.jstor.org/stable/43823419.

15 Ramnath, *Decolonizing Anarchism*, 91–92, https://files.libcom.org/files/Maia%20Ramnath%20-%20Decolonizing%20Anarchism.pdf; Ramnath, *Haj to Utopia*, 46, 95–96; Hummasti, *Finnish Radicals in Astoria*, 70–74.

16 Chief among them is Dr. Harish K. Puri, especially *Ghadar Movement: Ideology, Organisation & Strategy*.

17 See, for example, Sohi, *Echoes of Mutiny*; Ramnath, *Haj to Utopia*; and the many public talks and articles by Bellingham, Washington, historian Paul Englesberg; Vancouver, British Columbia, historians Sohan Pooni and Gurpreet Singh; and, regarding Astoria, Kartar Dhillon, "The Parrot's Beak," South Asian American Digital Archive, October 4, 2012, https://www.saada.org/tides/article/the-parrots-beak, and https://www.sikhpioneers.org/the-parrots-beak/.

18 Pashaura Singh Dhillon, Malwinder Singh Waraich, Darshan Tatla, Navneet Kaur, and Roomina Ahmed all generously assisted me with translations; all errors, however, are my own.

19 Ramnath, *Haj to Utopia*, 1–2.
20 Singh, "India and the Great War," 343.
21 Singh, "India and the Great War," 343.
22 Ramnath, *Haj to Utopia*, 35, 45–46, 72–73.
23 In 1946, the Luce-Celler Act deemed Indians racially eligible for naturalization, while also restricting immigrants to a mere one hundred per year.
24 I know of one descendant from that earlier community residing in Oregon.

CHAPTER 1

1   Historians' estimates range from a "few thousand" (Joan Jensen) to ten thousand (Maia Ramnath) in North America, with 6,656 to 6,800 in the United States (Maia Ramnath and Karen Leonard, respectively), and 9,000 in British Columbia (Nayan Shah). Jensen, *Passage from India*, 1; Leonard, *Making Ethnic Choices*, 24; Shah, *Stranger Intimacy*, 20; Ramnath, *Haj to Utopia*, 17.

2   Ogden, "Ghadar, Historical Silences, and Notions of Belonging," 174–175. There are many reasons why they were predominantly men: global labor opportunities favored men, the cost of travel was enormous, and women maintained the farms. Jensen, *Passage from India*, 25. The Canadian government also barred wives from entering the country. Puri, *Ghadar Movement*, 46.

3   Barber, "'We Were at Our Journey's End,'" 382–411; Wilm, "Old Myths, Turned on Their Heads," 326–351.

4   Wilm, "Old Myths, Turned on Their Heads"; Coleman, "'We'll All Start Even,'" 414–437.

5   Greg Nokes, "Black Exclusion Laws in Oregon," Oregon Encyclopedia, accessed April 13, 2023, https://www.oregonencyclopedia.org/articles/exclusion_laws/#. ZDhLTn2JJPY; Smith, "Oregon's Civil War," 167.

6   "Negroes" and "Mulattoes" were the terms used in the Oregon Constitution. Wong, *Sweet Cakes, Long Journey*, 30–33. The constitution was put to a popular vote, and 89 percent of voters—that is, white men—approved the exclusionary document.

7   Wong, *Sweet Cakes, Long Journey*, 35; Smith, "Oregon's Civil War," 172.

8   Smith, "Oregon's Civil War," 167.

9   Edward E. Baptist, *The Half Has Never Been Told* is one of many excellent books.

10 Chinese migrants arrived in California in the late 1840s, and the state became the center of anti-Chinese legislation and violence. See Pfaelzer, *Driven Out* (ix, 29–38). I'm indebted to Dr. Wong for this racial policy argument, particularly pages 47–60. This is not to say Oregon was without racial violence. See, for example, Greg Nokes, "Chinese Massacre at Deep Creek," Oregon Encyclopedia, accessed April 15, 2023, https://oregonencyclopedia.org/articles/chinese_massacre_at_deep_creek/#.WS3OUGjys2w; Ted W. Cox, "The Toledo Incident of 1925," Oregon Encyclopedia, accessed April 15, 2023, https://oregonencyclopedia.org/articles/toledo_incident_of_1925/#.WS3MZWjys2w.

11 Wong, *Sweet Cakes, Long Journey*, 30, 50.

12 Kolko, *The Triumph of Conservatism*, 280.

13 Wong, *Sweet Cakes, Long Journey*, 45, 176–178.

14 Wong, *Sweet Cakes, Long Journey*, 44–45.

15 Wong, *Sweet Cakes, Long Journey*, 45–47.

16 Wong, *Sweet Cakes, Long Journey*, 45–47, 51, 283 n58.

17 Wong, *Sweet Cakes, Long Journey*, 51.

18 Scott, "Labor Is Wealth," as quoted in Wong, *Sweet Cakes, Long Journey*, 54;
    some railroad building companies argued similarly. See Roediger and Esch, *The
    Production of Difference*, 75.

19 Wong, *Sweet Cakes, Long Journey*, 54–57.

20 Scott's stance was predicated on and supported the gradual disappearance of
    Chinese from the region through the effects of exclusion, the dearth of Chinese
    women, prohibition of marriage with whites, and the lack of civic status for
    many ethnically mixed children. Wong, *Sweet Cakes, Long Journey*, 59–60.

21 Wong, *Sweet Cakes, Long Journey*, 162.

22 Wong, *Sweet Cakes, Long Journey*, 11, 149, 159.

23 The act banned the entry and naturalization of migrating Chinese laborers and
    limited the entrance of businessmen and students. In effect until 1943, it was
    America's first federal law to exclude immigrants by an explicit racial criterion.
    Wong, *Sweet Cakes, Long Journey*, 6; Smith, "Oregon's Civil War," 157.

24 Wong, *Sweet Cakes, Long Journey*, 39.

25 Wong, *Sweet Cakes, Long Journey*, 145.

26 Wong, *Sweet Cakes, Long Journey*, 145.

27 Roediger and Esch, *The Production of Difference*, 10.

28 See chapters 2, 3, 7.

29 Barber, "We Were at Our Journey's End," 385–386.

30 Jensen, *Passage from India*, 9–10; Kazimi, *Undesirables*, 17.

31 Jensen, *Passage from India*, 24; Puri, *Ghadar Movement*, 11, 13–15; Sohi, *Echoes
    of Mutiny*, 14–15.

32 Sohi, *Echoes of Mutiny*, 2–3. The US colonization of Cuba and the Philippines
    began with the war of 1898.

33 Lee, "Hemispheric Orientalism," 33.

34 Jensen, *Passage from India*, 15–16, 59–62, 79, 83; Puri, *Ghadar Movement*, 15–
    16, 22.

35 Barber, "We Were at Our Journey's End," 389.

36 Thompson, *Making of American Whiteness*, 39, 40.

37 Myers, "Beyond the Psychological Wage," 6, 9.

38 Lake and Reynolds, *Drawing the Global Colour Line*, 2.

39 Thompson, "Expectation and Exclusion," 361; Wilm, "Old Myths, Turned on
    Their Heads," 329, 331, 336, 343, 345.

40 Thompson, *Making of American Whiteness*, 39.

41 Historian David Roediger argues that, in America, domestic chattel slavery
    bound "white" and "free" in labor rhetoric. Roediger, *Wages of Whiteness*, 20–21,
    31–32.

42 Thompson, *Making of American Whiteness*, 37.

43 Thompson, *Making of American Whiteness*, 1, 5.

44 Jonathan Hyslop's work, as cited, argues "white labourism" pervaded British
    colonies. Further, the specific political impact of Indian migrants in BC,
    especially among white laborers, is well documented. While I am not versed in
    Canadian labor history, a cursory review reveals others who consider whiteness
    an inter- and intra-racial issue. Historian Ruth A. Frager argues, "Class, ethnic,
    and gender issues have entwined historically in complex ways. If we are to
    understand more fully the development of working-class resistance to
    exploitation—and the limitations of this resistance—intra-class conflict must be
    taken seriously." "Labour History and the Interlocking Hierarchies of Class,

Ethnicity, and Gender: A Canadian Perspective," *International Review of Social History* 44, no. 2 (August 1999): 220.

45 Lake and Reynolds, *Drawing the Global Colour Line*, 6, 23.

46 Roediger and Esch illuminate the broadly imagined managerial architecture of this process in *The Production of Difference*.

47 There was active communication and organization within and across the global white labor movement. Hyslop, "The Imperial Working Class," 398–421; Lake and Reynolds, *Drawing the Global Colour Line*, 30–35.

48 As historian Patricia Limerick writes, this unprecedented intermixing of the world's people in the mines, lumber mills, and ranches of the West made the ethnic passions and divisions of the eastern United States resemble a mere family reunion. Limerick, *The Legacy of Conquest*, 260. America's rhetorical conflation of "white" and "free" endured after slavery's formal abolition and enveloped other nonwhite peoples. These beliefs and their underlying economic realities constructed and maintained a two-tier labor force and civic polity largely and enduringly defined by race. Roediger, *The Wages of Whiteness*, particularly 20–21, 31–32.

49 Hyslop, "The Imperial Working Class," 398–421.

50 Chang, quoting Stuart Hall, *Pacific Connections*, 80.

51 While my specific examples are from the United States—the focus of this book—I believe the basic argument applies to western Canada as well. The IWW operated in BC; Chang, *Pacific Connections*, 174, 176–177. More generally, Ruth A. Frager outlines parallel stratified labor constellations in "Labour History and the Interlocking Hierarchies of Class."

52 Cole, Struthers, and Zimmer, "Introduction," in *Wobblies of the World*, 4; Chang, *Pacific Connections*, 115, 146.

53 Chang, *Pacific Connections*, 95, 137.

54 Kipnis, *The American Socialist Movement*, 277, citing "A Letter from Japanese Socialists to Their Comrades in the United States," *Socialist Party Weekly Bulletin*, January 19, 1907; "Minutes of the National Executive Committee," March 2, 1907, "SP Official Bulletin," March and April 1907, quoted in Kipnis, page 277.

55 Lee, "Hemispheric Orientalism," 30. See also chapter 3 of this book.

56 Thompson, "Expectation and Exclusion," 361–363.

57 Barber, "We Were at Our Journey's End," 385. Underscoring the interrelationships among gender, class, race, and nation, Indian women were allowed to indenture in British colonies, but disallowed entry into Canada. Kazimi, *Undesirables*, 18; see, for example, Limerick, *Legacy of Conquest*, 58, 94, 124–129, 260–262, 268–273; and Saxton, *Indispensable Enemy*, 12–14, 16–17, 21–28.

58 Mahmud, "Cheaper Than a Slave," 218. The etymology of "coolie" underscores the sense of debasement accompanying wage labor and its racialized, global colonial construction. As Gaiutra Bahdaur writes, "'Coolie' comes from the Tamil word *kuli*, meaning wags or hire. It was first used beginning in the late sixteenth century, by Portuguese captains and merchants along the Coromandel Coast in India, who passed it on to the other Europeans to describe the men carrying loads at the docks. Gradually, 'coolie' meant someone paid to do menial work." Bahadur, *Coolie Woman*, xx.

59 McKeown, "Global Migration, 1846–1970," 155–189. McKeown argues that, globally, less than 10 percent of Indian migrants were indentured, that two

million Indians migrated as merchants or other non-laborers, and that migration expanded with the restrictions on and abolishment of indenture.

60 Arundhati Roy, "It's Hard to Communicate the Scale and the Shape of This Shadow Taking India Over," *Democracy Now!*, November 28, 2019, https://www.democracynow.org/2019/11/28/arundhati_roy_it_s_hard_to. In my mind, considering organized labor apart from the racialized citizenship and/or exclusion of African Americans, Chinese, Indians, or others significantly compromises any conclusions from such studies.

61 Anthony Farrington, interview by The British Library, drawn from his "Trading Places: The East India Company and Asia 1600–1834," published by The British Library, 2002, Sessions 1–5, accessed April 15, 2023, http://www.eablanchette.com/_supportdocs/session1.html. Farrington argues that the EIC became a prototype: "The profound changes in the world order that resulted in the subjection of most of Asia to European colonial rule, economic domination and varying degrees of political interference began in India." http://www.eablanchette.com/supportdocs/session5.html; Amartya Sen, "Illusions of Empire," *Guardian*, June 29, 2021, https://www.theguardian.com/world/2021/jun/29/british-empire-india-amartya-sen.

62 Sen, "Illusions of Empire."

63 Vatuk, *Thieves in My House*, 4; British Prime Minister Winston Churchill began his political career in, as he put it, "a lot of jolly little wars against barbarous peoples" in India, Sudan, and South Africa.

64 The British skillfully exploited a warrior tradition dating back to the Sikhs' persecution in the late 1600s. From 1857 to World War I, Sikhs made up 16–25 percent of its military forces, but less than 2 percent of its population. Service provided needed revenue for Sikhs and fostered pride and fealty to the Crown. Jensen, *Passage from India*, 6, 8; Sohi, *Echoes of Mutiny*, 16–17.

65 Kazimi, *Undesirables*, 21–24.

66 Vatuk, *Thieves in My House*, 5.

67 Kazimi, *Undesirables*, 22, 83.

68 Ramnath, *Haj to Utopia*, 39, 193.

69 Sohi, *Echoes of Mutiny*, 1.

70 Kazimi, *Undesirables*, 21–24.

71 Puri, *Ghadar Movement*, 23.

72 Ward, *White Canada Forever*, xxviii.

73 Jensen, *Passage from India*, 65.

74 Josh, *Baba Sohan Singh Bhakna*, 15.

75 Sohi, *Echoes of Mutiny*, 28; Lee, "Hemispheric Orientalism," 24.

76 Lee, "Hemispheric Orientalism," 19.

77 Takaki, *Strangers from A Different Shore*, 301.

78 Puri, *Ghadar Movement*, 42–43.

79 Puri, *Ghadar Movement*, 29–30.

80 Puri, *Ghadar Movement*, 27–30; Jensen, *Passage from India*, 75–78; Lee, "Hemispheric Orientalism," 21. The Continuous Journey was used against African Americans; Steve Schwinghamer, "The Colour Bar at the Canadian Border: Black American Farmers," Canadian Museum of Immigration at Pier 21, updated July 20, 2021, https://www.pier21.ca/research/immigration-history/the-colour-bar-at-the-canadian-border-black-american-farmers.

81 Jensen, *Passage from India*, 75–77; Sohi, *Echoes of Mutiny*, 27, 42.

82 Kazimi, *Undesirables*, 69; Puri, *Ghadar Movement*, 29; Sohi, *Echoes of Mutiny*, 30–31.

83 Puri, *Ghadar Movement*, 27; Sohi, *Echoes of Mutiny*, 27–28.

84 Jensen, *Passage from India*, 57–58; Sohi, *Echoes of Mutiny*, 18–22, 27.

85 Sohi, *Echoes of Mutiny*, 28.

86 Lee and Yung, *Angel Island*, 6–8.

87 Lee and Yung, *Angel Island*, 149–163; Sohi, *Echoes of Mutiny*, 28–34.

88 Puri, *Ghadar Movement*, 32–33; Sohi, *Echoes of Mutiny*, 184–197. See also chapters 5 and 6.

89 Lee, "Hemispheric Orientalism," 38.

90 Sohi, *Echoes of Mutiny*, 28–34.

91 Puri, *Ghadar Movement*, 34–35; Sohi, *Echoes of Mutiny*, 38–40.

92 Puri, citing Das, *Ghadar Movement*, 33.

93 Josh, citing O'Dwyer, *Baba Sohan Singh Bhakna*, xxiii.

94 Puri, quoting Swayne, *Ghadar Movement*, 31–32.

95 Puri, *Ghadar Movement*, 42–45.

96 Puri, *Ghadar Movement*, 42–43; Sohi, *Echoes of Mutiny*, 40–41, 84–85, 89–91.

97 Kazimi, *Undesirables*, 82–83.

98 Puri, *Ghadar Movement*, 45–46.

99 Kazimi, *Undesirables*, 82–83.

100 "Looking Back: Everett Mob Terrorizes Immigrant Mill Workers," *HeraldNet*, November 30, 2019, https://www.heraldnet.com/news/looking-back-everett-mob-terrorizes-immigrant-mill-workers/; "Hindus Leaving Everett To-Day," *Daily Province*, November 5, 1907, p. 11; "Hindus Are Leaving City: Aliens, Alarmed by Saturday's Demonstration, Are Taking Departure. Many Going to Portland," *Everett (WA) Herald*, November 4, 1907, np.

101 Puri, *Ghadar Movement*, 41–42.

102 Singh, *Why Mewa Singh Killed William Hopkinson?*, 10–11, 27.

103 Jensen, *Passage from India*, 51, 61.

104 Abbott, *The Great Extravaganza*, 59.

105 Robbins, *Landscapes of Promise*, 102, 234–236.

106 The children attended the Alderbrook public school, where Kapur made the honor roll. Dhillon, "Astoria Revisited," 1, 5.

107 Sawhney, *I Shall Never Ask for Pardon*, 81.

108 In July 1907, Bishn Singh, of Marhana, India, traveled by rail from Vancouver, BC, and then up the Columbia River by ship with about a dozen other men. In 1908 he purchased property in The Dalles from Joseph Huskey. Court records reveal he was prosecuted for fraud in 1909 and sentenced to two years in the Oregon State Penitentiary, but provide no further details. Troublingly, his prison photo provides one of the few photos of Indians in Oregon from these times. "Declarations of Intention," Bishn, Uttam, Hookam, Vir, Visawa, Bhola, Eson, Son, Sham, Talok, Jay, Sunder and Tebe Singh, along with Shib Diyal, "Ker," and "Kehru," Wasco, OR County Circuit Court, 1908; Wasco County, OR, Land title records, record 48:87; Oregon State Archives, Inmate Case Files, Box 5930-6072, File no. 5965.

109 A crew of Indians laid rails in the Coast Range, I believe for Andrew Hammond's enterprises, with a photo held by the Southern Oregon Historical Society, photo no. 001603, https://research.sohs.org/node/4079. For more on Hammond, see chapter 4.

110 *Portland City Directory* (Portland: R.L. Polk & Co., 1910), 1025. In the late 1990s and early 2000s, the cordage factory was the site of northwest Portland's Bridgeport Brewing.

111 Multnomah County Return of Marriage Record 12642, Oregon State Archives, Vital Statistics. Kahn was legally "white."

112 Misrow, "East Indian Immigration," 48, 57–59.

113 See chapters 2–4.

114 Kazimi, *Undesirables*, 52.

115 See chapters 3, 4, and 5.

116 Ogden, "The Telling Case of Dr. Bhagat Singh Thind," 6, 10, 12–13; see also chapters 5 and 6; the phrase "local racism has global implications" is borrowed from Kazimi.

117 Hochschild, *American Midnight*, 1–12.

118 See chapter 6.

CHAPTER 2

1 "Hindu Fears Knife," *Sunday Oregonian*, November 3, 1907, p. 11; "Charge Is Murder," *Morning Oregonian*, November 6, 1907, p. 6. I am using the name Harnam Singh from the "Hindu Fears Knife" article, which was seemingly reported with the aid of translator M. Ram. In "Charge Is Murder," the victim was referred to as Bingwan or alternatively Bhingwan Singh, who may instead have been the "unnamed" third companion of brothers Sporan and Harnam Singh. Harnam Singh is also the name used in the trial. See, for example, "Jury in Murder Case Still Out," *Morning Oregonian*, April 25, 1908, p. 8.

2 "Hindu Shot by Fellow Workman," *Morning Oregonian*, November 2, 1907, p. 13.

3 "Charge Is Murder."

4 "Charge Is Murder."

5 "Hindu Shot by Fellow Workman."

6 "Assault on Hindus Thirty Shots Fired," *Anaconda (MT) Standard*, November 2, 1907, p. 1.

7 "Hindu Shot by Fellow Workman"; "Hindu Fears Knife."

8 "Hindu Shot by Fellow Workman."

9 "Hindu Fears Knife."

10 "Charge Is Murder."

11 "Hindu Fears Knife"; "Charge Is Murder." Harnam Singh died November 5, 1907.

12 "Hindu Fears Knife"; "Hindu Shot by Fellow Workman."

13 "Hindu Shot by Fellow Workman"; "Charge Is Murder." The Jonsruds' first names are not included in this article.

14 "Bound Over for Murder," *Morning Oregonian*, November 14, 1907, p. 5. Vernon Hawes later returned to town from McMinnville and was charged. "Returns to the Sheriff," *Morning Oregonian*, November 9, 1907, p. 4.

15 "State's Homicide Record for 1907," *Morning Oregonian*, January 6, 1908, p. 4.

16 "Guilty of Murder Charge," *Morning Oregonian*, January 23, 1908, p. 12; "Begin Hindu Murder Trial," *Morning Oregonian*, April 23, 1908, p. 6.

17 "Guilty in Second Degree," *Sunday Oregonian*, April 26, 1907, 4. Harnam Singh's murder was also noted in the annual state records of homicides in Oregon in 1907: "State's Homicide Record for 1907."

18 Untitled, *Morning Oregonian*, April 27, 1908, p. 6.

19 Chalana, "Whither the 'Hindoo Invasion?'" 14–38.

20 Lake and Reynolds, *Drawing the Global Colour Line*, 181–182; Lee, "Hemispheric Orientalism,'" 19, 24, 26–27, 29–31; Jensen, *Passage from India*, 42.

21 Lake and Reynolds, *Drawing the Global Colour Line*, 2, 93, 180–181.

22 "Riot Cases Are Dismissed," *American Reveille*, September 21, 1907, p. 1; Paul Englesberg, "The Bellingham Anti-Hindu Riot," in *Our Stories: An Introduction to South Asian America*, ed. South Asian American Digital Archive (Philadelphia: SAADA, 2021), 31.

23 James Laidlaw, report, November 8, 1907, National Archives of the UK (NA): FO 371/360, General Correspondence from 1906–1966, United States, 1907, no. DSC0 2218.

24 Jensen, *Passage from India*, 51. Historian Paul Englesberg reports pockets of Indian Muslims persisted in Washington after 1907, a topic needing more research and analysis.

25 Jensen, *Passage from India*, 61.

26 This has an interesting parallel in the Chinese community, which, when faced with extensive violence in Tacoma in 1885, relocated in large numbers to Portland with the assistance of a wealthy Portland Chinese businessman. Wong, *Sweet Cakes, Long Journey*, 176, 178.

27 James Laidlaw, James Bryce, and Bernard Pelly, reports, September 1907, NA: FO 371/360, General Correspondence from 1906–1966, United States, 1907, no. DSC0 2161-2172.

28 Edward Grey, report, November 5, 1907, NA: FO 371/360, General Correspondence from 1906–1966, United States, 1907, no. DSC0 2199; Under Secy of State [illegible author], letter, December 10, 1907, NA: FO 371/360, General Correspondence from 1906–1966, United States, 1907, no. DSC0 2238."

29 James Laidlaw, report, November 8, 1907, NA: FO 371/360, General Correspondence from 1906–1966, United States, 1907, no. DSC0 2219.

30 Under Secy of State [illegible author], letter, December 10, 1907, NA: FO 371/360, General Correspondence from 1906–1966, United States, 1907, no. DSC0 2239.

31 Laidlaw, report, November 8, 1907, no. DSC0 2219.

32 "Looking Back: Everett Mob Terrorizes Immigrant Mill Workers," *HeraldNet*, November 30, 2019, https://www.heraldnet.com/news/looking-back-everett-mob-terrorizes-immigrant-mill-workers/; "Hindus Leaving Everett To-Day," *Daily Province*, November 5, 1907, p. 11; "Hindus Are Leaving City: Aliens, Alarmed by Saturday's Demonstration, Are Taking Departure. Many Going to Portland," *Everett (WA) Herald*, November 4, 1907, np. Citizenship application records document a small group of Sikh men who left Vancouver, BC, after its 1907 riots and, seemingly as a group, relocated to The Dalles, Oregon.

33 Bernard Pelly to James Laidlaw, November 3, 1907, NA: FO 371/360, General Correspondence from 1906–1966, United States, 1907, no. DSC0 2221.

34 James Laidlaw to Bernard Pelly, November 6, 1907, NA: FO 371/360, General Correspondence from 1906–1966, United States, 1907, no. DSC0 2223.

35 Marshfield is now known as Coos Bay, Oregon. James Laidlaw to James Bryce, November 19, 1907, NA: FO 371/360, General Correspondence from 1906–1966, United States, 1907, no. DSC0 2227.

36 In informal communications, historian Paul Englesberg notes that, after
    September 1907, US-Canada border crossing records show that Bellingham was
    no longer a destination, but Seattle, Tacoma, Portland, and especially San
    Francisco were. Manish Chalana writes, "The 1907 immigration
    report . . . showed that in that year, of the men heading for the Pacific Northwest,
    93% were planning to settle in Washington and only 7% in Oregon. Now, a mere
    three years later, most Indians in the area were in Oregon. The riots had
    ultimately hit both states, but their magnitude was greater in Washington, and
    clearly their impact was too." Chalana, "Whither the 'Hindoo Invasion?'" 21.

37 We do have a few patchy records of Indians' early presence. As early as 1906, the
    Portland City Directory (Portland: R.L. Polk & Co., 1882–1909), listed Hardit
    Singh and Karam Singh as living in town and working at a biscuit factory. By
    1907–1908, six names appear—Ganga Ram and ND Ram, both listed as laborers,
    along with Kishen, Natha, Ohaman, and Rangi Singh, all working at Portland
    Cordage Co. A 1906 notice in the *Astoria Daily Budget* reported the death by
    consumption of "Hindoo Sunday Singh" after an illness of several weeks. ("About
    Astoria," second column, *Astoria (OR) Daily Budget*, October 31, 1906, p. 6.)

38 Oregon, U.S., Arriving Passenger and Crew Lists, 1888–1963, searching "Singh"
    1900–1910, accessed May 16, 2023, https://www.ancestry.com/search/
    collections/1042/?name=_singh&count=50&name_x=_1. One man entered in
    1922, all fifty others after 1947; California, U.S., Arriving Passenger and Crew
    Lists, 1882–1959, "Singh," 1900–1910, accessed May 16, 2023, https://www.
    ancestry.com/search/collections/7949/?name=_singh&arrival=1900&arrival_
    x=10-0-0&count=50&name_x=_1&fh=450&fsk=MDs0NDk7NTA-61-.

39 Wong, *Sweet Cakes, Long Journey*, 150–151.

40 Octoroon refers to someone with one-eighth African ancestry, became an official
    US Census category in 1890, and reflects the obsession and supremacist practice
    of designating mixed-ethnicity people to a subordinate ethnicity.

41 See sources cited in the map of Ghadar planning meeting sites, chapter 2.

42 Wong, *Sweet Cakes, Long Journey*, 6, 31, 33–34, 47, 49–50, 51–60.

43 Abbott, *The Great Extravaganza*, 9, 52; Robbins, *Landscapes of Promise*, 197.
    Robbins's total attendance numbers includes both paid entrants (1,588,000) and
    the 966,000 courtesy passes, for a total of 2,554,000 attendees.

44 Carl Abbott, "The Booster City and Business Leaders," Oregon History Project,
    last modified 2014, https://www.oregonhistoryproject.org/narratives/lewis-and-
    clark-from-expedition-to-exposition-1803-1905/starting-a-new-century-the-
    lewis-and-clark-centennial-exposition-1905/
    the-booster-city-and-business-leaders/.

45 Abbott, *Great Extravaganza*, 9, 52; Robbins, *Landscapes of Promise*, 197.

46 Robbins, *Landscapes of Promise*, 196; Carl Abbott, "America's Pacific Vision,"
    Oregon History Project, last modified 2014, https://www.oregonhistoryproject.
    org/narratives/lewis-and-clark-from-expedition-to-exposition-1803-1905/
    starting-a-new-century-the-lewis-and-clark-centennial-exposition-1905/
    americas-pacific-vision/#.Y8HSgvrMJPY.

47 Robbins, *Landscapes of Promise*, 197.

48 Abbott, *Great Extravaganza*, 11; Carl Abbott, "Starting a New Century: The
    Lewis and Clark Centennial Exposition, 1905, Asia at the Fair," Oregon History
    Project, last modified 2014; https://oregonhistoryproject.org/narratives/lewis-
    and-clark-from-expedition-to-exposition-1803-1905/starting-a-new-century-
    the-lewis-and-clark-centennial-exposition-1905/asia-at-the-fair/#.WSRjl2jys2w.

49 Carl Abbott writes, "Portland more than doubled in size. . . . The city was far in front of its rivals and pulling away. Next in line were Astoria, Baker City, Pendleton, Salem, and The Dalles, but none had more than 10,000 residents." Abbott, "America's Pacific Vision." The state's population grew an unprecedented 63 percent between 1900 and 1910.

50 Abbott, *Great Extravaganza*, 59.

51 Scott, "The Momentous Struggle," 6. Japan's defeat of Russia in 1905 hastened the revolutionary upsurges in Russia in 1905, demonstrated an eastern country could defeat a European power, and set the stage for an intense intercolonial rivalry that for the West was only settled with Japan's defeat in World War II.

52 Portland sent lobbyists to Washington, DC, for funds. They used Scott's argument to garner congressional backing and were aided by Scott's political ally, Theodore Roosevelt. As one lobbyist argued to Congress, Portland's exposition was not merely a historical commemoration of Oregon's roots but was also pivotal to the Pacific trade and, thus, an "undertaking of national interest and importance." Abbott, *Great Extravaganza*, 17.

53 Interestingly, the Japanese and Russians, soon at war with one another, were next to each other at the fair.

54 Blee, "Completing Lewis and Clark's Westward March," 250–251.

55 The fair was open for four months, and 2.5 million people were estimated to have attended. This means there were, on average, 625,000 attendees per month, or 20,833 per day. With a 1905 population of around 90,000 people, 26 percent of Portland theoretically passed through fair gates daily. There were, however, many non-city and non-state residents in attendance. These calculations are meant only to aid in considering the impact of the fair on the city and surrounding areas.

56 Trafford, "Hitting the Trail," 158. Visuals on the fair, including the very disturbing zoo-like displays, can be accessed here: https://www.ohs.org/research-and-library/oregon-historical-quarterly/back-issues/upload/Trafford_Hitting-the-Trail_116_2_Summer-2015_spread.pdf.

57 "Whiteness" was and is an ever-shifting category including different people (Finns, Italians, Syrians, Jews) for different reasons (religion, skin tone, language) at different times and with differing acceptance, sometimes called "suspect whites."

58 Lal, "East Indians in British Columbia," 55, 56, quoting a government official (fn17), https://dx.doi.org/10.14288/1.0093725.

59 Goings, Barnes, and Snider, *The Red Coast*, 6, 10–11, 57–100. Employers also did targeted recruiting of foreign-born workers to ensure a massive and inexpensive labor force and as strikebreakers. When Indians recruited to break a strike were told by IWW-led strikers about their struggle, they not only refused to scab but worked to convince others to reject being similarly employed. "Lumber Workers Gaining Ground," *Industrial Worker* (Spokane, WA), April 18, 1912, p. 1. As Goings and colleagues argue on page 73, the propertied classes of the area embarked on a campaign to rid the area of peoples considered nonwhite, a campaign that was largely, but not completely, successful. The Survey of Race Relations (SRR) includes interviews conducted in 1924 at two Washington lumber mills in Aberdeen and Rochester, including "Mr. Kahn, Hindu foreman" and the foreman of N & M Lumber Co. employing "45 Orientals of which 21 are Japanese and 13 Hindus and 11 are Filipinos." Mr. Khan interview by R. L. Olson, July 28, 1924, Survey of Race Relations Records, Hoover Institution Library and Archives and Stanford Digital Repository, box 29, images 173–175, https://purl.stanford.edu/rx565ht0646; R. L. Olson, N. M. Lumber Co. interviews, July 22,

1924, box 29, images 178–184. Historian Paul Englesberg, utilizing census records, has documented Indians' presence in Grays Harbor. Across the country, Scotland Yard worked with Pinkertons in New York City attempting to track Indian revolutionary plots in 1908. James Laidlaw to James Bryce, November 3, 1908, NA: FO 371/563, General Correspondence from 1906–1966, United States, 1907, no. DSC0 3242-3243.

60 See, for example, James Laidlaw [to Primary Secy State Foreign Affairs?], June 26, 1907, NA: FO 371/359, General Correspondence from 1906–1966, United States, 1907, no. DSC0 2125–2126 regarding the "disloyal" Oregon Agricultural College student H. S. Chima and pundit Dr. N. Krishni's statements.

61 Sohan Singh Bhakna, "Sohan Singh Bhakna Ghadar Party Da Itihas," Desh Bhagat Yaadgar Library Special Collections, MSS no. 11227; Baba Harnam Singh Tundilat, "Answers to Questions Raised by Secretary, Ghadar Party History Sub-committee," "Notes on the History of the Ghadar Party," "Reply to the Question of History of Committee of Ghadar Party," Desh Bhagat Yaadgar Library Special Collections, MSS no. 11269. These are in Punjabi or Urdu, and excerpts were partially and informally translated for me by Oregonians Navneet Kaur and Roomina Ahmed.

62 Nayan Shah estimates that in Western Canada and the United States, single men accounted for fully 80 percent of population growth decade after decade during the first third of the twentieth century. Shah, *Stranger Intimacy*, 2.

63 Bell, *Lighting the Fires of Freedom*, 1.

64 Relevant is Nayan Shah's summary of what he terms the "three stabilizations" hindering historians' attempts to document "movement and change": "These three stabilizations are 1) permanence over transience, 2) the nuclear family household and 3) polarized sexuality," Shah, *Stranger Intimacy*, 6. Extant records of Indians in Oregon are largely the product of governmental tracking of ownership (businesses, land titles), population numbers (census records), or law and order (arrest or prison records). Astoria provided some exception to this, as Indians received more local press attention than other Columbia River communities, including Portland. Imaginatively, I have drawn on regional literature from British Columbia such as Nayar, *The Punjabis in British Columbia*, and studies of laborers and labor camps. I am most indebted to Sadhu Singh Dhami's semi-autobiographical *Maluka: A Novel*, based on the lives of Indian millworkers of British Columbia in the early 1920s. I cite specific pages where appropriate, but credit the work as a whole, especially pages 1–99. The majority of my information and analysis of the Chinese in Astoria and its social overlap with Indians is drawn from Chris Friday's *Organizing Asian American Labor*.

65 One aspect of the credit ticket system for Chinese laborers involved the Six Companies issuing a clearance on debts before a laborer could make the return trip to China. Batzell writes, "Although the huiguan of the Six Companies fulfilled important community functions, as an organization led by Chinese merchants they primarily 'sought to protect the interests of Chinese creditors,' an allegiance with enormous significance in a system of debt-financed labour mobilization. . . . The Six Companies were not the conspiratorial slave masters that racist rhetoric made them out to be, but the organization did represent the collective power of the merchant creditor elite in a regime of global labour mobilization based on debt." These were sizable debts, equivalent to paying transport costs of $120,000 for an average-income twenty-first-century American. Batzell, "Free Labour, Capitalism and the Anti-Slavery Origins," 153–158. Had Indians operated under the same credit ticket system in 1914, it would

212

NOTES TO PAGES 45–50

have posed an additional obstacle to the thousands who returned to India to attempt to overthrow British colonialism. Similarly, Indians in North America were not bound by the terms of Indian contract laborers throughout South America and the Caribbean.

66 "Punjab Rebellion Utterly Crushed," *Morning Oregonian*, November 27, 1916, p. 1; Harish Puri, *Ghadar Movement*, 9.

67 Puri, *Ghadar Movement*, 85.

68 [author], reports, January–February 1914, NA: FO 371/2154, General Correspondence from 1906–1966, United States, 1914, no. DSC0 9318, 9320-9349. There was also consular chatter, often peeved, over the assertion that newly arrived migrants turned to nationalists for assistance because consulate employees did little or nothing to assist them. R.S., report, April 4, 1912, NA: FO 371/1547, General Correspondence from 1906–1966, United States, 1912, no. DSC0 7970-7971.

69 In the US West, their itineracy was also more visible given the greater distances between towns and jobs unlike the densely populated American East Coast. Allerfeldt, *Race, Radicalism, Religion, and Restriction*, 98.

70 Leedom, *Astoria*, 119.

71 Indians were denied the vote in North America. They were denied in the United States because they were not citizens. In Canada, as their communities grew, voters stripped them from the vote in 1908. Jensen, *Passage from India*, 65. Many Ghadarites upheld the equality of women and respected leaders like Sohan Singh Bhakna, who, upon returning to India, established schools for girls and otherwise promoted equality of women in his village and the larger world. During World War I, several key Ghadar global organizers were women.

72 Dhami, *Maluka*, 2, 4, 19, 37.

73 Dhillon, "Astoria Revisited," 2, 4; Dhami, *Maluka*, 3.

74 Dhami, *Maluka*, 3–4, 7, 17.

75 Dhami, *Maluka*, 6.

76 Dhami, *Maluka*, 10.

77 Dhami, *Maluka*, 10, 17, 42–43.

78 Email correspondence from David Bhagat Thind to Liisa Penner, Clatsop County Historical Society archivist, March 6, 2006; Sawhney, *I Shall Never Ask for Pardon*, 78.

79 Transcript of Interview of Padma Chandra, November 18, 1972, Bancroft Special Collection, UC Berkeley, BANC MSS, 2002/78 CZ Box 4, 34, 41.

80 Dhami, *Maluka*, 11–17.

81 "Lumber Workers Gaining Ground," *Industrial Worker*, April 18, 1912, pp. 1–4. The article reads, in part, "Hindus are out of the mills and bosses are trying to get negroes to act as scabs. . . . The reason the Hindus worked in the first place was because there was no way in which to explain the situation to them. When an English speaking Hindu was found he made the situation clear to his countrymen and they all quit. The strikers are going to send a Hindu delegation in to persuade the Americans to quit scabbing."

82 Das was active in Oregon, especially during the St. Johns riot's aftermath, as detailed in chapter 3. Das's actions and presence in St. Johns were noted by Agent Hopkinson. See Hopkinson, report, January 12, 1912, NA: FO 371/1547, General Correspondence from 1906–1966, United States, 1912, no. DSC0 7945, 7948.

83 Chang, *Pacific Connections*, 134.

84 Not all Sikhs, or men of other faiths from India, wore turbans in North America. Many adopted the use of western hats over shorn hair. Their motivations in doing so were many: modernity, passing, or crafting new lives and selves. A lack of turban was not, and is not, a definitive indicator of a person's loss of faith.

85 Sawhney, *I Shall Never Ask for Pardon*, 78.

86 Indian training with meels influenced the United States, Europe, and England, including among young women during the health craze of the late Victorian era and into the 1920s. See, among other sources, Alter "Indian Clubs and Colonialism," 497–534, UTC photo at page 501.

87 Puri, *Ghadar Movement*, 129.

88 "Wrestling Date Set: Carlson to Meet Singh on March 14th," *Morning Astorian*, March 2, 1913, p. 3, notes Dodan as living in Astoria; "Wrestler Ready for Fray," *Morning Oregonian*, October 10, 1910, p. 10, notes Dodan as living in Astoria; while the October 7, 1911, *Seattle Star* describes Dodan Singh as "of Vancouver." In the *Astoria City Directory*, Dodan Singh is the only Singh listed in town that year, despite being one of many.

89 "O'Connell to Meet Singh," *Morning Oregonian*, September 20, 1910, p. 10; *Astoria City Directories*, 1906, 1908–1909, 1910, Clatsop County Historical Society. This is not conclusive, merely indicative. For example, the 1913 Directory lists only Dodan Singh, the wrestler, at the height of the Ghadarite organizing in Astoria and when it is known many Indians were in Astoria.

90 "Bout Is on Tuesday" *Sunday Oregonian*, October 9, 1910, Sports, p. 3; "Toe Hold Downs Hindu Grappler," *Oregon Daily Journal*, November 1, 1909, p. 10.

91 Regarding the culturally preferred place to train, Joseph S. Alter writes, "Earth, air, water and trees are the essential features which give an akhara [a place of practice] its aesthetic appeal." Perhaps the forests surrounding Astoria were a perfect setting for Dodan. Alter, *The Wrestler's Body*, 30.

92 "Wrestler Ready for Fray," 10.

93 "Astoria May Have Claim to Champion: Basanta Singh Is Certain to Give Ted Thyh a Busy Evening on January 17; Much Interest," *Morning Astorian*, January 11, 1920, p. 2. In Mills, *Subaltern Sports*, Mills's insightful opening essay succinctly defines subaltern, as "dominance without hegemony." He argues that in sports we find moments wherein the dominant relations are partially or momentarily upended and individual skills, prowess and guile rule rather than wealth, status or political manipulation (p. 1). Event spectators add to the impact and a broader takeaway moment of unexpected outcomes when a crowd's aspirations may be represented by one of the competitors. A spectacle's significance can reverberate beyond the confines of any one event, and may serve differing causes, whether progressive or regressive. I utilized Mills's framework to analyze wrestlers' brief gracing of Astoria's and regional newspapers.

94 Sohi, *Echoes of Mutiny*, 54, 55n28.

95 Author's conversation with family members, May 2010. On the centrality of internationalism to the Finnish socialist movement, see the Tyomies Society (Photographs) Records, Finnish American Collection, Immigration History Research Center, University of Minnesota.

96 Quoted in Shah, *Stranger Intimacy*, 242.

97 Untitled, *Astoria Daily Budget*, May 3, 1909, p. 6. I've been unable to track the exact outcome of this strike, although Indians continued to work for the mill until it was destroyed by fire in 1922. For evidence of this historical record, see

the Clatsop County Historical Society "Hindu file" records: "Complaint,"
February 28, 1920, Singh v. Lall, Clatsop County Circuit Court; City of Astoria
Police Ledger, July 1910–July 1916, unpaginated; also *Astoria Daily Budget*,
March 10, 1914, for Al Singh and Rola Singh's arraignment for assault on Sam
Hakin, a fellow workman; "Declaration of Intent" of Amin Chand Sherma,
March 2, 1911; Behari Lall Verma, August 31, 1910; [illegible] Singh, July 26,
1910; Behari Lal, July 13, 1910; S. Chhajju, June 15, 1921. Soba Singh and Pauline
Singh were married in 1919 in Vancouver, Washington, where their marriage
would not be subject to Oregon's miscegenation laws. Pauline resorted to racial
arguments in her filings, charging that her husband was "black" and demanding
alimony. They eventually reconciled. Source: Clatsop County Court documents
In Re Singh. Re the presence of children, see Dhillon, "Astoria Revisited," 7.

INTERLUDE

1 "O'Connell to Meet Singh," *Morning Oregonian*, September 20, 1910, p. 10.
2 "O'Connell to Meet Singh."
3 "O'Connell Goes to Astoria," *Morning Oregonian*, July 15, 1910, p. 8.
4 Alter, "Gama the World Champion," 5–6. For a more in-depth analysis of Indian
   wrestling, see Alter, "Subaltern Bodies and Nationalist Physiques," 45–72;
   "Indian Clubs and Colonialism: Hindu Masculinity and Muscular Christianity";
   "The Body of One Color," 49–72.
5 "Wrestler Ready for Fray," 10.
6 "Wrestler Ready for Fray," *Morning Oregonian*, October 10, 1910, p. 10.
7 "Match Is On Tonight," *Morning Oregonian*, October 11, 1910, p. 8.
   Consideration of weight differences was never acknowledged for a later wrestler,
   Basanta Singh, who consistently grappled above his weight class.
8 "Grappler Seeks Coin," *Morning Oregonian*, October 12, 1910, p. 8.
9 "Grappler Seeks Coin."
10 "Grappler Seeks Coin."
11 "Wrestling Match Off," *Oregon Daily Journal*, March 20, 1913, p. 15; "Water
   Under the Bridge," *Daily Astorian*, March 16, 1988.
12 Untitled, *Seattle Star*, October 7, 1911, p. 2.
13 "Mixed Bout Cause of Much Trouble," *Morning Oregonian*, February 16, 1922, p.
   12; "Basanta Victor at Marysville," *Sacramento Union*, July 8, 1920, p. 9; "Thye
   and Hindu Draw," *Morning Oregonian*, January 19, 1920, p. 10; "Foes Will Meet
   Again," *Sunday Oregonian*, December 31, 1922, p. 4; "Hindu Wrestler Is in
   Pendleton to See the 1922 Round-Up," *East Oregonian*, September 8, 1922, p. 1;
   "Grapplers of India Lauded by Native," *Morning Oregonian*, February 7, 1922, p.
   14; "Singh Olson Match Is Scheduled for Tomorrow at Alta," *East Oregonian*,
   March 9, 1922, p. 1; "Hindu Wrestler Will Meet Gustavo Again," *Daily East
   Oregonian*, March 18, 1922, p. 5.

CHAPTER 3

1 Abbott, *The Great Extravaganza*, 59; Carl Abbott, "America's Pacific Vision," Lewis and Clark: From Expedition to Exposition, 1803–1905, *Oregon History Project*, last modified 2014, https://oregonhistoryproject.org/narratives/lewis-and-clark-from-expedition-to-exposition-1803-1905/starting-a-new-century-the-lewis-and-clark-centennial-exposition-1905/americas-pacific-vision/.

2 Untitled, *St. Johns (OR) Review* (hereafter *Review*), July 12, 1907, p. 2.

3 The riot was on the night of Monday, March 21, 1910. Because the *Review* was a weekly, the first report of it was on Friday, March 25, 1910.

4 Portland Manufacturing Co.—notably the owner's son Thomas Autzen and an unnamed mill superintendent—produced plywood, a building material that revolutionized the industry. See Harrison Clark, "Plywood in Retrospect," *Portland Manufacturing Company* no. 1 (March 1967), https://www.apawood.org/data/Sites/1/documents/monographs/1-portland-manufacturing-co.pdf. Curiously, the *Review* did not suggest that "Hindus" were responsible for the fire. "Industry Goes Up in Smoke," *Review*, February 18, 1910, p. 1.

5 "Factory Is Burned," *Morning Oregonian*, February 15, 1910, p. 14.

6 "Big Doings in St. Johns," *Review*, March 25, 1910, p. 1.

7 "Big Doings in St. Johns." Newspaper accounts during the riot and trial report Gordon Dickey as working in several different mills in the area, including Willamette Pulp & Paper. I don't know if he changed jobs or the papers made errors. I am using the first reference to his employer, which was the St. Johns Lumber Mill.

8 "Hindu Riot Trial Will Open Today," *Morning Oregonian*, June 11, 1910, p. 14.

9 "More Arrests for Riots Promised," *Morning Oregonian*, March 24, 1910, p. 4.

10 "Big Doings in St. Johns."

11 "Big Doings in St. Johns."

12 "Big Doings in St. Johns." Also, as used by the reporter, "men" did not refer to Indian men, further revealing the bounds of community.

13 "Big Doings in St. Johns."

14 "Big Doings in St. Johns." The streetcar men who transported St. Johns' "Hindu problem" that evening were union men who won a long strike that began in late 1906 and had broad community support. See, for example, *Portland Labor Press*, "Carmen Are on Strike," December 17, 1906, p. 1; and, "Were Illegally Under Arrest," January 21, 1907, p. 1.

15 "21 Arrests Made; Hindu Accusers," *Morning Oregonian*, March 23, 1910, p. 5. See also "Big Doings in St. Johns."

16 "State Hurries Hindu Riot Case," *Morning Oregonian*, June 14, 1910, p. 12.

17 "State Hurries Hindu Riot Case."

18 I believe Kanshi Ram used the Americanized name of John Kim. The Kim/Ram name corresponds with Indian accounts of the riot and the role Kanshi Ram played in its aftermath. The *Oregonian* article on the frontispiece of this book agrees. "Punjab Rebellion Utterly Crushed," *Morning Oregonian*, November 27, 1916, p. 1.

19 "More Arrests for Riots Promised."

20 "21 Arrests Made"; "Hindus Roiled by Remark of Olson," *Morning Oregonian*, March 29, 1910, p. 12; "U.S. Is to Assist," *Sunday Oregonian*, May 1, 1910, p. 7. Office of the U.S. Attorney for the Judicial District of Oregon, 1907–1921, Box 1, Record 589, HMS/MLR Number: 7599, ARC Number: 5218591, Seattle Federal Records Center, Seattle, Washington.

21 "Hindus Roiled by Remark of Olson." The 1907 Boring case and its import is
    detailed in chapter 2. Dan J. Malarkey was hired by the British consul to assist in
    the prosecution of the murder of Harnam Singh, and resulted in convictions. See
    "Hindu Shot by Fellow Workman," *Morning Oregonian*, November 2, 1907, p. 13;
    "Begin Hindu Murder Trial," *Morning Oregonian*, April 23, 1908, p. 6; "Jury in
    Murder Case Still Out," *Morning Oregonian*, April 25, 1908, p. 8; "Jail for Father
    and Son," *Morning Oregonian*, April 29, 1908, p. 6.

22 "More Arrests for Riots Promised"; "Race War?," *Daily News* (Portland, OR),
    March 25, 1910, pp. 1–3.

23 "Hindus Arm, Are Arrested," *Morning Oregonian*, March 24, 1910, p. 4.

24 "Hindu Buy Guns and Are Arrested," *Daily News*, March 24, 1910, p. 1.

25 A weapons charge was pressed against only John Kim, as his gun was loaded.
    "Hindus Arm, Are Arrested." The spellings of names are given as they were
    printed in the newspaper.

26 "Race War?"

27 Untitled Editorial, *Review*, June 10, 1910, p. 6.

28 Untitled Editorial, *Review*, June 10, 1910. "The British lion must be appeased
    even if all the laws of Oregon be turned inside out to accomplish it."

29 St. Johns City Council records, Accession number 3700, March 22, 1910, City of
    Portland (OR) Archives and Records Center.

30 "More Arrests for Riots Promised."

31 "Politics Injected in Hindu Trouble," *Morning Oregonian*, March 25, 1910, p. 14.

32 "Politics Injected in Hindu Trouble."

33 "Three Men Held for Grand Jury," *Morning Oregonian*, March 26, 1910, p. 9.

34 "Politics Injected in Hindu Trouble."

35 "Three Men Held for Grand Jury."

36 "More Arrests for Riots Promised."

37 "Grand Jury Will Not Probe Riots," *Sunday Oregonian*, March 27, 1910, p. 4;
    "Three Men Held for Grand Jury."

38 "Three Men Held for Grand Jury."

39 "Hindus Roiled by Remark of Olson." To this writer's knowledge, no such
    accusations were made about white claims against Indians.

40 "Hindus Roiled by Remark of Olson."

41 "Three Men Held for Grand Jury." A new grand jury would be impaneled a few
    days later, on April 1.

42 "Hindu Makes Plea," *Morning Oregonian*, April 1, 1910, p. 14. Note: Das's first
    name is misspelled as Tasakuath.

43 Gould, *Sikhs, Swamis, Students, and Spies*, 187. Bellingham, Washington is about
    30 miles south of Vancouver, BC, and the US-Canada border.

44 Puri, *Ghadar Movement*, 42–43.

45 "Officials of St. Johns Under Fire," *Morning Oregonian*, April 19, 1910, p. 4;
    "Grand Jury Ready," April 23, 1910, p. 14.

46 "St. Johns Mayor and 8 Indicted," *Morning Oregonian*, April 27, 1910, p. 14.
    Based on his name, I am guessing Me Ha was Chinese. If so, that may mean that
    Me Ha was sharing quarters with the "Hindus." Across the US West, it was
    common that Chinese and Hindu laborers lived in the same parts of the city,
    given their shared racialized status. Continuing research and translation work is
    needed to document not just Me Ha, but the larger issues of intersections and
    collaboration between the communities.

47 "St. Johns Mayor and 8 Indicted."

48 On March 22, 1910, the *Daily News* recounted that Laidlaw swore out affidavits in the local justice court. "British Consul Swears Out 100 Arrest Warrants," *Daily News*, March 22, 1910, p. 1; "St. Johns' Mayor and 8 Indicted"; "Grand Jury Ready."

49 "Politics Injected in Hindu Trouble," *Morning Oregonian*, March 25, 1910, p. 14; "St. Johns' Mayor and 8 Indicted"; "Nine Are Indicted," *Review*, April 29, 1910, p. 1; "Indictment," April 26, 1910, State of Oregon v. Dickey, et al., Multnomah County Circuit Court, microfiche records accessed at Multnomah County Courthouse, Portland, OR.

50 "St. Johns' Mayor and 8 Indicted."

51 $700 in 1910 has a value of approximately $23,000, 110 years later.

52 "21 Arrests Made"; "More Arrests for Riots Promised"; "St. Johns' Mayor and 8 Indicted." The Greeks were eventually cleared.

53 "Grand Jury Ready"; "St Johns' Mayor and 8 Indicted."

54 "St. Johns' Mayor and 8 Indicted"; "Hindu Riot Trial Will Open Today"; "State Hurries Hindu Riot Case."

55 "Hindu Riot Trial Will Open Today."

56 "U.S. Is to Assist," *Sunday Oregonian*, May 1, 1910, sec. 2, p. 7.

57 The *Review* described a deputy arriving in St. Johns with a "washtub full of subpoenas." "Subpoenas Galore," *Review*, June 10, 1910, p. 1. For court records, see, "Motion and Affidavit on Behalf of Dickey," nd; "Affidavit on Behalf of Dickey," nd; "Certification of R.L. Stevens, Sheriff Multnomah County Oregon of Service of Subpoenas by JH Jones, Deputy," June 4, 1910; "Form CC9 Criminal Subpoena on behalf of the State of Oregon," June 2, 1910; "Affidavit of C.W. Garland," June 1, 1910; *Dickey*, MCCC.

58 Untitled, *Review*, June 10, 1910, p. 6.

59 "State Hurries Hindu Riot Case"; "Be It Remembered" entry by Judge John S. Cook, Presiding Judge of Dept. 4, June 13, 1910, *Dickey*, Multnomah County (OR) Circuit Court microfiche (hereafter MCCC); Ramnath, *Haj to Utopia*, 29; Sohi, *Echoes of Mutiny*, 52. My research, informed by a close reading of *Echoes* and a generous phone conversation with Dr. Sohi in November 2016, persuades me that, until Har Dayal's speaking tour in 1913, Oregon was not a focus of political police efforts.

60 "State Hurries Hindu Riot Case." The former was Mayor Cox.

61 "Dickey Poses as Hindus' Friend," *Morning Oregonian*, June 15, 1910, p. 14.

62 "State Hurries Hindu Riot Case."

63 "Jury Finds Dickey Guilty of Rioting, *Morning Oregonian*, June 16, 1910, p. 6.

64 "Jury Verdict," June 17, 1910, *Dickey*, MCCC.

65 Untitled, *Review*, June 17, 1910, p. 4.

66 I have no means of knowing whether or not Dickey was offered a deal by prosecutors for doing so.

67 J. J. Fitzgerald to James Laidlaw, December 14, 1911, NA: FO 371/1547, General Correspondence from 1906–1966, United States, 1912, no. DSC0 7914.

68 Dan J. Malarkey to James Laidlaw, March 29, 1922, Anti-Indian Riots in the State of Oregon, Commerce & Industry, Emigration B Proceedings, June 1911, file no. 65, 7–9; 12–16, National Archives of India. https://www.abhilekh-patal.in/jspui/handle/123456789/2749836?searchWord=anti-Indian&backquery=[location=123456789%2F1&query=%22anti-Indian%20riots%22&rpp=20&sort_by=dc.date.accessioned_dt&order=desc], accessed June 29, 2023.

69 Dan J. Malarkey to James Laidlaw, March 29, 1922. Malarkey claims that, had he been hired earlier by the British and thus been a part of the grand jury proceedings, the problem would not have occurred.

70 Reports, December 1911–January 1912, NA: FO 371/1547, General Correspondence from 1906–1966, United States, 1912, no. DSC0 7915–7917.

71 "Order," nd, *Dickey*, MCCC.

72 Untitled document, January 15, 1912, *Dickey*, MCCC; "Discharge of Bondsmen," February 6, 1911, *Dickey*, MCCC.

73 "Discharge of Bondsmen," February 6, 1911, *Dickey*, MCCC. Van De Bogard's pleading to charges might indicate that he did not receive, or received substantially less, financial support than Gordon Dickey.

74 J. J. Fitzgerald to James Laidlaw, December 14, 1911, NA: FO 371/1547, General Correspondence from 1906–1966, United States, 1912, no. DSC0 7914; Dan J. Malarkey to James Laidlaw, March 29, 1922; undated and untitled document, State v. Dunbar, C-1538, MCCC; "Bench Warrant," April 26, 1910, *Dickey*, MCCC; "Order of Dismissal," October 23, 1913, State v. Grovin, C-1509, MCCC. A bench warrant was issued for two of the others accused, and one case was dismissed for lack of prosecution by the state.

75 Brian Halvorsen, "List of Mayors of St. Johns, Oregon," last modified July 6, 2012, http:// en.wikipedia. org/wiki/User:Halvorsen_brian/List_of_mayors_of_St._Johns,_Oregon.

76 "The Hindu Situation," *Review*, April 8, 1910, p. 1; "Nine Are Indicted," *Review*, April 29, 1910, p. 1; "Council Proceedings," *Review*, February 10, 1911, p. 1; Untitled, *Review*, June 30, 1911, p. 1; Untitled, *Review*, July 14, 1911, p. 1; "Commercial Club Meet," *Review*, November 24, 1911, p. 1; "Local News," *Review*, November 15, 1912, p. 3.

77 "Hindu Riot Case Ended," *Morning Oregonian*, March 6, 1912, p. 12.

78 *Supplement to the Review*, March 8, 1912. Ofc. Dunbar similarly petitioned for the city to pay his legal fees, but I do not know if it was approved. "Council Proceedings," *Review*, March 15, 1912, p. 1; "Council Proceedings," *Review*, April 5, 1912, p. 1.

79 One example is the front page, "Mayor, Justice, Police Indicted," *Los Angeles Herald*, April 27, 1910, p. 1, reporting on the indictments of the St. Johns city officials.

80 "The Hindu Invasion," *Collier's Weekly*, March 26, 1910, p. 15, https://www. saada.org/item/20101217-157.

81 Herman Scheffauer, "The Tide of Turbans," *Forum* 43 (June 1910): 616–618; "The Hindu, The Newest Immigration Problem," *Survey*, October 1910, p. 2, https:// www.saada.org/item/20110808-293.

82 Sohi, *Echoes of Mutiny*, 28–34. Exclusionists pressured for North's removal, and he eventually was removed.

83 Chandrasekhar, "Indian Immigration in America," 138–143; Scheffauer, "Tide of Turbans," 616–618; "The Hindu Invasion," 15; "The Hindu: The Newest Immigration Problem," 2–3. For comparison, in 1907, often noted as the peak year for European immigration, more than 1.2 million persons entered the United States, and by 1910, some 13.5 million immigrants called the United States home. Olivia B. Waxman, "Ellis Island's Busiest Day Ever Was 110 Years Ago. Here's Why," *Time*, April 17, 2017, https://time.com/4740248/ellis-island-busiest-day/; "U.S. Immigrant Population and Share over Time, 1850–Present,"

Migration Policy Institute, accessed April 2, 2023, https://www.migrationpolicy. org/programs/data-hub/charts/immigrant-population-over-time.

84 "The Hindu Situation."

85 "Big Doings in St. Johns."

86 "The Hindu Situation."

87 "[Dickey] Affidavit," June 4, 1910, *Dickey*, MCCC.

88 "Undertaking," March 27, 1910, *Dickey*; "Undertaking of Bail before Indictment," March 28, 1910, *Dickey*, MCCC.

89 "Big Doings in St. Johns."

90 "Hindu Riot Trial Will Open Today."

91 "Big Doings in St. Johns"; "Three Men Held for Grand Jury."

92 "Grand Jury Will Not Probe Riots."

93 "Hindu Riot Trial Will Open Today."

94 After the 1907 violence, mill owners went before the Bellingham City Council and claimed they would "gladly welcome any provision which will insure them white men to take the places of Hindus employed in the mills now." Owner Fred J. Wood stated to the council that "the only way to eliminate this trouble is to not employ a single Hindu in our mills. "Mill manager L. O. Waldo concurred but insisted "it would be useless to attempt to depend upon the white men who work first in one mill and then after a few days go to the nearest mill in the same city, where they will stay but a few days also." He went on to add that "I admit that the Hindu laborer is the most undesirable citizen in our mill, . . . but we must have full crews of men to run the mill. We cannot get white men who will remain steadily at their work. A large number are transient and work only for 'whiskey money' leaving the company in the lurch just at the time that their services are most desired." "Hindus March Back to Mills Under Guard," *Bellingham (WA) Herald*, September 5, 1907, p. 2. This same rationale and language was used by railroad magnates to justify the unpopular hiring of Chinese laborers. Roediger and Esch, *The Production of Difference*, 73–75.

95 Wilkerson, *Caste*, 181.

96 L. T. Paye "The Anti Hindu Riot in St. Johns, Washington [*sic*]," *White Man* 1, no. 1 (June 1910), Special Collections of the Knight Library, University of Oregon, Eugene, gathered from personal notes generously shared by Nayan Shah. I am uncertain where the *White Man* was published, but given that it places St. Johns in Washington, I assume it was not in Oregon. It also appears to have been a one-issue wonder.

97 "Jap Labor Unsatisfactory," *Portland Labor Press* (hereafter *PLP*), March 2, 1906, p. 2; "Complete Platform of the Champion of Statement 1," *PLP*, March 30, 1906; *PLP*, July 6, 1906, p. 2; *PLP*, February 11, 1907, p. 2; "Labor Notes," *PLP*, July 20, 1906, p. 6.

98 "News of Here and There," *PLP*, October 28, 1909, p. 6.

99 "Notes of Local Labor," *PLP*, February 10, 1910, p. 6.

100 "News Notes of Here and There," *PLP*, February 10, 1910, p. 8.

101 "Report on Portland Federated Trades," *PLP*, July 15, 1907, p. 2.

102 *PLP*, February 11, 1910, p. 4.

103 Sohi, *Echoes of Mutiny*, 223 n28.

104 Regarding Spokane Free Speech fight: "IWW Yearbook: 1910," University of Washington IWW History Project, https://depts.washington.edu/iww/ yearbook1910.shtml; Portland IWW chapters had their own press in 1914 and again in 1925–1926: "IWW Newspapers," https://depts.washington.edu/iww/

newspapers.shtml; a detail of IWW actions: "IWW Strikes, Campaigns, Arrests 1906–1920 (Maps)," https://depts.washington.edu/iww/map_events.shtml; the IWW had six additional chapters in Oregon, including one in Astoria: " IWW Local Unions 1906–1917 (Maps)," https://depts.washington.edu/iww/map_locals.shtml, all accessed May 19, 2023.

105 Chang, *Pacific Connections*, 135, quoting the *Industrial Worker,* November 31, 1912.

106 Chang, *Pacific Connections*, 143.

107 Chang, *Pacific Connections*, 136.

108 For more on this critique, see Chang, *Pacific Connections*, 127–130. Chang references a larger and important literature on the topic that is outside the scope of this project. See Sinha, *Colonial Masculinity*; and Gouda, "Good Mothers, Medeas, or Jezebels," in *Domesticating the Empire*.

109 Chang, *Pacific Connections*, 135–140.

110 Chang, *Pacific Connections*, 144.

111 Chang, *Pacific Connections*, 146.

112 Chang, *Pacific Connections*, 118.

113 Chang, *Pacific Connections*, 117, 166, 176.

114 Limerick, *Legacy of Conquest*, 99.

115 Allerfeldt, *Race, Radicalism, Religion, and Restriction*, 100.

116 Allerfeldt, *Race, Radicalism, Religion, and Restriction*, 96. Allerfeldt further writes, at page 102, "It was not only political, demographic and social events that changed the attitudes toward the immigrant worker. . . . It is notable that the Northwestern support for an open-door immigration policy diminished as mechanization developed and an increasingly sedentary workforce emerged— removing the necessity for a volatile, unreliable and increasingly undesirable 'foreign' workforce."

117 See Shah's *Stranger Intimacy* for more detailed discussion of this with respect to Indians in North America.

118 Allerfeldt, *Race, Radicalism, Religion, and Restriction*, 98. For laborers in the PNW, home ownership (40 percent) and marriage (80 percent) rates were higher than many towns in New England. Perhaps here is where a $.10 wage differential might have made a difference.

119 Kazimi, *Undesirables*, 51.

120 G. L. Perrine, "Perrine on Hinduism," *Review*, June 24, 1910, p. 4.

121 Beyond the *PLP*, this was also on full display in Portland's *Daily News*. One of Hyslop's breathtaking examples of this strident trade unionism with a hard racial twist is a banner carried by miners in a 1922 strike in South Africa: "Workers of the World, Fight and Unite for a White South Africa." Hyslop, "The Imperial Working Class."

122 "Riot Cases Are Dismissed," *American Reveille*, September 21, 1907, p. 1. That no prosecution occurred was also seemingly despite the mayor's wishes. "Mayor Determined to Have Rioters Punished," *Bellingham Herald*, September 21, 1907, p. 3.

123 On the formation of the political police force, see Puri, *Ghadar Movement*, 42–43; and Sohi, *Echoes of Mutiny*, 39–44, 84–85, 89–91. On the Continuous Journey provision, see Joan M. Jensen, *Passage from India*, 75.

124 Dan J. Malarkey to James Laidlaw, March 29, 1922. Malarkey claims that, had he been hired earlier by the British and thus been a part of the grand jury proceedings, the problem would not have occurred.

125 Some precedence for Oregon authorities' prosecution of, and British involvement in, the St. Johns rioters can be discerned in the response to the Boring murder trial of 1907. See chapter 2 for more on Boring.

126 Bernard Pelly, "Report Re Attack on Hindus at Bellingham," September 9, 1907, NA: FO 371/360, General Correspondence from 1906–1966, United States, 1907, no. DSC0 2177. St. Johns officially became part of Portland soon after the trials concluded. While economics was the primary motivation for the merger, it is possible that the small town's chastening regarding ethnic policy was part of the terms of St. Johns' admission.

127 Prior to June 2021, my research regarding Consul Laidlaw was limited to records held in the Pacific Northwest. In June 2021, Dr. David C. Atkinson, Purdue University History Department, and author of *The Burden of White Supremacy: Containing Asian Migration in the British Empire and the United States* (Chapel Hill: University of North Carolina Press, 2017), generously shared Washington, DC, National Archives and Records Administration (NARA) records with me. Those included extensive correspondence between Laidlaw and his British superiors and with the US State Department. These both confirmed and provided important new insights to the local story, including how and why the mayor's case was abandoned and confirmation of Laidlaw's important role for his government. My 2019 article in *Oregon Historical Quarterly* on St. Johns did not have the benefit of the intelligence records (Ogden, "White Right and Labor Organizing," 488–517).

128 Untitled, *Review*, May 6, 1910, p. 4.

129 See chapter 2.

130 Report, NA: FO 371/1547, General Correspondence from 1906–1966, United States, 1912, No. 7921.

131 Report, NA: FO 371/1547, General Correspondence from 1906–1966, United States, 1912, Nos. 7926-7934, spellings as in the originals.

132 Report, NA: FO 371/1547, General Correspondence from 1906–1966, United States, 1912, Nos. 7921–7925.

133 Hopkinson, report, NA: FO 371/1547, General Correspondence from 1906–1966, United States, 1912, no. DSC0 7948.

134 Bhakna, *Jeewan Sangam*, sec. 6, p. 10 (informal translation from Urdu to English for the author by Professor Malwinder Waraich in March 2017 via email).

CHAPTER 4

1 Bhakna, *Jeewan Sangam*, sec. 6, pp. 10–11 (informal translation from Urdu to English for the author by Pashaura Singh Dhillon and Professor Malwinder Waraich, March and April 2017 via email).

2 Bhakna, *Jeewan Sangam*, sec. 6, p. 12.

3 Sohi, *Echoes of Mutiny*, 45–46; Puri, *Ghadar Movement*, 52.

4 Deol, *The Role of the Ghadar Party*, 56. Note: Dr. Deol has been accused of plagiarism; his book is not considered inaccurate. Given my lack of language skills, I am utilizing Dr. Deol's English-language work.

5 Deol, *The Role of the Ghadar Party*, 56–57; Sohi, *Echoes of Mutiny*, 54.

6 Sawhney, *I Shall Never Ask for Pardon*, 76–80, 85–86.

7 Bhakna, *Jeewan Sangam*, sec. 6, p. 11.

8 Bhakna, *Jeewan Sangam*, sec. 6, p. 10.

9 Josh, *Baba Sohan Singh Bhakna*, 17–18.

10 Josh, *Baba Sohan Singh Bhakna*, 14. Everyday Indians could not carry weapons after the 1857 Mutiny in India. Despite being targets in America, the country was seen by some, but not all, as a place where all things were possible given it was not ruled by the British.

11 Regarding these "webs of empire," see Ballantyne, *Between Colonialism and Diaspora*, 31.

12 Bhakna, *Jeewan Sangam*, sec. 6, p. 10.

13 Gramsci, *Selections from the Prison Notebooks*, 323.

14 Puri, *Ghadar Movement*, 53, 54; Jensen, *Passage from India*, 22–23; Ramnath, *Haj to Utopia*, 22–23. The nature of that union is debated. A. C. Bose, for example, argues intellectuals were simply filling an empty vessel or utilizing the "raw material" of laborers. Bose, *Indian Revolutionaries Abroad*, 48.

15 A movement is never the work of one person. Puri, *Ghadar Movement*, 63; Brown, *Har Dayal*, 137; Sawhney, "Pandurang Khankhoje," in *The Ghadr Movement and India's Anti-Imperialist Struggle*, 75–86; Ramnath, *Haj to Utopia*, 30–31, 45–47, 63–64, 67, 178, 183–184.

16 Puri, *Ghadar Movement*, 16.

17 This included the attempted or successful deportations of Chagan Khairaj Varma, Kaka Husain Rahim, Bhagwan Singh Gyanee, and Teja Singh. Sohi, *Echoes of Mutiny*, 85–87.

18 Sohi, *Echoes of Mutiny*, 85; Bose, "Taraknath Das (1884–1958)," 85–86.

19 Puri, *Ghadar Movement*, 47. A group of medal-wearing Sikh veterans attended and pledged fealty to the duke and king.

20 Ramnath, *Haj to Utopia*, 62.

21 Josh, *Baba Sohan Singh Bhakna*, 32.

22 "Let Him Revolt," *Morning Oregonian*, December 13, 1913, p. 8.

23 Ramnath, *Haj to Utopia*, 62.

24 Puri, *Ghadar Movement*, 33.

25 Takaki, *Strangers from a Different Shore*, 301.

26 Puri, *Ghadar Movement*, 2, 53; Jensen, *Passage from India*, 22–23.

27 Puri, *Ghadar Movement*, 52, 59.

28 Josh, *Baba Sohan Singh Bhakna*, 25; Puri, *Ghadar Movement*, 59. Puri notes that Oregon was not the only place looking for leadership, citing a letter from Canada to a Lahore newspaper seeking "a great Indian political leader . . . to educate and unite all Indians and 'take the lead here for India.'" Puri, *Ghadar Movement*, 58 n23.

29 Ramnath, *Haj to Utopia*, 125; Sohi, *Echoes of Mutiny*, 50.

30 Brown, *Har Dayal*, 18–19, 69; Sohi, *Echoes of Mutiny*, 22–23.

31 Sohi, *Echoes of Mutiny*, 23; Puri, *Ghadar Movement*, 55–59. Dayal was known for his broad interests and also his wide emotional and philosophical swings. For a more in-depth examination of these, see Brown, *Har Dayal*, especially 85–126.

32 Brown, *Har Dayal*, 127.

33 Puri, *Ghadar Movement*, 59; Ramnath, *Haj to Utopia*, 32, quoting DCI at fn67.

34 Ramnath, *Haj to Utopia*, 20.

35 Brown, *Har Dayal*, 104–115.

36 Brown, *Har Dayal*, 131. As Puri writes, Dayal's "salute to the bomb thrower" "evidently was an echo of the anarchist theory of 'propaganda by deed,' which is born of desperation in the absence of a mass movement. Soon [in Oregon],

however, Har Dayal was to awaken to the opportunity of organizing a mass movement." Puri, *Ghadar Movement*, 58.

37 Brown, *Har Dayal*, 117.

38 Brown, *Har Dayal*, 117–120.

39 Brown, *Har Dayal*, 120, 127.

40 Puri, *Ghadar Movement*, 53.

41 Josh, *Baba Sohan Singh Bhakna*, 26; Puri, *Ghadar Movement*, 59. At 59 n26, Puri addresses the timing of meetings in Oregon. Hard dates from Astoria newspapers set Har Dayal's appearance in Astoria in late May/early June 1913. As Harish Puri argues, preamble meetings likely happened earlier in May in St. Johns and then other enclaves, enabling Har Dayal to stay in Oregon and help guide the efforts. Puri's logic puts political police reports, contemporaneous newspaper accounts and striking while the iron is hot into alignment.

42 Puri, *Ghadar Movement*, 60.

43 Puri, *Ghadar Movement*, 60.

44 Josh, *Baba Sohan Singh Bhakna*, 26.

45 Puri, *Ghadar Movement*, 60–61. Their self-description as "brave" draws on the "brave Sikh fighting tradition" is reflected in Ghadar poetry (chapter 5) and frequently discussed in Ghadar histories. But it is also worth noting their self-description as "prosperous." My review of Hammond payroll records from 1917 to 1920, the only records, seemingly all that survived the 1922 Hammond mill fire, bears this out. Indians are in the mid- to upper-middle range of the pay scale. Importantly, those are wartime records when labor was scarce and Hammond's materials were in heavy demand. Misrow writes that Oregon wages were some of the best for Indians in the North American west. Misrow, "East Indian Immigration on the Pacific Coast," 48, 57–59.

46 The March St. Johns meeting contrasts sharply with a February 1913 meeting in Vancouver, BC. There the community elected to send a delegation to ask London to allow families to join men in Canada. Colonial authorities refused to speak with them. Josh, *Baba Sohan Singh Bhakna*, 18–22.

47 Josh, *Baba Sohan Singh Bhakna*, 24, 26; Puri, *Ghadar Movement*, 60.

48 Deol, *The Role of the Ghadar Party*, 56–57.

49 Puri, *Ghadar Movement*, 61. By explicitly targeting only the British, Dayal sought to preserve Ghadar's relative organizational freedom vis-à-vis the US government.

50 Puri, *Ghadar Movement*, 65–66.

51 Puri, *Ghadar Movement*, 61.

52 Parmanand later joined Ghadar. Sohi, *Echoes of Mutiny*, 55, 181.

53 Deol, *The Role of the Ghadar Party*, 59–60; Puri, *Ghadar Movement*, 61–62; Isemonger and Slattery, *An Account of the Ghadr Conspiracy*, 14. In various Ghadri memoirs and historical accounts, this town is alternately called Wina or Winans. In my 2012 *Oregon Historical Quarterly* article ("Ghadar, Historical Silences, and Notions of Belonging," 164–197), I reported it as Winans, a small enclave of Indians south of Hood River, Oregon. I now believe that Wauna is the correct name. Wauna was (and is) not so much a town, as it was a large mill about 45 miles east (upriver) of Astoria. Wauna could draw from nearby Indian communities such as Cathlamet, Goble, Clatskanie, and Svenson.

54 Isemonger and Slattery, *An Account of the Ghadr Conspiracy* (10), based on the testimony of informant Nawab Khan, and allegedly a principal in the Seaside group.

55 Sohi, *Echoes of Mutiny*, 89–90.

56 Sohi, *Echoes of Mutiny*, 84–88.

57 Report, FO 371/1547, General Correspondence from 1906–1966, United States, 1912, nos. 7947–7948.

58 Report, FO 371/1547, General Correspondence from 1906–1966, United States, 1912, nos. 7950, 7953.

59 Sohi, *Echoes of Mutiny*, 89–90.

60 The impact of religious leaders was mixed and changed over time and place. Some leaders guarded against apostasy. Many temples became critical sites in the North American West, Singapore, and the Philippines, for nurturing and spreading a revolutionary message.

61 Puri, *Ghadar Movement*, 51.

62 Sohi, *Echoes of Mutiny*, 40–41, 84–85, 89–91, 102.

63 Sohi, *Echoes of Mutiny*, 53.

64 Sohi, *Echoes of Mutiny*, 147. In 1914, there were a series of murders in Vancouver involving political police agents and radical activists, culminating in the shooting of Hopkinson himself in the courthouse in October. See chapter 1.

65 Sohi, *Echoes of Mutiny*, 90–91; Brown, *Har Dayal*, 138. Even then, both Brown and Sohi note that Hopkinson's interest continued to be focused on deporting Dayal as an anarchist, not as a leader of a laborers' movement. My research, informed by a close reading of *Echoes* and a generous phone conversation with Dr. Sohi in November 2016, persuades me that until Har Dayal's speaking tour in 1913, Oregon was not a focus of political police efforts.

66 Half were foreign-born. "Interesting Figures in Population Survey," *Morning Astorian*, May 10, 1914, p. 9.

67 Deur, "The Making of Seaside's 'Indian Place,'" 538–541.

68 William Lang, "Oregon Treaty, 1846," Oregon Encyclopedia, accessed February 4, 2023, https://www.oregonencyclopedia.org/articles/oregon-treaty/#. Y97duMhKhPY.

69 Friday, *Organizing Asian American Labor*, 6, 8; Hummasti, *Finnish Radicals in Astoria*, 17.

70 Untitled, *Astoria Daily Budget*, October 31, 1906, p. 6. There was also a small article, "Sing No More," in the *Morning Astorian*, November 1, 1906, p. 5. "Four Strange Strangers," *Morning Astorian*, on August 18, 1906, p. 5, reported on four Hindus arriving in Astoria from Portland, and noted "several . . . domiciled and are at work in this city."

71 "Hindoos to Burn Body of Deceased Countryman," *Astoria Daily Budget*, November 1, 1906, p. 5.

72 "Hindoos to Burn Body"; "Cremated by Hindoo Rites," *Astoria Daily Budget*, November 1, 1906, p. 1; "Rauma Singh's Cremation," *Daily Astorian*, August 21, 1981, p. 6. Historian Regan Watjus, in a May 2016 NW Labor Conference presentation, reported a Chinese funerary ceremony that also included local white Astoria authorities.

73 Alborn, "The Hindus of Uppertown," 13.

74 "Cremated by Hindoo Rites"; "Rauma Singh's Cremation."

75 Untitled article, *Astoria Daily Budget*, November 3, 1906, p. 6.

76 Regan Watjus presentation, March 14, 2015, Pacific Northwest Labor History Association Mini Conference, Astoria, Oregon.

77 Friday, *Organizing Asian American Labor*, 11; Leedom, *Astoria*, 68.

78 Leedom, *Astoria*, 68–69.

79 Friday, *Organizing Asian American Labor*, 2; Leedom, *Astoria*, 70–71.

80 Friday, *Organizing Asian American Labor*, 2, 15, 18, 56–57, 73–74.

81 Marconeri, "Chinese-Americans in Astoria, Oregon: 1880–1930," 34, citing the *Morning Oregonian*, September 10, 1918. By 1943, when exclusion was lifted, about a hundred Chinese Astorians remained, the last of their buildings demolished for a highway.

82 Friday, *Organizing Asian American Labor*, 2, 58; Leedom, *Astoria*, 70–71.

83 Friday, *Organizing Asian American Labor*, 18–19.

84 Their attackers believed the 1882 Exclusion Act had not effectively curbed Chinese immigration and consequently threatened "white" jobs. Friday, *Organizing Asian American Labor*, 26, 57–58; regarding the impact of the national campaign on Astoria, see Friday, *Organizing Asian American Labor*, 2–3, 18–19, 82–87; Pfaelzer, *Driven Out*.

85 See chapters 1 and 2 for a fuller discussion, drawing on Marie Rose Wong's *Sweet Cakes, Long Journey*, of northwestern Oregon's racial policy.

86 Friday, *Organizing Asian American Labor*, 58, citing *Weekly Astorian*, February 10, 1886, p. 4; "Regarding the Canneries," *Daily Morning Astorian*, February 11, 1886, p. 2.

87 Don McIntosh, "A Look Back: Astoria's Radical Immigrant Labor Past," *Northwest Labor Press*, April 1, 2015, https://nwlaborpress.org/2015/04/look-back-astorias-radical-immigrant-labor-past/; for more on their personal and work lives, see Friday, *Organizing Asian American Labor*, 55, 63, 67–68; Marconeri, "Chinese-Americans in Astoria," 34.

88 "Like Kan Yuen Low's noodles and Chop Suey on Bond Street," Advertisement, *Astoria Daily Budget*, April 11, 1906, p. 2.

89 Friday, *Organizing Asian-American Labor*, 59–63; Marconeri, "Chinese-Americans in Astoria," 31, 33–34, 36–37. In the wake of the 1882 Exclusion Act, the opera house constructed in 1883 closed and people moved to seats dubbed "China Heaven," high above the European American audience. Friday, *Organizing Asian American Labor*, 63.

90 Friday, *Organizing Asian American Labor*, 65–67; Marconeri, "Chinese-Americans in Astoria," 34.

91 Friday, *Organizing Asian American Labor*, 66, quoting the *Daily Astorian*. As discussed in chapter 2, Indian workers did not have a similar controlling labor hierarchy within their community.

92 Friday, *Organizing Asian American Labor*, 66–67.

93 Friday, *Organizing Asian American Labor*, 67. There was much political interaction between Indians and Chinese nationalists, particularly in San Francisco.

94 Friday, *Organizing Asian American Labor*, 57.

95 Friday, *Organizing Asian American Labor*, 57.

96 There are numerous articles. See, for example, "Chinese Exclusion: Astoria Central Labor Council Is in Favor of It," *Astoria Daily Budget*, April 10, 1906, p. 5; "A Whopper!! The People's Verdict Is that 'The Chinese Must Go!,'" *Astoria Daily Budget*, October 3, 1893, p. 1; "Do Not Delay: The Chinese Must Go beyond Any Question of Doubt," *Astoria Daily Budget*, October 4, 1893, p. 1; "Councilman Lewis' Reason," *Astoria Daily Budget*, March 7, 1894, p. 1; "Registration of Chinese," *Astoria Daily Budget*, January 9, 1894, p. 4; "Coolie Exclusion Act Signed by Roosevelt," *Astoria Daily Budget*, February 20, 1907; "Astoria Labor Council Petitions Astoria Water Commission and Public Library to Replace Chinese Janitors with White Men," *Astoria Daily Budget*, April 3,

1906, p. 6; "Citizens Complain about Nuisance of Gardens," *Astoria Daily Budget*, October 8, 1907, p. 2.

97 Friday, *Organizing Asian-American Labor*, 34.

98 The Chinese developed their own labor hierarchy of respect and earning potential, paralleling that of whites. Friday, *Organizing Asian American Labor*, 30–32.

99 Saxton, *Indispensable Enemy*, 74–77; Friday, *Organizing Asian American Labor*, 21. As noted in chapter 3, both historians argue that a distinction can be made between industries where employment of Asian laborers directly displaced Euro-Americans, and industries where Asian employment expanded opportunities for Euro-American laborers, especially in the upper tiers. Friday argues the latter was the case with the salmon canning industry.

100 In 1886, the Knights of Labor organized eighteen Astoria cannery owners to exclude Chinese workers. The agreement never held, and in the effort's wake, the town's Knights dwindled into insignificance. McIntosh, "A Look Back." Some years later, and seemingly without recognizing the irony, nearby cities that had expelled Chinese laborers petitioned Astoria employers to temporarily resupply them.

101 Friday, *Organizing Asian American Labor*, 58, quoting the *Weekly Astorian*.

102 Gordon, "Economic Phoenix," 600; "Hindu Alley Men Were Peaceable," *Daily Astorian*, Centennial 1873–1973, April 26, 1973, p. 9B.

103 Leedom, *Astoria*, 119.

104 Gordon, "Economic Phoenix."

105 Goings, "Red Harbor"; city council, 5, 10, 57, 120; newspapers, 5, 13, 44, 76, 101, 104, 106, 135, 220; boycotts, 158, 211–212, 226–227. Area towns were the site of violent encounters between mill owners and laborers.

106 Albert Johnson coauthored the 1924 Johnson Reed Act that banned Indian and most other non-European immigration for more than thirty years (see chapter 7). Goings, Barnes, and Snider, *The Red Coast*, 14, 77–85. See also, Henry, "Home Defender."

107 Leedom, *Astoria*, 119.

108 "Hindu Alley Men Were Peaceable," *Daily Astorian*, Centennial 1873–1973 April 26, 1973, p. 9B, claimed that Andrew Hammond recruited directly from India. However, Greg Gordon, author of *When Money Grew on Trees: A. B. Hammond and the Age of the Timber Baron* does not corroborate this, either in his writings or in response to this writer's inquiry.

109 Ancestry (searching for anyone born in India), 1910 US Census, https://www. ancestry.com/search/collections/7884/?birth=_india_5112&birth_x=_1-0&count=50&residence=_astoria-clatsop-oregon-usa_61799&residence_x=_1-1-a&fh=100&fsk=MDs5OTs1MA-61--61-; Leedom, *Astoria*, 119.

110 Ancestry (searching for anyone born in India), 1910 US Census.

111 Ancestry, 1910 US Census, searching "Khan." https://www.ancestry.com/search/collections/7884/?name=_khan&count=50&name_x=1_1&residence=_astoria-clatsop-oregon-usa_61799&residence_x=_1-1-a.

112 Untitled, *Astoria Daily Budget*, May 3, 1909, p. 6; Alborn, "The Hindus of Uppertown," 15.

113 Leedom, *Astoria*, 119.

114 Hummasti, *Finnish Radicals in Astoria*, 8–10.

115 Hummasti, *Finnish Radicals in Astoria*, 8–9, 17.

116 Friday, *Organizing Asian American Labor*, 68.

117 Goings, "Red Harbor," 163–168.

118 Hummasti, *Finnish Radicals in Astoria*, 12–14. My analysis of the effect of the Russian-Japanese war on Astoria Finns is based on reading the *Astoria Daily Budget*'s almost daily front page coverage of the conflict from roughly December 1904 through March of 1905. See, for example, *Astoria Daily Budget* January 4, 1905, p. 1, and January 23, 1905, p. 1. Regarding the global political impact of Japan's defeat of Russia, see Lake and Reynolds, *Drawing the Global Colour Line*, 2, 93, 163, 166–168; regarding its more specific effect on diasporic Indians, see Price, "'Orienting' the Empire"; Deol, *The Role of the Ghadar Party*, 26; Bose, *Indian Revolutionaries Abroad*, 7.

119 Goings, "Red Harbor," 175–177. Finns were one group categorized as "suspect whites" in the United States.

120 Goings, "Red Harbor," 178; Sohi, *Echoes of Mutiny*, 192.

121 Hummasti, *Finnish Radicals in Astoria*, 1, 3, 7; Goings, "Red Harbor," 28, 179–180.

122 Hummasti, *Finnish Radicals in Astoria*, 19–24.

123 The Finnish Socialist Federation defined itself as "foreign language organization[s] within the Socialist Party of America (SPA)." While affiliated with the national, English-speaking SPA, the Astoria SSK and other groups like it operated with a large degree of organizational autonomy. Hummasti, *Finnish Radicals in Astoria*, 35–37.

124 Astoria's Finnish socialists were sometimes called "fish captain" socialists, partly as a nod to their membership. For some, it was a comment on the politics advocated by Astoria's and other Finnish socialist locals; most were not firebrand revolutionaries. Much of the Astoria SSK's work to acclimate Finns into mainstream American life through providing language and citizenship lessons and by forming co-ops and other organizations to aid economic stability and success. Focused on the democratic process, they lobbied for legal protections and programs now often taken for granted, including unemployment insurance and benefits for injured workers and the aged, work that aided workers lives but did not challenge fundamental societal power relations. Still, federal and local government and police hounded socialists, legally and otherwise. This was even more pronounced during World War I and after the establishment of the Soviet republic. Nationally, many government officials and the public viewed socialist organizations and their members (often immigrants) as moral, political, and economic threats to US society. Several members of the Astoria SSK were sentenced to McNeil Island Penitentiary for inciting rebellion among US soldiers and sailors during World War I. However conservative they were judged, and despite acts of suppression, the men and women of Astoria's SSK contributed a socialist message of the unity of all working people in opposition to the nativists and xenophobes making headlines and wreaking havoc in the US West. Goings, "Red Harbor," 241; "The Finnish Socialists of Astoria, "A Look Back: Astoria's Radical Immigrant Labor Past," NW Labor Press.org, accessed January 24, 2023, https://nwlaborpress.org/2015/04/look-back-astorias-radical-immigrant-labor-past/.

125 Hummasti, *Finnish Radicals in Astoria*, 40, 50.

126 Hummasti, *Finnish Radicals in Astoria*, 41, 57.

127 Johnson, *They Are All Red Out Here*, 121–122.

128 Hummasti, *Finnish Radicals in Astoria*, 54; Johnson, *They Are All Red Out Here*, 122.

129 Hummasti, *Finnish Radicals in Astoria*, 44–46; Hummasti, "World War I and the Finns of Astoria," 334–349.

130 As Hummasti notes, "Possessed of such a hall, the ASSK was the center of Finnish social activity in Astoria for years to come." It became a major center of Finnish cultural activities—dances, language schools, orchestras, choirs, plays and the like. Further, it was the center of socialist educational activities in the form of classes and speakers. Hummasti, *Finnish Radicals in Astoria*, 70–74.

131 Goings, "Red Harbor," 181–183.

132 Goings, "Red Harbor," 182, 212–213.

133 Sawhney, *I Shall Never Ask for Pardon*, 109.

134 Sohan Pooni, interview with the author, January 2014, Surrey, BC.

135 Per the testimony of #43 from First Conspiracy Case as informally translated by Sohan Pooni for this author on March 18, 2017. Harnam Singh of Bridal Veil was reportedly ill and not in attendance.

136 Isemonger and Slattery, *An Account of the Ghadr Conspiracy*, xv. Sarabha, a Sikh UC Berkeley student, is consciously referencing the multiple religious traditions (Muslim, Hindu, Zoroastrian) among Ghadarites and recasting them within a revolutionary frame (namaz is Muslim; Sandhya and Rama Hindu, puja from Hinduism and Buddhism; Khuda is originally Zoroastrian).

137 Isemonger and Slattery, *An Account of the Ghadr Conspiracy*, 13. They report the chant as in Bengali, but the placards as being in English, and thus intended for the townspeople. While I am not certain that was the case, it makes sense the banners would be in English, especially given Munshi Ram's event notice to the townspeople just a few days prior.

138 *Astoria Daily Budget*, May 30, 1913, CCHS "Hindu" archive file.

139 Isemonger and Slattery, *An Account of the Ghadr Conspiracy*, 13.

140 Untitled, *Astoria Daily Budget*, June 2, 1913, p. 6.

141 "Hindu Scholar Coming," *Morning Astorian*, May 30, 1913, CCHS "Hindu" archive file.

142 Untitled, *Astoria Daily Budget*, June 3, 1913, p. 6; untitled, *Astoria Daily Budget*, June 2, 1913, p. 6; "British Rule Is Oppressive," *Astoria Daily Budget*, June 5, 1913, p. 2.

143 Untitled Editorial, *Morning Astorian*, June 7, 1913, p. 2.

144 "Troubles of India," *Weekly Astorian*, June 4, 1913, p. 5; "Conditions in India," *Weekly Astorian*, June 5, 1913, p. 5.

CHAPTER 5

1 Deol, *The Role of the Ghadar Party*, 56–57, 60. Puri, *Ghadar Movement*, 65–66; Gurpreet Singh, "Rebellious Rhymes," in *Interpreting Ghadar*, 34.

2 Josh, *Baba Sohan Singh Bhakna*, 27.

3 Josh, *Baba Sohan Singh Bhakna*, 28. The $2,000 (roughly $64,000 a century-plus later) came from laborers. Jensen, *Passage from India*, 183.

4   Tatla, "A Fateful Encounter?," 53.

5   Ramnath, *Haj to Utopia*, 37–38; Sohi, *Echoes of Mutiny*, 57, 59.

6   Ramnath, *Haj to Utopia*, 44.

7   Ramnath, *Haj to Utopia*, 37–38, 44; Sohi, *Echoes of Mutiny*, 59–60; Sohan Pooni, interview with the author, Surrey, BC, January 2014.

8   Harnam Singh, *Notes on the History of the Ghadar Party*, 12–15. as informally translated from Urdu for the author by Roomina Ahmed.

9   Thind arrived in Seattle, Washington, in July of 1913, and made his way to Astoria after Ghadar's founding (see chapter 7). https://bhagatsinghthind.com/wp-content/uploads/2023/03/British-Intelligence-on-the-Activities-of-Bhagat-Singh-Thind-1916-1925.pdf.

10 Sohi, *Echoes of Mutiny*, 57.

11 Ramnath, *Haj to Utopia*, 46, 64, 66, 95–96; Sohi, *Echoes of Mutiny*, 57, 82, 91, 98.

12 Ramnath, *Haj to Utopia*, 39–40.

13 Sohi, *Echoes of Mutiny*, 57. Vancouver, BC, was home to the first.

14 Puri, *Ghadar Movement*, 37, 53; Sohi, *Echoes of Mutiny*, 24–25; Deol, *The Role of the Ghadar Party*, 61.

15 Ramnath, *Haj to Utopia*, 39.

16 Ramnath, *Haj to Utopia*, 38–39.

17 Ramnath, *Haj to Utopia*, 39–40.

18 Ramnath, *Haj to Utopia*, 38–40. Reportedly, Kartar Singh Sarabha translated the Urdu editions into Gurmukhi. Singh, "Rebellious Rhymes," 31.

19 Ramnath, *Haj to Utopia*, 41–43.

20 Tatla, "A Sikh Manifesto?," 2; Sohi, *Echoes of Mutiny*, 60.

21 Ramnath, *Haj to Utopia*, 41, 43; Sohi, *Echoes of Mutiny*, 60.

22 Tatla, "A Sikh Manifesto?," 5, referencing Ramnath. Ramnath, *Haj to Utopia*, 41.

23 Shason, "Evolving Utopias."

24 Tatla, "A Sikh Manifesto?," 5.

25 Tatla, "A Sikh Manifesto?," 6.

26 Tatla, "A Sikh Manifesto?," 4.

27 Tatla, "A Sikh Manifesto?," 13.

28 Singh, "Rebellious Rhymes," 36.

29 Singh, 36, "Rebellious Rhymes," citing Rahi.

30 Singh, 37, "Rebellious Rhymes," citing Rahi.

31 Singh, 37, "Rebellious Rhymes," citing Rahi.

32 Tatla, "A Sikh Manifesto?," 14–16.

33 Tatla, "A Sikh Manifesto?," 15.

34 Tatla, "A Sikh Manifesto?," 17.

35 Shason, "Evolving Utopias," 90.

36 Shason, "Evolving Utopias," 90. Holi, known as a festival of love and unity, is celebrated across India. As Shason writes, "the soldiers are given the choice of adorning their hands with the . . . coloured-powder of the *holi* festival celebrations instead of soiling them with their own blood and the blood of foreign victims." Shason, "Evolving Utopias," 91.

37 Shason, "Evolving Utopias," 78, among many sources.

38 Ramnath, *Haj to Utopia*, 37, 41, 43.

39 Ramnath, *Haj to Utopia*, 36.

40 Hochschild, *American Midnight*.

41 Sohi, *Echoes of Mutiny*, 88.

42 Sohi, *Echoes of Mutiny*, 82–83. Sohi documents a convergence of British and US interests. Historian Joan Jensen leans more toward viewing US government anti-Ghadar actions as the result of pressure by the British on US officials, which certainly did occur. Jensen, "The 'Hindu Conspiracy.'"

43 Puri, *Ghadar Movement*, 75. Besides banning so-called idiots and imbeciles, the 1907 law (amended in 1910) prohibited the immigration of "persons who have been convicted of or admit having committed a felony or other crime or misdemeanor involving moral turpitude; polygamists, or persons who admit their belief in the practice of polygamy, anarchists, or persons who believe in or advocate the overthrow by force or violence of the Government of the United States, or of all government, or of all forms of law, or the assassination of public officials; persons coming for immoral purposes," Immigration Act of 1907, 34 Stat. 898, (1907), http://www.historycentral.com/documents/immigrationact.html.

44 Shason, "Evolving Utopias," 89.

45 "Slaughter Urged by Dyal," *Morning Oregonian*, November 27, 1916, p. 2, https://oregonnews.uoregon.edu/lccn/sn83025138/1916-11-27/ed-1/seq-2/.

46 Puri, *Ghadar Movement*, 83.

47 Ramnath, *Haj to Utopia*, 47; Sohi, *Echoes of Mutiny*, 100.

48 Ramnath, *Haj to Utopia*, 47.

49 Puri, *Ghadar Movement*, 68, 148.

50 Ramnath, *Haj to Utopia*, 71–72.

51 Puri, *Ghadar Movement*, 150.

52 Ramnath, *Haj to Utopia*, 70–71, 89; Hochschild, *American Midnight*, 2; Sohi, *Echoes of Mutiny*, 196–197.

53 Isemonger and Slattery, *An Account of the Ghadr Conspiracy*, x.

54 Sohi, *Echoes of Mutiny*, 153; Kazimi, *Undesirables*, 133. Gajendra Singh puts the troop count at 1.7 million. Singh, "India and the Great War," 343.

55 "World War I," Mahatma Gandhi's Writings, Philosophy, Audio, Video, and Photographs, accessed July 13, 2020, https://www.mkgandhi.org/biography/wrldwar1.htm#:~:text=World%20War%20I%20When%20World%20War%20I%20broke,his%20Indian%20friends%20to%20raise%20an%20ambulance%20unit.

56 Anu Kumar, "100 Years On, Remembering the Hindu-German Conspiracy to Violently Overthrow the British Raj," *Scroll.In*, April 10, 2018, https://scroll.in/magazine/870835/100-years-on-remembering-the-hindu-german-conspiracy-to-violently-overthrow-the-british-raj, referenced December 5, 2020.

57 Sohi, *Echoes of Mutiny*, 68–69, 73: "Rai always stipulated that, in fighting on behalf of the empire, Indians were fighting for their own freedom. He expected that Indian military service would ensure that their interests could not be ignored once the war was over." Rai was partly trying to counter British influence on US authorities and demonstrate Indians' abilities, a stance that complicated his relationship with many Ghadris. Postwar Rai reassessed his position. Rai's colleague and friend, W. E. B DuBois, also argued that World War I was a time for African Americans to prove their worth and urged enlistment, a position he also came to regret. (Marcus Garvey opposed what he called the "white man's war.") There were other complicating issues. President Wilson promoted the United States as a change agent for colonized peoples. Indians in the United States also had to tread carefully about criticizing an American ally—the British—at a time of war. For more on Lajpat Rai, see Puri, "Lajpat Rai in USA

1914–1919," in *Lala Lajpat Rai in Retrospect*, 65–80, https://theprg.files.
wordpress.com/2009/07/puri-lala-lajpat-rai.pdf.

58 "Transcript from Enlisted Record for Bhagat Singh Thind," July 1918, *South Asian American Digital Archive*, https://www.saada.org/item/20160807-4603.

59 "Letter from Bhagat Singh Thind to His Father," December 21, 1914, *South Asian American Digital Archive*, https://www.saada.org/item/20110805-280.

60 Puri, *Ghadar Movement*, 76–81. There is debate as to whether Gurdit Singh chartered the ship in order to test the Continuous Journey provision or whether it was, as he publicly claimed, simply a business venture that utilized passenger fares to offset the cost of shipping goods.

61 Puri, *Ghadar Movement*, 27–30, 77. For an extended meditation on the *Komagata Maru*, see Ali Kazimi's film, *Continuous Journey* (Peripheral Visions, 2004), and his book, *Undesirables: White Canada and the Komagata Maru, An Illustrated History*.

62 Sohi, *Echoes of Mutiny*, 134, 143–144, 149; Ramnath, *Haj to Utopia*, 49.

63 British Columbia was the only province in Canada with a significant population of Indians, and both the populace and its politicians often felt that the country's central government in Ottawa did not adequately understand or sympathize.

64 Sohi, *Echoes of Mutiny*, 134–144; Kazimi, *Undesirables*, 123–130.

65 Sohi, *Echoes of Mutiny*, 108.

66 Sohi, *Echoes of Mutiny*, 112, 139, 144, 149.

67 Sohi, *Echoes of Mutiny*, 110–117.

68 Sohi, *Echoes of Mutiny*, 149.

69 Gurpreet Singh, "Rebellious Rhymes," 38.

70 Ramnath, *Haj to Utopia*, 48–49; Sohi, *Echoes of Mutiny*, 149–150; see Isemonger and Slattery, *An Account of the Ghadr Conspiracy*, 46–47, for possible details on this work.

71 Puri, *Ghadar Movement*, 80.

72 Isemonger and Slattery, *An Account of the Ghadr Conspiracy*, 59.

73 Isemonger and Slattery, *An Account of the Ghadr Conspiracy*, 53.

74 Puri, *Ghadar Movement*, 80; Sohi, *Echoes of Mutiny*, 145–146.

75 Isemonger and Slattery, *An Account of the Ghadr Conspiracy*, 58. Khalsa Diwan Societies were Sikh organizations, usually associated with *gurdwaras*, with a history in both British Columbia and the United States of advocating for Indian rights, including for non-Sikhs. In the early twentieth century, it was an important organization advocating for immigrants in North America.

76 Puri, *Ghadar Movement*, 81, quoting *Ghadr*.

77 Isemonger and Slattery, *An Account of the Ghadr Conspiracy*, 48; Ramnath, *Haj to Utopia*, 49–50.

78 Ramnath, *Haj to Utopia*, 49.

79 "Local News of the Lower Columbia District, *Astoria Daily Budget*, August 6, 1914, p. 6.

80 Isemonger and Slattery, *An Account of the Ghadr Conspiracy*, 54.

81 Isemonger and Slattery, *An Account of the Ghadr Conspiracy*, 57.

82 Sohi, *Echoes of Mutiny*, 146.

83 Puri, *Ghadar Movement*, 85; Ramnath, in *Haj to Utopia* (51), also writes that the eight thousand represented some two-thirds of Ghadar's overseas membership; Sohi, *Echoes of Mutiny*, 153.

84 Ramnath, *Haj to Utopia*, 50.

85 Sohi, *Echoes of Mutiny*, 150.

86 Ramnath, *Haj to Utopia*, 5.

87 Ramnath, *Haj to Utopia*, 35, 45–46.

88 Ramnath, *Haj to Utopia*, 72–73.

89 Ramnath, *Haj to Utopia*, 73; Sohi, *Echoes of Mutiny*, 100, 183.

90 Ramnath, *Haj to Utopia*, 2–5.

91 Puri, *Ghadar Movement*, 83.

92 Ramnath, *Haj to Utopia*, 72–73.

93 Ramnath, *Haj to Utopia*, 71. What, for example, are the political implications on supporting people in Germany's colonies?

94 Sohi, *Echoes of Mutiny*, 166–167.

95 Ramnath, *Haj to Utopia*, 75.

96 Ramnath, *Haj to Utopia*, 73, 75; Sohi, *Echoes of Mutiny*, 154.

97 Ramnath, *Haj to Utopia*, 74.

98 See chapter 6.

99 Sohi, *Echoes of Mutiny*, 153.

100 See chapter 6.

101 Puri, *Ghadar Movement*, 3.

102 Puri, *Ghadar Movement*, 85. Puri's project in *Ghadar Ideology* is to critique Ghadar from the standpoint of organization and ideology versus ascribing their defeat to "the spy killed it." Puri, *Ghadar Movement*, 5.

103 "Indians: Do Not Lose the Opportunity," was the July 27, 1914, *Ghadr* headline. Puri, *Ghadar Movement*, 82, 150–151.

104 Ramnath, *Haj to Utopia*, 62.

105 Sohi, *Echoes of Mutiny*, 101.

106 Bhakna actually had two widowed mothers, both of whom were involved in his life. His father married again after his first wife was unable to bear children and provide an heir for the family property. Josh, *Baba Sohan Singh Bhakna*, xii–xiii, 1–2, 11–13; Singh, "Sohan Singh Bhakna," 194, 198.

107 Josh, *Baba Sohan Singh Bhakna*, 11.

108 Sohi, *Echoes of Mutiny*, 54–55; Puri, *Ghadar Movement*, 57.

109 Josh, *Baba Sohan Singh Bhakna*, 18; Ogden, "Ghadar, Historical Silences, and Notions of Belonging," 183–184.

110 Shason, "Evolving Utopias," 61, citing Bajaj.

111 Josh, *Baba Sohan Singh Bhakna*, xxi.

112 Shason, "Evolving Utopias," 61.

113 Sohi, *Echoes of Mutiny*, 18–19.

114 David Thind, interview by the author, December 4 and 5, 2015, on his father's intent to become a US citizen upon leaving India. Ogden, "The Telling Case of Dr. Bhagat Singh Thind," 9–10, 25–26, 29.

115 Ralph Waldo Emerson, "Self Reliance," in *Essays: First Series* (1841), accessed April 11, 2021, https://emersoncentral.com/texts/essays-first-series/self-reliance/.

116 Amritsar is home to Sikhism's most sacred shrine. Washington marriage license 34346 (Spokane, WA, December 22, 1923), Ancestry.com Washington Marriage Records, 1854–2013, accessed June 13, 2017, http://search.ancestry.com/cgi-bin/sse.dll?_phsrc=yeA2&_phstart=successSource&usePUBJs=true&gl=34&gsfn=Bhagat%20Singh&gsln=Thind&gss=angs-g&so=2. Judge Wolverton's Memo of October 18, 1920, in Thind's Oregon citizenship case gives his arrival date as July

4, 1913. In 1919, the Department of Labor Immigration Service issued a certificate dating Thind's arrival in Seattle aboard the *Minnesota* as June 24, 1913. Either date places him in the United States after Ghadar's Astoria founding.

117 Bhagat Singh Thind, "Life at Hindoo Alley (Astoria, Oregon)," accessed February 25, 2023, https://bhagatsinghthind.com/about/life-at-hindoo-alley-astoria-oregon/. While this resource was useful and informative, I cross-referenced information from the family website with other sources.

118 Bhagat Singh Thind, "Family in India," accessed February 25, 2023, https://bhagatsinghthind.com/about/family-in-india/.

119 Thind, "Life at Hindoo Alley (Astoria, Oregon)"; Sohi, *Echoes of Mutiny*, 108–109. Thind's time in the Philippines was not simply a means for financing a long and costly trip, but also an attempt to defeat US immigration officers in San Francisco and Seattle who declined Indians on numerous pretexts. Indians argued that by entering the Philippines, they had entered US territory and should therefore pass unmolested into the continental United States. US immigration officers excluded many who pursued this route, but not Bhagat Singh Thind.

120 "Letter from Bhagat Singh Thind to His Father," December 21, 1914, South Asian American Digital Archive, https://www.saada.org/item/20110805-280.

121 For more on Thind's beliefs and life post-verdict, see Ogden, "The Telling Case of Bhagat Singh Thind."

122 Sohi, *Echoes of Mutiny*, 2–4.

CHAPTER 6

1 Sohi, *Echoes of Mutiny*, 181–182, 186–187.

2 Sohi, *Echoes of Mutiny*, 164.

3 Sohi, *Echoes of Mutiny*, 162.

4 Sohi, *Echoes of Mutiny*, 154.

5 Many entered India by way of unanticipated routes to elude authorities. Puri, *Ghadar Movement*, 84.

6 Sohi, *Echoes of Mutiny*, 171–172; Puri, *Ghadar Movement*, 85.

7 Puri's and Ramnath's work analyze Ghadar's organizational and ideological strengths and weaknesses, including how much men changed from their overseas sojourn. Their full analysis is outside the scope of this manuscript, but provides a more nuanced answer to Ghadar's immediate defeat beyond, as Puri puts it, "the spy wrecked it." Puri, *Ghadar Movement*, 5.

8 Puri, *Ghadar Movement*, 62.

9 Sohan Singh Bhakna quoted in Sohi, *Echoes of Mutiny*, 159.

10 Puri, *Ghadar Movement*, 85; Sohi, *Echoes of Mutiny*, 171.

11 Puri, *Ghadar Movement*, 86, 158; Sohi, *Echoes of Mutiny*, 158, 160, 181–182; Gurpreet Singh writes, "People like Sarabha ensured that nobody participated in these acts for personal benefits." Singh, "Rebellious Rhymes," in *Interpreting Ghadar*, 39.

12 Puri, *Ghadar Movement*, 154–155.

13 Puri, *Ghadar Movement*, 86–87, 156; Sohi, *Echoes of Mutiny*, 158–159.

14 Sohi, *Echoes of Mutiny*, 162; Puri, *Ghadar Movement*, 94.

15 Sohi, *Echoes of Mutiny*, 162–163.

16 Singh, "India and the Great War," 352.

17 Sohi, *Echoes of Mutiny*, 162; Ramnath, *Haj to Utopia*, 192. The participation of Japanese troops is important, given many Indian revolutionaries hoped for a Pan-Asian unity, and that Japan would counter Western colonial powers, especially after Japan's 1905 defeat of Russia.

18 Sohi, *Echoes of Mutiny*, 162–163.

19 Gurpreet Singh, "Rebellious Rhymes," 39.

20 Gajendra Singh, "India and the Great War," 350.

21 It had already been postponed from November. Puri, *Ghadar Movement*, 154; Sohi, *Echoes of Mutiny*, 163.

22 Sohi, *Echoes of Mutiny*, 163.

23 Bose attempted to assassinate Viceroy Hardinge a few years earlier. Sohi, *Echoes of Mutiny*, 164.

24 Sohi, *Echoes of Mutiny*, 160, 178.

25 Sohi, *Echoes of Mutiny*, 159, 180–181, 208.

26 Sohi, *Echoes of Mutiny*, 182.

27 Puri, *Ghadar Movement*, 167.

28 Puri, *Ghadar Movement*, 88.

29 Gajendra Singh, "India and the Great War," 343–344.

30 Gajendra Singh, "India and the Great War," 343.

31 Gajendra Singh, "India and the Great War," 344, 351. Sohi, *Echoes of Mutiny*, 166.

32 Gajendra Singh, "India and the Great War," 352.

33 Gajendra Singh, "India and the Great War," 352.

34 Gajendra Singh, "India and the Great War," 352–353.

35 Sohi, *Echoes of Mutiny*, 173; Gajendra Singh, "India and the Great War," 344–345. Gajendra Singh argues, "Colonial officials were unable to react to the demands of moderate nationalists after the First World War, because they were haunted by the specter of what had occurred during the conflict. . . . The years were remarkable for the array of revolutionary conspiracies that threatened British rule. The movements were small in comparison to Congress but were imbued with a startling dynamism and scope," 345.

36 Sohi, *Echoes of Mutiny*, 173.

37 Dignan, "The Hindu Conspiracy," 60, 75. Rai supported a peaceful transfer of power to Indian self-rule, even arguing that such change represented Britain's best defense against the global rising tide of Bolshevism and its Indian adherents, former Ghadris among them. Sohi, *Echoes of Mutiny*, 199.

38 Sohi, *Echoes of Mutiny*, 205–206. In 1931, young Bhagat Singh (not to be confused with American Bhagat Singh Thind) was executed for attempting to avenge Scott's murder of Rai. Explicitly inspired by the Ghadris before him, and with widespread public support, Bhagat Singh transformed his trial into an indictment of British rule and a call for Indians' need for revolution.

39 The Immigration Act of 1917, also known as the Asiatic Barred Zone, was passed on February 5, 1917. Kritika Agarwal "Shadows of the Past: Trump's Executive Order on Immigration and the Asiatic Barred Zone," South Asian American Digital Archive, February 5, 2017, https://www.saada.org/tides/article/shadows-of-the-past.

40 Ngai, *Impossible Subjects*, 42; Salyer, "Baptism by Fire," 851.

41 Hochschild, *American Midnight*, 60–61.

42 Hochschild, *American Midnight*, 3, 137–139, 230, 243–244.

43 Sohi, *Echoes of Mutiny*, 3.

44 Sohi, *Echoes of Mutiny*, 101, 197.

45 Ngai, *Impossible Subjects,* 18.

46 Sohi, *Echoes of Mutiny,* 88–89. British consular records contain numerous references to Indo-American citizenship and to Taraknath Das in particular. See, for example, National Archives Public Record Office (NA): FO 371/2154, General Correspondence from 1906–1966, United States, 1914, nos. 9404-09; NA: FO 371/359, General Correspondence from 1906–1966, United States, 1907, no. 2130; NA: FO 371/1547, General Correspondence from 1906–1966, United States, 1912, nos. 7964-66.

47 Sohi, *Echoes of Mutiny,* 90–93; Puri, *Ghadar Movement,* 75.

48 Hess, "The 'Hindu' in America," 61, 65; Ngai, *Impossible Subjects,* 41, wherein she writes that US Attorney General Charles Bonaparte instructed court clerks to refuse Japanese citizenship petitions. Despite these instructions, during the 1900s and 1910s, several hundred Japanese and South Asian Indians became naturalized citizens.

49 Ngai, *Impossible Subjects,* 41.

50 Hess, "The 'Hindu' in America," 61; Dignan, "The Hindu Conspiracy," 60. The impact of western nativists on US immigration officials and policy began with Chinese immigration.

51 Coulson, *Race, Nation, and Refuge,* 54.

52 Jensen, "The 'Hindu Conspiracy,'" 74; Ramnath, *Haj to Utopia,* 89.

53 Plowman, "The British Intelligence Station in San Francisco," 1.

54 Jensen, "The 'Hindu Conspiracy,'" 73.

55 Sohi, *Echoes of Mutiny,* 167. The *Annie Larsen,* having missed all connections and fully loaded with weapons, ultimately docked in Aberdeen, Washington. A second scheme to run weapons through Siam and Burma was coordinated out of New York and Chicago, and similarly never materialized except as fodder for the German-Indian conspiracy. Sohi, *Echoes of Mutiny,* 169.

56 Plowman, "The British Intelligence Station in San Francisco," 12.

57 Hochschild, *American Midnight,* 7.

58 Jensen, "The 'Hindu Conspiracy,'" 67–68.

59 Jensen, "The 'Hindu Conspiracy,'" 74.

60 Jensen, "The 'Hindu Conspiracy,'" 74–75.

61 Jensen, "The 'Hindu Conspiracy,'" 75.

62 Jensen, "The 'Hindu Conspiracy,'" 76.

63 This involved German actions to disrupt American war production or, as the article wrote, "conspiracies to blow up ammunition plants and ships and for the steamship Sacramento coaling case," "Consul of Germany and His Aid [*sic*] Indicted," *New York Times,* February 19, 1916, p. 1, https://www.nytimes.com/1916/02/09/archives/consul-of-germany-and-his-aid-indicted-franz-bopp-and-baron-schack.html.

64 Jensen, "The 'Hindu Conspiracy,'" 73–74.

65 "Judge Hunt to Hear Bopp Case," *San Francisco Examiner,* November 14, 1916, p. 3.

66 Dignan, "The Hindu Conspiracy," 73.

67 Sohi, *Echoes of Mutiny,* 184–185.

68 Jensen, "The 'Hindu Conspiracy,'" 79; President Wilson's April 2, 1917, speech to Congress seeking a declaration of war, US President, "Making the World 'Safe for Democracy,'" 65th Cong., 1st sess., 1917, S. Doc. 5, https://historymatters.gmu.edu/d/4943/.

69 Sohi, *Echoes of Mutiny*, 184.

70 Plowman, "The British Intelligence Station in San Francisco," 9.

71 Jensen, "The 'Hindu Conspiracy,'" 79–80.

72 Jensen, "The 'Hindu Conspiracy,'" 80.

73 Jensen, "The 'Hindu Conspiracy,'" 80; Sohi, *Echoes of Mutiny*, 184.

74 Gajendra Singh, "India and the Great War," 352–353.

75 Dignan, "The Hindu Conspiracy," 57.

76 Sohi, *Echoes of Mutiny*, 185.

77 Jensen, "The 'Hindu Conspiracy,'" 80–82.

78 Sohi, *Echoes of Mutiny*, 190.

79 Jensen, "The 'Hindu Conspiracy,'" 81–82.

80 Hochschild, *American Midnight*, 159–160; Sohi, *Echoes of Mutiny*, 192.

81 Ramnath, *Haj to Utopia*, 91–92; Sohi, *Echoes of Mutiny*, 186, 189, 195. I am indebted to Sohi's entire explication of this trial, especially pages 186–197.

82 Plowman, "The British Intelligence Station in San Francisco," 7.

83 Plowman, "The British Intelligence Station in San Francisco," 4, 8–12.

84 Forty-two had been indicted but only twenty-nine stood trial. The remainder fled to countries outside US or British reach, including a number who escaped to Mexico. Sohi, *Echoes of Mutiny*, 186.

85 "Von Brincken Pleads Guilty in Hindoo Plot," *San Francisco Chronicle*, December 6, 1917, pp. 1, 3.

86 Ramnath, *Haj to Utopia*, 92; Sohi, *Echoes of Mutiny*, 186–188.

87 Sohi, *Echoes of Mutiny*, 187.

88 Sohi, *Echoes of Mutiny*, 192.

89 Sohi, *Echoes of Mutiny*, 187. Dayal was in Europe, not on trial.

90 Sohi, *Echoes of Mutiny*, 192, 204.

91 Sohi, *Echoes of Mutiny*, 190. Chakravarty appealed to that parallel directly, but was not the only or first to do so. T. Das sounded the same theme in his *Oregonian* editorial in the midst of the St. Johns riot trials (chapter 3) and in his citizenship case.

92 Sohi, *Echoes of Mutiny*, 191.

93 Sohi, *Echoes of Mutiny*, 191.

94 Ramnath, *Haj to Utopia*, 94; Sohi, *Echoes of Mutiny*, 194.

95 "Two Hindus Slain in Federal Court," *New York Times*, April 24, 1918, p. 1.

96 Plowman, "The British Intelligence Station in San Francisco," 13.

CHAPTER 7

1 Sohi, *Echoes of Mutiny*, 68; Jensen, "The 'Hindu Conspiracy,'" 76.

2 Declaration of Intention of Citizenship, January 17, 1917, Ancestry.com, https://www.ancestry.com/discoveryui-content/view/46211:2530?tid=&pid=&queryId=db93c2d60402b9a2d5c00e4b52e5f45b&_phsrc=axs280&_phstart=successSource. For more on Thind and his wife Chint Kaur, see Ogden, "The Telling Case of Dr. Bhagat Singh Thind," 10, 23–24. Most Indian men left their wives at home, given the expense of travel, the hardships, and proscriptions against women's entrance into North America. Bhagat's son, David Thind, reported that upon leaving India Bhagat never intended to return, and his father

knew this, citing the four "nevers" instructions from his father, directing his son to never beg or borrow, commit adultery, smoke or partake of any intoxicating drinks or drugs, and to never live in the past. David Thind, interview with author, December 4 and 5, 2015.

3 Kritika Agarwal, "Shadows of the Past: Trump's Executive Order on Immigration and the Asiatic Barred Zone," South Asian American Digital Archive, February 5, 2017, https://www.saada.org/tides/article/shadows-of-the-past.

4 Sohi, *Echoes of Mutiny*, 3.

5 David Thind, interview with author, December 4 and 5, 2015.

6 Sohi, *Echoes of Mutiny*, 174.

7 de la Garza, *Doctorji*, 14, referencing British surveillance records formerly posted on the Thind family website: "British Intelligence Files," Dr. Bhagat Singh Thind website, accessed February 23, 2023, https://bhagatsinghthind.com/%20about/british-intelligence-files/#.

8 "Transcript from Enlisted Record for Bhagat Singh Thind," July 22, 1918, South Asian American Digital Archive, https://www.saada.org/item/20160807-4603; "All U.S., Veterans Administration Master Index, 1917–1940, Results for Singh," accessed March 11, 2023, https://www.ancestry.com/search/collections/61861/?name=_singh&count=50&residence=_oregon-usa_40; https://www.ancestry.com/search/collections/61861/?name=_khan&count=50. Not all "Khans" can be assumed to be from India.

9 "Young India (October 1918)," South Asian American Digital Archive, accessed February 23, 2023, https://www.saada.org/item/20110923-378.

10 "Petitioner's Ex. 2, Memorandum from 1st Lt. Walter A. Grayson," United States v. Bhagat Singh Thind, 21-USDC, Box 3299, Portland Civil, Criminal and Admin Case Files, 1911–1922, Folder 9341, NARA Sand Point, WA.

11 "Petitioner's Ex. 4, letter from President of the Examining Board," January 18, 1913, *Thind*.

12 Hochschild, *American Midnight*, 32; Sohi, *Echoes of Mutiny*, 6, 66, 102–103, 200.

13 Hochschild, *American Midnight*, 74.

14 Hochschild, *American Midnight*, 96–102.

15 Hochschild, *American Midnight*, 82.

16 Hochschild, *American Midnight*, 60–61.

17 Hochschild, *American Midnight*, 60–61.

18 Hochschild, *American Midnight*, 85.

19 Salyer, "Baptism by Fire," 851.

20 Salyer, "Baptism by Fire," 852.

21 Ngai, *Impossible Subjects*, 42; Salyer, "Baptism by Fire," 850–851.

22 Salyer, "Baptism by Fire," 852–853.

23 Salyer, "Baptism by Fire," 853.

24 Ngai, *Impossible Subjects*, 42 n73.

25 "Oregon Petition for Citizenship, May 6, 1919," Ancestry.com, https://www.ancestry.com/discoveryui-content/view/65850:2530?tid=&pid=&queryId=6e00bb6dab5b9ad543abbf55dcd82208&_phsrc=axs292&_phstart=successSource.

26 Gajendra Singh, "India and the Great War," 352; Ngai, *Impossible Subjects*, 42; Salyer, "Baptism by Fire," 848, 861–862. "But although Indian soldiers were to be differentiated from the majority of the colonized populace because of the near-European qualities, sipahis remained almost but not quite white."

27 Salyer, "Baptism by Fire," 854.

28 Salyer, "Baptism by Fire," 861.
29 Salyer, "Baptism by Fire," 864.
30 Salyer, "Baptism by Fire," 854, 856, 858, 861.
31 A month later, Bureau of Naturalization Commissioner Crist issued a memo confirming Asian servicemen were entitled to citizenship per the act. Subsequently, agents could advocate against naturalizations in courtrooms, but could not invoke the act. With the act now moot, courts returned to determining petitioners' racial eligibility per Section 2169 of the Revised Statute. Salyer, "Baptism by Fire," 861.
32 "Oregon Petition for Citizenship, May 6, 1919," Ancestry.com.
33 Wong, *Sweet Cakes, Long Journey*, 115, 141, 143–144. See chapters 2 and 3 regarding the prosecution of anti-Indian vigilantes.
34 Helquist, *Marie Equi*, 181.
35 Helquist, *Marie Equi*, 143, 153, 156, 160.
36 "Oregon Petition for Citizenship, May 6, 1919," Ancestry.com.
37 For more on Mannix, see "Manuscripts, Detectives Reports on Thomas Mannix," MSS 1073; Oregon Historical Society Research Library; "Death Ends Career of Thomas Mannix," *Morning Oregonian*, March 16, 1932, Vertical file: Biography "'M' Folder," Oregon Historical Society Research Library.
38 Salyer, "Baptism by Fire," 861.
39 Wong, *Sweet Cakes, Long Journey*, 145. In an earlier case, Wolverton ruled a Syrian applicant was a "free white person," and thus eligible for citizenship, a decision upheld by SCOTUS. Coulson, *Race, Nation, and Refuge*, 58.
40 "Judge Wolverton's Opinion," United States v. Bhagat Singh Thind, U.S. Supreme Court Transcript of Record with Supporting Pleadings, MOML US Supreme Court Records and Briefs, 1832–1978, np; Haney López, *White by Law*, 61–62.
41 Coulson, *Race, Nation, and Refuge*, 57.
42 Judge's Memo at, 2, *Thind*.
43 "Petitioner's Ex. 3, LLLL membership card," *Thind*, 21-USDC, Box 3299, Portland Civil, Criminal and Admin Case Files, 1911–1922, Folder 9341, NARA Sand Point, WA. Seattle march details previously available at http://www.bhagatsinghthind.com/brit_intel.php, accessed March 15, 2015.
44 Haney López, *White by Law*, 5, 35–55. Haney López argues that courts' differing rulings arose from using science (as it were) or "common knowledge" in deciding what constituted whiteness. Doug Coulson argues that the commonsense language is always a court's guide. He argues that in *Thind*, British imperial politics intervened and upended the "common knowledge" of whiteness from *Ozawa* to *Thind*. Coulson, *Race, Nation, and Refuge*, 45–88.
45 "Judge Wolverton's Memo" at 3, *Thind*.
46 "Certificate from U.S. Circuit Court of Appeals for the Ninth Circuit," MOML US Supreme Court Records and Briefs, 1832–1978, np.
47 "Lester W. Humphreys' Bill of Complaint in Equity with Affidavit Exhibit of V.W. Tomlinson, Naturalization Examiner," January 8, 1921, *Thind*.
48 Judge Wolverton's March 28, 1921, Order, *Thind*.
49 Helquist, *Marie Equi*, 163.
50 Helquist, *Marie Equi*, 176.
51 Helquist, *Marie Equi*, 171, 204–205; United States Department of the Interior, National Park Service, *National Register of Historic Places Continuation Sheet*, sec. 8, pp. 6–7, accessed March 8, 2023, https://npgallery.nps.gov/GetAsset/f26eacc5-4c66-4f71-b8b9-b84f0bcaae19.

52 Hochschild, *American Midnight*, 52–53, 60.

53 Hochschild, *American Midnight*, 84.

54 Hochschild, *American Midnight*, 96–97; Helquist, *Marie Equi*, 143.

55 Hochschild, *American Midnight*, 53, 82–84, 96–97.

56 *Sunday Oregonian*, February 6, 1921, sec. 3, p. 43, and *Morning Oregonian*, January 31, 1921, p. 1. The Democratic Party supported slavery.

57 *Sunday Oregonian*, July 13, 1919, p. 14. Like attorney Mannix, Humphreys died relatively young in 1929, while on a fishing trip, suspected to have been murdered by a jealous law partner.

58 "Legion Would Ban All Immigrants," *Morning Oregonian*, September 19, 1919, p. 6.

59 Published by the *Portland Telegram*, on August 2, 1921, one day after the photographed gathering, "KKK Meets with Oregon Leaders, 1921," Oregon History Project, https://www.oregonhistoryproject.org/articles/historical-records/kkk-meets-with-portland-leaders-1921/#.ZAp_9kPMJPZ.

60 "KKK in Oregon," Oregon History Project, accessed April 23, 2023, http://oregonhistoryproject.org/articles/historical-records/portland-kkk/#.VgMKD8tViko.

61 "Haney Quits Post as U.S. Attorney," *Morning Oregonian*, October 29, 1919, p. 16; "Old Friend Is On Job," *Morning Oregonian*, October 31, 1919, p. 17; "Haney Quits as US Attorney for Oregon," *East Oregonian*, October 28, 1919, p. 1.

62 "Lester W. Humphreys' Bill of Complaint in Equity," January 8, 1921, *Thind*.

63 Ngai, *Impossible Subjects*, 41.

64 Smith, "Race, Nationality, and Reality," 1.

65 Smith, "Race, Nationality, and Reality," 1.

66 "All Citizenship Records for Singh," Ancestry.com, accessed March 15, 2023, https://www.ancestry.com/search/categories/img_citizenship/?name=_singh&event=1915&count=50&keyword=naturalization+petition&name_x=_1. One of those cases was for Rakha Singh Gherwal of Linnton, noted above. Gherwal also enlisted in the US military, sought citizenship after his discharge, and, like Thind, became a spiritual teacher. He was not, to this writer's knowledge, associated with Ghadar.

67 Appellate Judge William Ball Gilbert, a former state representative and longtime Oregon attorney who taught at area law schools, was arguably familiar with Western Oregon's racial policy, given the prominence of Justice Deady. Senior member and San Francisco–based Judge William W. Morrow was involved in the watershed *Wong Kim Ark* case, ruling that children born in the United States to Chinese nationals were citizens. Besides his role in *Bopp*, Judge William Henry Hunt, the court's newest member, a Montana practitioner and governor of Puerto Rico, was intimately familiar with the politics of colonial possessions. "Federal Judicial History," Federal Judicial Center, accessed December 15, 2020, https://www.fjc.gov/history.

68 Per the *Examiner*, Hunt's reassignment was because the district court docket and judges were overscheduled. Plowman, "The British Intelligence Station in San Francisco," 6; "Judge Hunt to Hear Bopp Case," *San Francisco Examiner*, November 14, 1916, p. 3; "Three Selected to Try German Officers," *San Francisco Call*, December 4, 1916, https://cdnc.ucr.edu/?a=d&d=SFC19161204.2.11&e=-en-20-1-txt-txIN-1. See chapter 6 for more on *Bopp*.

69 Section 2169, Revised Statutes, provides that the provisions of the Naturalization Act "shall apply to aliens, being free white persons, and to aliens of African

nativity and to persons of African descent." Smith, "Race, Nationality, and Reality," 2.

70 The 1857 *Dred Scott v. Sandford* case held that no person of African ancestry could claim US citizenship. In 1896 *Plessy v. Ferguson* enshrined racial segregation through its "separate but equal" standard; overturned in law, if not in life, by the 1954 case *Brown v. Board of Education*. The 2013 *Shelby County v. Holder* case gutted key provisions of the Voting Rights Act, the opening gambit in America's Black voter suppression efforts. "Landmark United States Supreme Court Cases," American Bar Association, accessed June 7, 2023, https://www. americanbar.org/groups/public_education/programs/constitution_day/ landmark-cases/; "Shelby County v. Holder," Cornell Law School, accessed June 7, 2023, https://www.law.cornell.edu/supct/cert/12-96.

71 Hess, "The 'Hindu' in America," 41; Sohi, *Echoes of Mutiny*, 88–89, 191. Sohi's entire book is a comprehensive exploration of the US government's interest in targeting Indian activists and US government collusion with British authorities.

72 I am indebted to Doug Coulson's argument on this point. His book, generous conversations and correspondence significantly changed my thinking regarding the connection of Ghadar and *Thind*. Coulson, *Race, Nation, and Refuge*, 45–88. I would also acknowledge Haney López's brief but encouraging correspondence to pursue these linkages. While Thind continued to support Ghadar, characterizing him as "the heart and soul of Ghadar" in Oregon is contextualized by most Ghadris having left the state. Also, by his own declaration, Thind arrived in Seattle in July 1913—a month after Ghadar's founding—meaning Thind was not a Ghadar founder. I do believe that Thind *represented the threat* of Ghadar to the British government. My research also indicates that Thind wanted citizenship and a future in America and made the arguments, including defending caste and racial purity, to do so. David Thind argues his father came to the United States with the intention of becoming an attorney, spiritual leader, and citizen (David Thind, interview with author, December 4 and 5, 2015). Thind reported the same to the *Oregonian* after the Supreme Court verdict ("Hindu Will Make Citizenship Fight"). See Ogden, "The Telling Case of Dr. Bhagat Singh Thind."

73 Regarding general British concerns regarding Indo-American citizenship, see Dignan, "The Hindu Conspiracy," 72–76. Regarding British concealment of its role in the San Francisco trial, see Plowman, "The British Intelligence Station in San Francisco," 13.

74 Hochschild, *American Midnight*, 132.

75 Dignan, "The Hindu Conspiracy," 75–76.

76 Ngai, *Impossible Subjects*, 10.

77 Jamiles Lartey and Sam Morris, "How White Americans Used Lynchings to Terrorize and Control Black People," *Guardian*, April 26, 2018, https://www. theguardian.com/us-news/2018/apr/26/lynchings-memorial-us-south-montgomery-alabama; Hochschild, *American Midnight*, 251–256.

78 Ngai, *Impossible Subjects*, 19.

79 Haney López, *White by Law*, 35–77; Hochschild, *American Midnight*, 1–12.

80 Ngai, *Impossible Subjects*, 38.

81 "'Exhibit A,' Bhagat Singh Thind's Statement Regarding His Race. Anthropology of Races," in Thomas Mannix, *US v. Bhagat Singh Thind U.S. Supreme Court Transcript of Record with Supporting Pleadings*, MOML US Supreme Court Records and Briefs, 1832–1978, 20, 22, 34.

82 Koshy, "Morphing Race into Ethnicity," 164–165.

83   Haney Lopéz, *White by Law*, 1.
84   Smith, "Oregon's Civil War," 167, 171.
85   Koshy, "Morphing Race," 167.
86   Haney López, *White by Law*, 36, 51–52; Koshy, "Morphing Race," 166–167.
87   Haney López, *White by Law*, 57–61.
88   Haney López, *White by Law*, 62.
89   Mannix, "Brief for the United States, Statement of the Case," U.S. v. Bhagat Singh Thind U.S. Supreme Court Transcript of Record, 9–15.
90   Mannix, "'Exhibit A,'" *Thind*, 34. See also Mannix, "Brief of Respondent," *Thind*, 20, 22.
91   Snow, "The Civilization of White Men," in *Race, Nation, and Religion in the Americas*, 276.
92   Mannix, *Thind U.S. Supreme Court Transcript of Record*, 34.
93   Mannix, "Exhibit A," *Thind*, 20–22.
94   Mannix, "Exhibit A," *Thind*, 34. See also Mannix, "Brief of Respondent," *Thind*, 20, 22.
95   Haney López, *White by Law*, 180–182.
96   Koshy, "Morphing Race," 173.
97   Ngai, *Impossible Subjects*, 46.
98   Haney López, *White by Law*, 65–67.
99   Jensen, *Passage from India*, 257, 259, 265.
100 Ngai, *Impossible Subjects*, 46–47.
101 Haney López, *White by Law*, 65; Ngai, *Impossible Subjects*, 49.
102 Aaron Goings, "Johnson, Albert (1869–1957)," History Link, accessed March 23, 2023, https://www.historylink.org/File/8721; Hochschild, *American Midnight*, 50–51.
103 Ngai, *Impossible Subjects*, 7.
104 The US Department of State Office of the Historian now wanly acknowledges the purpose of the act was "to preserve the ideal of American homogeneity." "The Immigration Act of 1924 (The Johnson-Reed Act)," United States of America, Department of State, Office of the Historian, accessed June 25, 2023, http://history.state.gov/milestones/1921-1936/immigration-act. The twin process embodied in immigration and naturalization laws profoundly shaped the United States. As legal scholar Ian Haney López so succinctly put it, "The racial composition of the US citizenry reflects in part the accident of world migration patterns. Even more, it reflects the conscious design of US immigration and naturalization laws." Haney López, *White by Law*, 27.
105 This was an American tradition. As Mae Ngai writes, "in the mid nineteenth century, American nationalism revived the mythology of Anglo-Saxonism, ascribing a racial origin to (and thus exclusive ownership of) the democratic foundations of the nation." Ngai, *Impossible Subjects*, 42.
106 Haney López, *White by Law*, 31.
107 "Final Decree of Chas. E. Wolverton," June 26, 1926, *Thind*. Thind gained citizenship in 1937. Ogden, "The Telling Case of Dr. Bhagat Singh Thind," 33.
108 Jensen, *Passage from India*, 257, 259, 265.
109 Ratification and Confirmation of Naturalization of Certain Persons of the Hindu Race: Part 1, Before the Senate Comm. on Immigration, 69th Cong., 2nd sess. (December 9, 1926).

110 Ratification and Confirmation of Naturalization of Certain Persons of the Hindu Race; Haney López, *White by Law*, 64–65; Jensen, *Passage from India*, 259; on the larger issue of "fraud" and its use in American naturalization cases, 257–265; Kritika Agarwal, "Living in a Gilded Cage: Vaishno Das Bagai's Disillusionment with America," *Tides Magazine*, South Asian American Digital Archive, August 6, 2014, https://www.saada.org/tides/article/living-in-a-gilded-cage.

111 Nicolosi, "'We Do Not Want Our Girls to Marry Foreigners,'" 15–16.

112 Hidemitsu Toyota, a World War I veteran of Japanese descent, had his status rescinded by the Supreme Court. Salyer, "Baptism by Fire," 865–866.

113 Ngai, *Impossible Subjects*, 49.

114 See chapter 1 for details on British stratagems.

115 For Bhagat Singh Thind life outcomes post-verdict, see Ogden, "The Telling Case of Dr. Bhagat Singh Thind."

116 Jensen, "The 'Hindu Conspiracy,'" 268. Tagore's vow to never return to the United States after the *Thind* verdict came despite his son's attendance at a US college, his many American friends, and having previously praised the US government for its international leadership.

117 Hess, "The 'Hindu' in America," 67–68.

118 "Indians in USA," *Tribune*, June 21, 2023, p. 6.

EPILOGUE

1 "How Were India-Pakistan Partition Borders Drawn?" *Aljazeera*, https://www.aljazeera.com/news/2022/8/12/infographic-how-were-the-india-pakistan-partition-borders-drawn. When I had the privilege of visiting Punjab in 2014, it was a rare person of a certain age who did not offer a family story of horrific loss from the time of partition.

2 In the Punjabi short story, "The Exchange of Lunatics," governmental officials transfer the inhabitants of insane asylums to their new and "proper" countries, a concept lost on the patients who cannot understand their inability to ever return home to their farms and former Sikh, Muslim, or Hindu neighbors, friends, or family. The story's dark humor resides in exactly what, or who, in the story is insane. Munto, "The Exchange of Lunatics/Toba Tek Singh," in *Land of the Five Rivers*, 1–14.

3 Brown, *Har Dayal Hindu Revolutionary and Rationalist*, 220, 234.

4 Brown, *Har Dayal Hindu Revolutionary and Rationalist*, 268–271.

5 Ogden, "The Telling Case of Dr. Bhagat Singh Thind." New Thought was a religious healing movement that claimed that "'spirit,' 'mind,' or human thought had the power to shape matter, overcome heredity, and mold desire." Satter, *Each Mind a Kingdom*, 9.

6 Ogden, "The Telling Case of Dr. Bhagat Singh Thind," 32–33.

7 Post–World War II, America's web of international racial profiling laws began to unravel as comparison to Germany's master race narrative proved too close for comfort. Moreover, the country's structural exclusion of and violence against African Americans, and the many nonwhite peoples denied citizenship within its borders, stood as an obstacle to US authorities ingratiating themselves as a force for democracy with formerly colonized countries. The 1952 McCarren Walter Act began the government's move away from excluding immigrants based simply on country of origin, with quotas officially withdrawn in 1965.

8 The Black Panther Party has been my frequent frame. Much like Ghadar, it was also a group that "lost." Yet I know the impact the Panthers have had on my life

and generation. Inheritors and enhancers of Marcus Garvey and Malcolm X, they are also proud ancestors of the many Black Lives Matter heroes.

9   Gajendra Singh argues, "Colonial officials were unable to react to the demands of moderate nationalists after the First World War, because they were haunted by the specter of what had occurred during the conflict. . . . The years were remarkable for the array of revolutionary conspiracies that threatened British rule. The movements were small in comparison to Congress but were imbued with a startling dynamism and scope" (chief among these was Ghadar). In short, British intransigence against the more modest nationalist demands set the stage for the 1920s noncooperation movement. Gajendra Singh, "India and the Great War," 345. Ghadris and their revolutionary offshoots were not simply noncooperation activists; many, for example, became communists aligned with the global communist movement and other such radical movements, and agitated amid the broad movements.

10 Suresh K, "Arundhati Roy on Gandhi—III," December 15, 2020, https://www.kesuresh.com/2020/12/arundhati-roy-on-gandhi-iii.html.

11 While I write this in a period of global extremist demagogues' ascendance, it's worth repeating that the historic crimes against Indian personhood and nationhood described in this book were carried out by mainline, democratic British and American leaders, many of whom remain revered.

12 "AP Wins Pulitzer for Exposing NYPD's CIA-Linked Intel Program, Leading Widespread Spying on Muslims," *Democracy Now*, April 17, 2012, https://www.democracynow.org/2012/4/17/ap_wins_pulitzer_for_exposing_growth; "The First Hate-Crime Attack after 9/11," BBC, September 11, 2021, https://www.bbc.com/news/av/world-us-canada-58531179.

13 "More Than 9,000 Anti-Asian Incidents Have Been Reported since the Pandemic Began," NPR, August 12, 2021, https://www.npr.org/2021/08/12/1027236499/anti-asian-hate-crimes-assaults-pandemic-incidents-aapi.

14 Morrison, *Beloved*, 61.

15 "Suchness," reprinted with the permission of Amarjit Chandan, and as it appeared in *MPT, The Best of World Poetry*, no.1 (2016): 80–81.

Bibliography

Abbott, Carl. *The Great Extravaganza: Portland and the Lewis and Clark Exposition.* 3rd ed. Portland: Oregon Historical Society Press, 2004.

Alborn, Denise. "The Hindus of Uppertown." *Cumtux* 10, no. 1 (Winter 1989): 13–18.

Allerfeldt, Kristofer. *Race, Radicalism, Religion, and Restriction: Immigration in the Pacific Northwest, 1890–1924.* Westport, CT: Praeger Publishers, 2003.

Alter, Joseph S. "The Body of One Color: Indian Wrestling, the Indian State, and Utopian Somatics." *Cultural Anthropology* 8, no. 1 (February 1993): 49–72.

———. "Gama the World Champion: Wrestling and Physical Culture in Colonial India." *Iron Game History* 4, no. 2 (October 1995): 3–9.

———. "Indian Clubs and Colonialism: Hindu Masculinity and Muscular Christianity." *Comparative Studies in Society and History* 46, no. 3 (July 2004): 497–534.

———. "Subaltern Bodies and Nationalist Physiques: Gama the Great and the Heroics of Indian Wrestling." *Body & Society* 6, no. 2 (June 2000): 45–72.

———. *The Wrestler's Body: Identity and Ideology in North India.* Berkeley: University of California Press, 1992.

Bahadur, Gaiutra. *Coolie Woman: The Odyssey of Indenture.* Chicago: University of Chicago Press, 2013.

Ballantyne, Tony. *Between Colonialism and Diaspora: Sikh Cultural Formations in an Imperial World.* Durham, NC: Duke University Press, 2006.

Baptist, Edward E. *The Half Has Never Been Told: Slavery and the Making of American Capitalism.* New York: Basic Books, 2014.

Barber, Katrine. "'We Were at Our Journey's End': Settler Sovereignty Formation in Oregon." *Oregon Historical Quarterly* 120, no. 4 (Winter 2019): 382–411.

Batzell, Rudi. "Free Labour, Capitalism and the Anti-Slavery Origins of Chinese Exclusion in California in the 1870s." *Past and Present* 225, no. 1 (September 2014): 143–186.

Bell, Janet Dewart. *Lighting the Fires of Freedom: African American Women in the Civil Rights Movement.* New York: The New Press, 2018.

Bhakna, Baba Sohan Singh. *Jeewan Sangam.* Edited by Malwinderjit Singh Waraich and Sita Ram Bansal. Barnala, India: Tarakbharti Parkashan, 1967.

Blee, Lisa. "Completing Lewis and Clark's Westward March: Exhibiting a History of Empire at the 1905 Portland World's Fair." *Oregon Historical Quarterly* 106, no. 2 (Summer 2005): 232–253.

Bose, Arun Coomer. *Indian Revolutionaries Abroad, 1905–1922: In the Background of International Developments.* Allahabad: Indian Press Private Ltd., 1971.

Bose, Neilesh. "Taraknath Das (1884–1958), British Columbia, and the Anti-Colonial Borderlands." *BC Studies* 204 (Winter 2019/20): 67–88.

Brown, Emily C. *Har Dayal: Hindu Revolutionary and Rationalist.* Tucson: University of Arizona Press, 1975.

Chalana, Manish. "'Whither the 'Hindoo Invasion'? South Asians in the Pacific Northwest of the United States, 1907–1930." *International Journal of Regional and Local History* 16, no. 1 (April 2021): 14–38.

Chandrasekhar, Sripati. "Indian Immigration in America." *Far Eastern Survey* 13, no. 15 (July 1944): 138–143.

Chang, Kornel. *Pacific Connections: The Making of the U.S.–Canadian Borderlands.* American Crossroads. Berkeley: University of California Press, 2012.

Cole, Peter, David Struthers, and Kenyon Zimmer. "Introduction." In *Wobblies of the World: A Global History of the IWW*, edited by Peter Cole, David Struthers, and Kenyon Zimmer, 1–26. London: Pluto Press, 2018.

Coleman, Kenneth R. "'We'll All Start Even': White Egalitarianism and the Oregon Donation Land Claim Act." *Oregon Historical Quarterly* 120, no. 4 (Winter 2019): 414–437.

Comstock-Skipp, Jaimee K. "Art Deco Sartorientalism in America: Persian Urban Turbans and Other Versions." *Chitrolekha International Magazine on Art and Design* 1, no. 3 (2011): 19–24.

Coulson, Doug. *Race, Nation, and Refuge: The Rhetoric of Race in Asian American Citizenship Cases.* Albany: State University of New York Press, 2017.

de la Garza, Amanda. *Doctorji: The Life, Teachings, and Legacy of Dr. Bhagat Singh Thind.* Santa Barbara, CA: Studio E Books, 2010.

Deol, Gurdev Singh. *The Role of the Ghadar Party in the National Movement.* Delhi: Sterling Publishers, 1969.

Deur, Douglas. "The Making of Seaside's 'Indian Place': Contested and Enduring Native Spaces on the Nineteenth Century Oregon Coast." *Oregon Historical Quarterly* 117, no. 4 (Winter 2016): 536–573.

Dhami, Sadhu Singh. *Maluka: A Novel.* Liverpool: Lucas Publications, 1987.

Dhillon, Kartar. "Astoria Revisited: A Search for the East Indian Presence in Astoria." *Cumtux* 15, no. 2 (Spring 1995): 2–9.

Dignan, Don K. "The Hindu Conspiracy in Anglo-American Relations during World War I." *Pacific Historical Review* 40, no. 1 (February 1971): 57–76.

Foner, Eric. *Free Soil, Free Labor, Free Men: The Ideology of the Republican Party before the Civil War.* New York: Oxford University Press, 1995.

Friday, Chris. *Organizing Asian American Labor: The Pacific Coast Canned-Salmon Industry, 1870–1942.* Philadelphia: Temple University Press, 1994.

Goings, Aaron A. "Red Harbor: Class, Violence, and Community in Grays Harbor, Washington." PhD diss., Simon Fraser University, 2011.

Goings, Aaron, Brian Barnes, and Roger Snider. *The Red Coast: Radicalism and Anti-Radicalism in Southwest Washington.* Corvallis: Oregon State University Press, 2019.

Gordon, Greg. "Economic Phoenix: How A. B. Hammond Used the Depression of 1893 and a Pair of Defunct Oregon Railroads to Build a Lumber Empire." *Oregon Historical Quarterly* 109, no. 4 (Winter 2008): 598–621.

———. *When Money Grew on Trees: A. B. Hammond and the Age of the Timber Baron.* Norman: University of Oklahoma Press, 2014.

Gouda, Frances. "Good Mothers, Medeas, or Jezebels: Feminine Imagery in Colonial and Anticolonial Rhetoric in the Dutch East Indies, 1900–1942." In *Domesticating the Empire: Race, Gender, and Family Life in French and Dutch Colonialism*, edited by Julia Clancy-Smith and Frances Gouda, 236–254. Charlottesville: University Press of Virginia, 1998.

Gould, Harold A. *Sikhs, Swamis, Students, and Spies: The India Lobby in the United States, 1900–1946.* New Delhi: Sage Publications, 2006.

Gramsci, Antonio. *Selections from the Prison Notebooks.* New York: International Publishers, 1971.

Haney López, Ian. *White by Law: The Legal Construction of Race.* New York: New York University Press, 2006.

Heatherton, Christina. "University of Radicalism: Ricardo Flores Magón and Leavenworth Penitentiary." In "Las Américas Quarterly," special issue, *American Quarterly* 66, no. 3 (September 2014): 557–581.

Helquist, Michael. *Marie Equi: Radical Politics and Outlaw Passions.* Corvallis: Oregon State University Press, 2015.

Henry, Chris. "Home Defender: Albert Johnson's Pursuit of Immigration Restriction as a Means of Combating Radicalism." Senior thesis, St. Martins University, 2013.

Hess, Gary R. "The 'Hindu' in America: Immigration and Naturalization Policies and India, 1917–1946." *Pacific Historical Review* 38, no. 1 (February 1969): 59–79.

Hill, Joe. *I.W.W. Little Red Songbook: Nineteenth Edition from 1923 with All of the Classic Hits.* Portland, OR: Microcosm Publishing, 2019.

Hochschild, Adam. *American Midnight: The Great War, a Violent Peace, and Democracy's Forgotten Crisis.* Boston: Mariner Books, 2022.

Hummasti, Paul George. *Finnish Radicals in Astoria, Oregon, 1904–1940: A Study in Immigrant Socialism.* Scandinavians in America. New York: Arno Press, 1979.

———. "World War I and the Finns of Astoria, Oregon: The Effects of the War on an Immigrant Community." *International Migration Review* 11, no. 3 (Autumn 1977): 334–349.

Hyslop, Jonathan. "The Imperial Working Class Makes Itself 'White': White Labourism in Britain, Australia, and South Africa before the First World War." *Journal of Historical Sociology* 12, no. 4 (December 1999): 398–421.

Isemonger, F. C., and J. Slattery. *An Account of the Ghadr Conspiracy (1913–1915).* Meerut, India: Archana Publications, 1998.

Jensen, Joan M. "The 'Hindu Conspiracy': A Reassessment." *Pacific Historical Review* 48, no. 1 (February 1979): 65–83.

———. *Passage from India: Asian Indian Immigrants in North America.* New Haven, CT: Yale University Press, 1988.

Johnson, Jeffrey A. *They Are All Red Out Here: Socialist Politics in the Pacific Northwest, 1895–1925.* Norman: University of Oklahoma Press, 2008.

Josh, Sohan Singh. *Baba Sohan Singh Bhakna, Life of the Founder of the Ghadar Party.* New Delhi: People's Publishing House, 1970.

Kazimi, Ali. *Undesirables: White Canada and the Komagata Maru: An Illustrated History.* Vancouver: D&M Publishers, 2012.

Kipnis, Ira. *The American Socialist Movement 1897–1912.* New York: Columbia University Press, 1952.

Kolko, Gabriel. *The Triumph of Conservatism: A Reinterpretation of American History, 1900–1916.* New York: The Free Press of Glencoe, 1963.

Koshy, Susan. "Morphing Race into Ethnicity: Asian Americans and Critical Transformations of Whiteness." *Boundary 2* 28, no. 1 (Spring 2001): 153–194.

Lake, Marilyn, and Henry Reynolds. *Drawing the Global Colour Line: White Men's Countries and the International Challenge of Racial Equality.* Cambridge, UK: Cambridge University Press, 2008.

Lal, Brij. "East Indians in British Columbia, 1904–1914: An Historical Study in Growth and Integration." Master's thesis, University of British Columbia, 1976.

Lee, Erika. "Hemispheric Orientalism and the 1907 Pacific Coast Race Riots." *Amerasia Journal* 33, no. 2 (September 2007): 19–47.

Lee, Erika, and Judy Yung. *Angel Island: Immigrant Gateway to America*. Oxford: Oxford University Press, 2010.

Leedom, Karen L. *Astoria: An Oregon History*. Pittsburgh, PA: The Local History Company, 2008.

Leonard, Karen Isaksen. *Making Ethnic Choices: California's Punjabi Mexican Americans*. Philadelphia: Temple University Press, 1994.

Limerick, Patricia Nelson. *The Legacy of Conquest: The Unbroken Past of the American West*. New York: W.W. Norton & Company, 1987.

Mahmud, Tayyab. "Cheaper Than a Slave: Indentured Labor, Colonialism and Capitalism." *34 Whittier Law Review* 215 (2013): 215–243.

Mannix, Thomas. *U.S. v. Bhagat Singh Thind U.S. Supreme Court Transcript of Record with Supporting Pleadings*. MOML US Supreme Court Records and Briefs, 1832–1978.

Marconeri, Cynthia J. "Chinese-Americans in Astoria, Oregon: 1880–1930." *Cumtux* 13, no. 3 (Summer 1993): 30–39.

McKeown, Adam. "Global Migration, 1846–1970." *Journal of World History* 15, no. 2 (June 2004): 155–189.

Mills, James H., ed. *Subaltern Sports: Politics and Sport in South Asia*. Anthem South Asian Studies. London: Anthem Press, 2005.

Misrow, Jogesh C. "East Indian Immigration on the Pacific Coast." Master's thesis, Stanford University, 1915.

Morrison, Toni. *Beloved*. New York: Alfred A. Knopf, 1990.

———. *Playing in the Dark: Whiteness and the Literary Imagination*. Cambridge, MA: Harvard University Press, 1992.

Munto, Saadat Hassan. "The Exchange of Lunatics/Toba Tek Singh." In *Land of the Five Rivers*, edited by Khushwant Singh and Jaya Thadani, 1–14. Bombay: Jaico Publishing House, 1965.

Myers, Ella. "Beyond the Psychological Wage: Du Bois on White Dominion." *Political Theory* 47, no. 1 (2019): 6–31.

Nayar, Kamala Elizabeth. *The Punjabis in British Columbia: Location, Labour, First Nations, and Multiculturalism*. Vol. 2, McGill-Queen's Studies in Ethnic History. Montreal: McGill-Queen's University Press, 2012.

Ngai, Mae M. *Impossible Subjects: Illegal Aliens and the Making of Modern America*. Princeton, NJ: Princeton University Press, 2003.

Nicolosi, Ann Marie. "'We Do Not Want Our Girls to Marry Foreigners': Gender, Race, and American Citizenship." In "Gender and Social Policy: Local to Global," special issue, *NWSA Journal* 13, no. 3 (Autumn 2001): 1–21.

Ogden, Johanna. "Ghadar, Historical Silences, and Notions of Belonging: Early 1900s Punjabis of the Columbia River." *Oregon Historical Quarterly* 113, no. 2 (Summer 2012): 164–197.

———. "The Telling Case of Dr. Bhagat Singh Thind." *Oregon Historical Quarterly* 124, no. 1 (Spring 2023): 6–19.

———. "White Right and Labor Organizing in Oregon's 'Hindu' City." In "White Supremacy & Resistance," special issue, *Oregon Historical Quarterly* 120, no. 4 (Winter 2019): 488–517.

Pfaelzer, Jean. *Driven Out: The Forgotten War against Chinese Americans*. New York: Random House, 2007.

Plowman, Matthew Erin. "The British Intelligence Station in San Francisco during the First World War." *Journal of Intelligence History* 12, no. 1 (2013): 1–20.

Price, John. "'Orienting' the Empire: MacKenzie King and the Aftermath of the 1907 Race Riots." In "Refracting Pacific Canada," special issue, *BC Studies* 156/157 (Winter/Spring 2007/2008): 53–81.

Puri, Harish K. *Ghadar Movement: Ideology, Organisation & Strategy*. Amritsar, India: Guru Nanak Dev Press, 1983.

———. "Lajpat Rai in USA 1914–1919: Life and Work of a Political Exile." In *Lala Lajpat Rai in Retrospect: Political, Economic, Social, and Cultural Concerns*, edited by J. S. Grewal and Indu Banga, 65–80. Chandigarh, India: Panjab University Publication Bureau, 2000.

Ramnath, Maia. *Decolonizing Anarchism: An Antiauthoritarian History of India's Liberation Struggle*. Anarchist Interventions 3. Chico, CA: AK Press, 2012.

———. *Haj to Utopia: How the Ghadar Movement Charted Global Radicalism and Attempted to Overthrow the British Empire*. California World History Library 19. Berkeley: University of California Press, 2011.

Robbins, William G. *Landscapes of Promise: The Oregon Story, 1800–1940*. Seattle: University of Washington Press, 1997.

Roediger, David R. *The Wages of Whiteness: Race and the Making of the American Working Class*. Haymarket Series. London: Verso, 2007.

Roediger, David R., and Elizabeth D. Esch. *The Production of Difference: Race and the Management of Labor in U.S. History*. Oxford: Oxford University Press, 2012.

Salyer, Lucy E. "Baptism by Fire: Race, Military Service, and U.S. Citizenship Policy, 1918–1935." *Journal of American History* 91, no. 3 (December 2004): 847–876.

Satter, Beryl. *Each Mind a Kingdom: American Women, Sexual Purity, and the New Thought Movement, 1875–1920*. Berkeley: University of California Press, 2001.

Sawhney, Savitri. "Pandurang Khankhoje: An Important Combatant in the Movement." In *The Ghadr Movement and India's Anti-Imperialist Struggle*, edited by Dr. Prithvi Raj Kalia. Winnipeg: Progressive Peoples' Foundation of Edmonton, 2013.

———. *I Shall Never Ask for Pardon: A Memoir of Pandurang Khankhoje*. New Delhi: Penguin Books India, 2008.

Saxton, Alexander. *The Indispensable Enemy: Labor and the Anti-Chinese Movement in California*. Berkeley: University of California Press, 1975.

Scheffauer, Herman. "The Tide of Turbans." *Forum* 43 (June 1910): 616–618.

Scott, Harvey. "The Momentous Struggle for Mastery of the Pacific." *Pacific Monthly* 14, no. 1 (June–December 1905): 3–12.

Shah, Nayan. *Stranger Intimacy: Contesting Race, Sexuality, and the Law in the North American West*. Berkeley: University of California Press, 2012.

Shason, Jan-Paul. "Evolving Utopias: An Overview of Three Representative Punjabi Works from 1890s, 1910s & 1930s." Master's thesis, University of British Columbia, 2009.

Singh, Gajendra. "India and the Great War: Colonial Fantasies, Anxieties and Discontent." *Studies in Ethnicity and Nationalism* 14, no. 2 (October 2014): 343–361.

Singh, Gurpreet. "Rebellious Rhymes: Understanding the History of Radical South Asian Immigrants on the West Coast of North America through the Ghadar Narrative." In *Interpreting Ghadar: Echoes of Voices Past, Ghadar Centennial Conference Proceedings*, edited by Satwinder Kaur Bains, 21–44. Abbottsford, BC: Centre for Indo-Canadian Studies, University of the Fraser Valley, October 2013.

———. "Sohan Singh Bhakna: A Life for Social Justice and Freedom for the Wretched and Poor." In *The Ghadr Movement and India's Anti-Imperialist Struggle*, edited by Dr. Prithvi Raj Kalia. Winnipeg: Progressive Peoples' Foundation of Edmonton, 2013.

———. *Why Mewa Singh Killed William Hopkinson?: Revisiting the Murder of a Canadian Immigration Inspector.* Punjabi: Chetna Parkashan, 2013.

Singh, Baba Harnam Tundilat. *Notes on the History of the Ghadar Party.* Desh Bhagat Accession No. 19144 (Urdu).

Sinha, Mrinalini. *Colonial Masculinity: The "Manly Englishman" and the "Effeminate Bengali" in the Late Nineteenth Century.* Studies in Imperialism. Manchester, UK: Manchester University Press, 1995.

Smith, Marian L. "Race, Nationality, and Reality: INS Administration of Racial Provisions in U.S. Immigration and Nationality Law since 1898." *Prologue Magazine* 34, no. 2 (Summer 2002).

Smith, Stacey L. "Oregon's Civil War: The Troubled Legacy of Emancipation in the Pacific Northwest." *Oregon Historical Quarterly* 115, no. 2 (Summer 2014): 154–173.

Snow, Jennifer. "The Civilization of White Men." In *Race, Nation, and Religion in the Americas*, edited by Henry Goldschmidt and Elizabeth McAlister, 259–280. Oxford: Oxford University Press, 2004.

Sohi, Seema. *Echoes of Mutiny: Race, Surveillance, and Indian Anticolonialism in North America.* Oxford: Oxford Press, 2014.

Takaki, Ronald. *Strangers from a Different Shore: A History of Asian Americans.* Boston: Little, Brown and Company, 1989.

Tatla, Darshan S. "A Fateful Encounter? Sikh Interaction with the Hindu Elite on the Pacific Coast of North America." *Journal of Sikh & Punjāb Studies* 26, nos. 1/2 (Spring/Fall 2019): 35–60.

———. "A Sikh Manifesto? A Reading of the Ghadar Poetry." *Punjab Past and Present* 44, no. 1 (April 2013): 61–81.

Thompson, Carmen P. "Expectation and Exclusion: An Introduction to Whiteness, White Supremacy, and Resistance in Oregon History." *Oregon Historical Quarterly* 120, no. 4 (Winter 2019): 358–367.

———. *The Making of American Whiteness: The Formation of Race in Seventeenth-Century Virginia.* Philosophy of Race. Lanham, MD: Lexington Books, 2023.

Trafford, Emily. "Hitting the Trail: Live Displays of Native American, Filipino, and Japanese People at the Portland World's Fair." *Oregon Historical Quarterly* 116, no. 2 (Summer 2015): 158–195.

Trouillot, Michel-Rolph. *Silencing the Past: Power and the Production of History.* Boston: Beacon Press, 1995.

Vatuk, Ved Prakash. *Thieves in My House: Four Studies in Indian Folklore of Protest and Change.* Varanasi: Vishwavidyalaya Prakashan, 1969.

Ward, W. Peter. *White Canada Forever: Popular Attitudes and Public Policy toward Orientals in British Columbia.* 3rd ed. Vol. 8, McGill-Queen's Studies in Ethnic History. Montreal: McGill-Queen's University Press, 2002.

Wilkerson, Isabel. *Caste: The Origins of Our Discontents.* New York: Random House, 2020.

Wilm, Julius. "Old Myths, Turned on Their Heads: Settler Agency, Federal Authority, and the Colonization of Oregon." *Oregon Historical Quarterly* 123, no. 4 (Winter 2022): 326–357.

Wong, Marie Rose. *Sweet Cakes, Long Journey: The Chinatowns of Portland, Oregon.*
    Seattle: University of Washington Press, 2004.

ARCHIVES

Clatsop County Historical Society
Desh Bhagat Yadgar Library Special Collections
National Archives and Records Administration
National Archives of India
Oregon Historical Society
Oregon State University Special Collections and Research Center
City of Portland (OR) Archives and Records Center
South Asian American Digital Archive (www.saada.org)
University of Oregon, Special Collections of the Knight Library
Whatcom County Historical Society

Index